ATLANTIC STUDIES ON SOCIETY IN CHANGE

NO. 77

A Joint Publication with the
Committee for Danubian Research, Inc.

War and Society in East Central Europe
Volume XXX

Wartime American Plans for a New Hungary

Documents from the U.S. Department of State, 1942-1944

Edited with an Introduction by
Ignác Romsics

Social Science Monographs, Boulder, Colorado
Atlantic Research and Publications,
Highland Lakes, New Jersey

Distributed by Columbia University Press, New York
1992

EAST EUROPEAN MONOGRAPHS, NO. CCCLIV

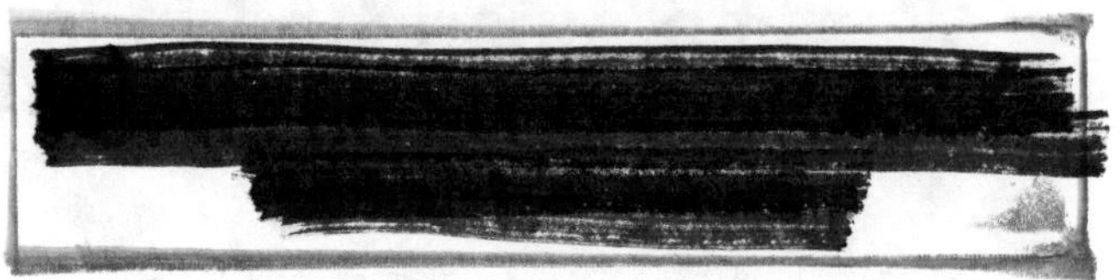

Library of Congress Catalog Card Number 92-82611
ISBN 0-88033-251-4
Printed in the United States of America

To my wife, Éva
and
to my son, Gergő

Table of Contents

Chapter III. Summaries and Recommendations

Part Three: Political Reorganization of Hungary

Part Four: Final Summaries and Recommendations

Preface to the Series

The present volume is a component of a series that, when completed will constitute a comprehensive survey of the many aspects of East European society. The bulk of the publication costs for this book were covered by a generous grant from the Committee for Danubian Research, Incorporated.

The books in the series' volumes deal with the peoples whose homelands lie between the Germans to the west, the Russians to the east and, the Mediterranean and Adriatic seas to the south. They constitute a particular civilization, one that is at once an integral part of Europe, yet substantially different form the West. The area is characterized by a rich variety in language, religion, and government. The study of this complex subject demands a multidisciplinary approach and, accordingly, our contributors to the series represent several academic disciplines. They have been drawn from the universities and other scholarly institutions in the United States and Western Europe, as well as East and Central Europe. The editor of the present volume is a distinguished historian, and Associate Professor of History at the Eötvös Loránd University of Budapest (ELTE).

The editors, of course, take full responsibility for ensuring the comprehensiveness, cohesion, internal balance, and scholarly quality of the series. We cheerfully accept this responsibility and intend this work to be neither a justification nor condemnation of the policies, attitudes, and activities of any persons involved. At the same time, because the contributors represent so many different disciplines, interpretations, and schools of thought, our policy in this, as in the past and future volumes, is to present their contributions without major modifications.

Acknowledgments

This volume has been put together with help from many quarters. First of all, it was the György Soros – Hungarian Academy of Sciences Foundation which enabled me to do research in the United States in the first half of 1991. Atlantic Research and Publications, Inc., or more precisely, Professor Peter Pastor, undertook the organization of my trip, and the management of my day-to-day research activities there. His guidance and assistance have been invaluable. I would like to express my appreciation also to the officials and associates of the Library of Congress, the National Archives, the Franklin D. Roosevelt Library at Hyde Park, and the Yale University Sterling Memorial Library. Their helping hand made the data gathering process much easier.

The first people with whom I discussed my notions about the Advisory Committee on Post-War Foreign Policy as its work related to Hungarian affairs were my Washington friends, Enikő Molnár-Basa, András Ábrahám, Sándor Taraszovics, and two Hungarian friends temporarily in Washington at the time, Miklós Dérer and Tamás Hofer. I would like to take this opportunity to convey my gratitude for their apt suggestions and constructive criticism.

I also wish to thank those who have helped, in Budapest, in the editing phase of the work: Éva D. Pálmai, for translating into English the preface, the introduction and the editorial notes; László Sebők for reproducing the maps, and Olga Novotta, for the typing.

Göd, 1991.

Foreword

Three weeks after Pearl Harbor, on December 28, 1941, President Roosevelt approved the Department of State's setting up the Advisory Committee on Post-War Foreign Policy. Its task, as its name suggests, was to work out the policies that would guide the U.S. in the postwar task of negotiating peace. Officially, the Committee continued to function until the summer of 1943; in fact, however, it carried on its work until the end of the war, though under other names. In about three years, the Advisory Committee and its successors wrote thousands of reports and situation analyses, which served as the basis of presentations heard and discussed by hundreds of committees and sub-committees.

The accumulated material, reports of fact-finding missions, analyses, presentations, minutes and recommendations, altogether about thirty-five running meters of documents, was deposited in the National Archives by the State Department in 197O. The collection, which came to two hundred and eighty boxes, was catalogued as the Notter File, and made available to researchers in 1974. It is difficult to overestimate the value of the collection to anyone interested in the personalities who shaped U.S. foreign policy during the war and in the immediate postwar period, to whoever wants to understand the concerns of these people, and the way their minds worked. It is indicative of the thoroughness of the material that there are close to eight hundred pages dealing with Hungary alone. As for its documentary value, we might note that in the early '80's, Japanese researchers had copies made of most of the material dealing with Japan. The purpose of this volume is to present the various points of view that emerged in the course of the Advisory Committee's discussions of the future of Hungary and its place in the proposed "Mid-European Union" and to give an idea of its recommendations. About a third of the relevant documents have been included, those deemed to be most significant, and those most conducive to the reader's drawing his own conclusions about the nature of the postwar Hungary envisioned by U.S. foreign policy makers.

The material I selected during the time spent at the National Archives in the first half of 1991. I first called attention to this extraordinary collection at lectures held at the Kossuth House in Washington, D.C., at Montclair State College, and at Rutgers University, the meeting place of the Hungarian Allumni Association. Subsequently, brief interviews on the subject were aired on Hungarian Radio and on Hungarian Television, and an article in the November 1991 issue of Valóság followed. This, however, is the first time that the documents themselves are published.

The documents contained in the volume are grouped thematically into four units. Part One deals with plans for the "Mid European Union." Part Two with Hungary s proposed frontiers; and Part Three with what would be a desirable form of postwar government in Hungary. Part Four contains the recommendations actually submitted to the Secretary of State and the President.

Following the convention of source publications, we are publishing the documents *verbatim et literatim*, correcting only the obvious typing errors. For the sessions of the Territorial Subcommittee, we have not only the minutes of each of the meetings, but also the "Summaries and Recommendations" prepared in connection with the major issues discussed. In view of the importance of these issues, we shall publish both types of documents, separated by asterisks, as they relate to a particular question. In cases where the minutes of a certain meeting deal with issues unrelated either to Hungary or Eastern Europe, we shall publish only the part of the document that applies. That the document is fragmentary shall be indicated both in its title, and by the use of omission marks [....] within the text itself. Certain of the documents have notes; these shall be included at the end of the document, numbered with Arabic numerals as in the original. My own editorial notes shall be distinguished by asterisks, and the notes themselves be given as footnotes. Some of the records refer to documents or maps not included in the volume. Most of the former can be found in the National Archives, but not so all the maps. Of the tentative maps drawn up for the Advisory Committee, we have included the five that are the most informative, and the best visual aids to understanding the documents themselves. Three further maps, specifically drawn for this volume, have also been included: one a regional map of historical Hungary; one showing the borders recommended by the U.S. delegation to the 1919 peace talks; and one showing the territorial revisions of the years 1938 to 1941. There is an index to facilitate cross reference to personal and geographic names, and an introduction to advise the reader on the composition of the Advisory

Committee, on the background of the issues discussed, and on why it was that the events of 1945 to 1947 could thwart the American plans for a postwar settlement.

I am only too aware of the fact that what this volume is about is not "history" in the sense that the Crusades or other politically indifferent faits accomplis of even the more recent past are history. Its links to the present are obvious; some of the documents could have been written today. This, however, is no reason for not making these documents public. History is something that we must learn to live with – we Hungarians, as well as our neighbors. The historian's only task is to discover the evidence for how things were, and to make it available to all. If, in the process, certain sore points are touched upon, that is not his fault, but the work of history. Though the converse is just as true: it's his work, but the fault of history.

I. R.

INTRODUCTION

Introduction

1. *The Composition of the Advisory Committee*

The Advisory Committee first met on February 12, 1942. Unlike the Inquiry, the committee charged with working out United States peace proposals in the course of the First World War, the Advisory Committee included not just scholars and university professors,[1] but also leading associates of the Department of State. Another difference was that it was responsible to the Secretary of State, not to the President. The chairman of the Committee, accordingly, was Secretary of State Cordell Hull, its deputy-chairman was Undersecretary of State Sumner Welles, while the person who actually ran the day-to-day workings of the Committee was Leo Pasvolsky (1893-1953), an economist of Russian descent, and one of Hull's advisers. The Advisory Committee spent its first meeting setting up six subcommittees, the most important of which were the Political Subcommittee and the Territorial Subcommittee. The former, whose sessions were generally chaired by either Hull or Welles, dealt with global and regional political issues, thus, for instance, with what kind of collective security organization should be set up in place of the League of Nations, with inter-state relations throughout the world, and specifically, with Soviet-American relations. The latter, the Territorial Subcommittee, was charged with mapping the regions of the world made most unstable by potential territorial and ethnic disputes, and suggesting border revisions that might eliminate or at least minimize these tensions.[2]

The chairman of the Territorial Subcommittee, and one of the key figures of the Advisory Committee as a whole, was Isaiah Bowman (1878-1950), a veteran of the Inquiry, and a professor of geography. As president of the National Geographic Society from 1915 to 1935, Bowman had travelled the world over, his interest in geopolitics making him an avid student of international relations, his specialty at Johns Hopkins University after 1935.[3]

The other key figure of the Advisory Committee was Hamilton Fish Armstrong (1893-1973), the member of the above two subcommittees most versed in European affairs, and the editor of Foreign Affairs, the semi-official quarterly of the Department of State. Armstrong, whose job as editor since 1922 had gained him an extraordinary range of contacts, was particularly knowledgeable about Eastern Europe. His first experience of the region was between 1918 and 1922, as military attaché to the United States embassy in Belgrade. Though after that Foreign Affairs kept him in New York for most of the year, he still travelled extensively in Europe, and counted Józef Piłsudski, Eduard Beneš, Tomaš Masaryk, Albert Apponyi, Pál Teleki, István Bethlen, Iuliu Maniu, Nicolae Titulescu and Nikola Pašić among his personal acquaintances. He spent the summer of 1931 in Yugoslavia, mostly Dubrovnik. His good will toward these countries was recognized in the form of medals of honor by the Yugoslav state in 1919, and by the Romanian in 1924.[4]

Of the high-ranking Committee members associated with the Department of State, Sumner Welles (1892-1961) was particularly interested in Europe, as was Adolf A. Berle (1895-1971). Berle had majored in history and law at Harvard, and, as one of the youngest members of the 1919 peace delegation, had been consulted on Russian and Northeastern European affairs. His having joined with those members of the Inquiry who protested that the American delegations' "permissiveness" had allowed a number of unjust measures to pass seemed, for a while, to have put an end to his diplomatic career. During the 1920's, he ran a law practice, and also taught at Harvard and Columbia. After 1932, he was an adviser to Roosevelt, and was appointed Deputy Secretary of State in 1938. He had the job of preparing for peace, and thus, of keeping in touch with émigré politicians and governments-in-exile. This was how he came to know Tibor Eckhardt, a leader of the opposition forces in Hungary, sent abroad in 1940, and János Pelényi, the Hungarian ambassador to Washington, who had resigned over Hungary's declaration of war on the United States in 1941. He not only came to know them, but — unlike Armstrong, whose contacts were mostly the politicians of the former Little Entente and within the democratic branch of the Hungarian exiles — Berle sympathized with the views Eckhardt and Pelényi expressed in connection with the postwar future of Eastern Europe.[5]

Other names that we come across in reading the minutes of the various subcommittee sessions are those of Anne O'Hare McCormick (1882-1954), foreign policy analyst of the New York Times and the first woman journalist to win the Pulitzer Prize; Herbert Feis (1893-1972), economist, economic consultant to the Department of State at the time, and later one of the best-known historians of the war and cold war years, and Cavendish W. Cannon (1895-1962), a career diplomat, and head of the State Department's Southeast European Section in 1944-1945.

The Advisory Committee and its various subcommittees had a research staff to help them in their work. Initially, this staff consisted of junior members of the Department of State. By the summer of 1942, however, thirty graduate students who had just received their Ph.D. degrees or were just about to — historians, political scientists, economists, librarians, cartographers, and so on — were recruited specifically for this job. The research staff, or, as it was officially known, the Division of Special Research, consisted of fifty-five people at the end of 1942, of ninety-six in mid-1943, and of seventy-seven when it was terminated in 1944. The de facto head of the research staff was a youngish career diplomat, Harley Notter (1903-1950); he was also secretary to the Advisory Committee. His lieutenant, and also the head of the group of research staffers working on territorial issues, was Philip E. Mosely (1905-1972), a Harvard graduate, and a specialist in East European history. In the early 1930's, Mosely, then a young teaching assistant, spent two years in the Soviet Union; the years 1935-36 saw him spend a number of months in the Balkans. It was at that time that he also visited Transylvania. Except for Armstrong, Mosely was the member of the Advisory Committee most familiar with the Danube region. Other members of the research staff working on Eastern Europe, and thus on Hungary, were Harry N. Howard (1902-1987), John C. Campbell (1911-). Cyril E. Black (1915-1969), and Thomas F. Power (1916-1988). All of them young historians at the start of their careers, in the postwar years they were to follow their boss, Philip E. Mosely, in making a name for themselves in the postwar decades as the chief East-European experts, Balkan experts and Kremlinologists of the United States.[6]

2. *The "Mid-European Union" and Hungary*

The idea of a confederation of "eastern," "east-central" or "central" European states — the terms interchangeably used by American experts for the region lying between the Baltic Sea in the north and the Adriatic in the south, with Germany as its western frontier and the Soviet Union as its eastern — was first raised in the United States in the fall of 1918, once the fate of the Habsburg Monarchy was sealed. Its chief advocate was Herbert A. Miller, professor of sociology at Oberlin College, and a friend of Tomaš Masaryk's, who subsequently did so much to help Oscar Jászi, the Hungarian democrat forced into exile after 1919, feel at home in the United States.

The "Mid-European Union" envisioned by Masaryk and Miller was to stretch from the Baltic Sea to the Adriatic, its chief function being to serve as a counterweight to Pan-German aspirations.[7] Once the United States delegation withdrew from the Paris peace talks, however, and particularly after President Woodrow Wilson lost the 1921 election and isolationism became the order of the day, the idea was shelved, until Hitler's *Drang nach Osten* gave it a new urgency. Plans for closer political and economic cooperation between the states of the Danube region were proposed by George Messersmith, former United States ambassador to Vienna and then Deputy Secretary of State, in 1937-38, and subsequently, in 1939, by Robert D. Coe, who had the East Central European desk in the Department of State.[8]

Sumner Welles was the first powerful supporter of the idea within the State Department, but, on the evidence of John F. Montgomery, the United States ambassador to Budapest at the time, and of Archduke Otto von Habsburg, President Roosevelt himself "was planning a Danubian Confederation to unify the Danube region".[9] By 1942, the time the Advisory Committee started its work, postwar economic and political cooperation between the countries of Eastern Europe was taken for granted, and it was only natural that the Political Subcommittee, in charge of regional planning, should give it considerable attention. Eight entire sessions were devoted to the matter in the spring and summer of 1942, and the issue was returned to periodically in 1943 and 1944. Of the concrete proposals discussed, four were considered particularly carefully: those of Wladislaw Sikorski, of Edvard Beneš, of Otto von Habsburg, and the plan jointly worked out by Tibor Eckhardt and János Pelényi. Sikorski, the head of the London-based Polish government-in-exile, advocated a loose, primarily economic confederation of all the states lying between the Baltic Sea and the Adriatic, and Germany and the Soviet Union. Beneš's idea, which enjoyed the support of a number of the exiled politicians of the countries concerned, was two confederations: a Balkan federation centering on Yugoslavia and Greece, and a Central European federation centering on Poland and Czechoslovakia. The Yugoslav-Greek pledge of cooperation of January 15, 1942, and the Polish-Czechoslovak agreement of January 19 of the same year seemed to have laid the groundwork for such a system. Archduke Otto's proposal was a Danubian federation of the lands of the former Habsburg Monarchy, one in which dynastic and national aspirations were reconciled in the spirit of the twentieth century. Though this never concretely specified, it was clear that he himself was to be the Habsburg at the helm of this federation. The Eckhardt-Pelényi proposal envisioned three loosely-knit federative units, the Balkan, the Polish-Baltic, and the Danubian — the last much like the Danubian Union envisioned by Archduke Otto, consisting of Austria, Hungary, Bohemia, Slovakia, Transylvania and perhaps Croatia.[10]

The Political Subcommittee examined the above proposals from two salient points of view: security and economic viability. The security consideration meant that they wanted the new federation to be proof against a possible German or Russian attack, and even a joint Russo-German aggression, as in 1939. As Undersecretary of State Welles noted at the first, May 9 session of the Political Subcommittee which he chaired, "If such an organization can be established, it would be a counterpoise to both Russia and Germany."[11] It was noted that international security was by no means independent of the issue of peace in the region, and some argued that a federative solution was desirable precisely from the point of view of world peace.

The other main consideration, economic rationality, involved establishing a unit of the size optimal for a domestic market, so that a functional economy might serve to alleviate some of the social tensions endemic to the region, and become the basis of a functioning democracy. As Sumner Welles put it:

> The people of Eastern Europe must be given the opportunity to achieve at last those standards of existence which modern civilization regards as minimum. The experience of the past twenty-five years has shown clearly that objective cannot be attained so long as the whole economy of the East European nations is fractionalized, and so long as the economic policies practiced during the past quarter of a century persist. ...Without a higher living standard, ...these vast areas will continue to be a primary source of danger to the peace and order of the world.[12]

Both security and economic considerations argued for the Subcommittee's taking a stand for as large and as strong a units possible already at its very first sitting. Pasvolsky maintained that what would be ideal was for the region to be self-sufficient, like the United States. There were, however, geographic impediments to this. The areas that were to join in the confederation were only partly complementary in their economies, and thus the constituent units would continue to be obliged to trade with nations outside the federation as well. The goal, in any case, was autarky as far as possible, and this meant treating the region as one, and not broken into smaller units. Armstrong felt that security considerations pointed in the same direction, and "presented the view that it is of importance to organize these areas in the strongest possible way. This, he said, is a fundamental part of the establishment of peace in Europe."[13] Pasvolsky's stand for as large and as strong a unit as possible effectively ruled out the Eckhardt-Pelényi plan for a tripartite region, and also Archduke Otto's proposal, which had left out the Balkans and the Polish-Baltic Sea region. What remained was Sikorski's suggestion, and perhaps Beneš's. But Armstrong adduced very concrete arguments against Otto's proposal over and above the security and viability points of view. Unlike Sumner Welles, who wanted at least to give "the conception of the reconstitution of Austria-Hungary" due consideration, Armstrong was categorical in his rejection: "...This would be going back to something which it had been necessary to destroy at the end of the last war — it would be a re-creation of a principal factor in creating the last war." But even if the Department of State were receptive to the Habsburg plan, he added, the majority of the nations concerned were certain not to be.

Armstrong must have been very persuasive, and the majority on the Committee probably shared his views, for the possibility of a Habsburg restoration was never again discussed. Armstrong was no less categorical in his repudiation of the Eckhardt-Pelényi plan, and one must concede that his point was well made: "...The motive of Eckhardt's proposals seemed to be that of trying to restore as much of Austria-Hungary (especially Hungary) as possible. Transylvania, for example, was included." The Sikorski plan, he noted, "was a little less self-seeking," for "the larger the group, the less power Poland would necessarily have."[14]

Another point at issue in connection with the proposed federation was its precise nature and organization, i.e. the measure of autonomy the member states would retain, and the competence of the organs of central government. The majority on the Subcommittee agreed that given the legacy of national conflict and non-cooperation in the region, confederation was, at best, a long-range goal; initially, what was realistic was a loose federation of sorts. The issue arose as to how far it was necessary or feasible to carry economic cooperation over into the political sphere. Some of the members would have been content to see no more than a tariff and currency union for a start. Others insisted on the need for close political cooperation as well, arguing that in the twentieth century, there could be no economic cooperation without political coordination.

The Political Subcommittee dealt very little with the matter of borders, leaving it to the Territorial Subcommittee to do so. It did, however, declare that the confederation must aim to bring about "cohesive national groups," and that possibly, border adjustments would need to be made to this end. Furthermore, the creation of smaller national units than the ones existing at the time was not out of the question.[15] The points on which the Political Subcommittee had reached a consensus as of June 19, 1942, were outlined in a few pages by the research staff, the gist of which reads as follows:

> The regional organization should have the form not of a federation but of a union of independent and sovereign states, cooperating for limited objectives through common non-legislative institutions, loosely rather than tightly organized. Provisionally the union is considered as including all states of Central and Eastern Europe between Russia and Germany from and including Estonia on the North to Austria on the West and Greece on the South.

The loose federation was to be headed by a Political Council, which was to include two delegates from every country: the prime minister, and the speaker of the house, or their proxies. Initially, the Political Council was to have minimal jurisdiction, but its competence was to grow in time. The Economic Council was to another joint institution, its task being to coordinate economic cooperation within the federation, and trade with non-member states. A Court of Appeal was to decide in case of dispute among the members. Though every member state was to maintain independent foreign relations and security forces of its own, the outline included the setting up of a joint defensive force as well.[16] The Political Subcommittee returned to the Mid-European Union issue at several sessions in late 1942 and early 1943. One reason for this was that they had "polled" the émigré politicians of the region, and had found little enthusiasm for a plan that wanted to see the entire region become one federal unit. As Anne O'Hare McCormick reported to the Subcommittee:

> All of these persons had favored a federation, but all had differed as to its territorial extent. In the Danubian area,... it was felt that if the Balkans were brought into the same federation, their low standard of living would tend to drag down that of the Danubian area. On the other hand, the Balkans also felt that federation with the Danubian area would be disadvantageous to them.[17]

That a federation embracing the entire region would indeed, be problematic was the conclusion arrived at also by Notter, Mosley, and other members of the research staff. They concluded their analysis of February 10, 1943, by pointing out that an Eastern Europe spreading from Finland to Greece was illusory in the extreme: the areas involved looked back on no common history, were heterogeneous in respect of culture and religion, and, in fact, had absolutely nothing in common besides their backwardness and subjection to Germany. With no internal cohesion to bind it, they noted, it was very dubious if this test-tube baby of a federation would prove in any way viable. Notter and his group believed the federation would stand no real chance unless the victorious allies or some international body were to assume protectorate over it "for an indefinite period."[18]

The Political Subcommittee sought to bridge the chasm between its own recommendations and the reservations of the exiles and its own research staff by espousing, as of early 1943, also "a possible but less desirable alternative," a plan calling for two East European federations, a "Balkan" and a "northern" union.[19] This, naturally raised other problems, such, for instance, as where Austria and Hungary were to belong, and even Croatia and Slovenia, in the absence of a unified Yugoslavia. Since the "Danubian countries" as such belonged organically neither to the Balkan unit nor the Polish-Czech unit, a number of people began to toy with the idea of a South German-Austrian-Danubian unit,[20] which, of course, was tantamount to the rehabilitation of the Eckhardt-Pelényi, and the Otto von Habsburg proposals. As of the summer of 1943, the Political Subcommittee was able to come up with no unanimous stand on this matter. After that, it no longer wanted to, for it would have been senseless to force a decision on a matter which, more and more obviously, would fall to the Soviet Union to decide on and not the United States or Great Britain.

It was in December of 1941, on the occasion of Foreign Secretary Anthony Eden's visit to Moscow, that Stalin first informed his Western allies that one of the Soviet Union's goals is to restore the borders agreed in the Molotov-Ribbentrop Pact, in short, to reannex certain parts of Finland, the Baltic States, Eastern Poland, and Bessarabia. Stalin also mentioned that he regards Eastern Europe and the western half of Central Europe as likewise of immediate interest to the Soviet Union, and that it might be best to divide Europe in British and Soviet spheres of influence.[21] The British and the Americans refused to sign a secret agreement as to the postwar territorial division of spoils, and publicly insisted that territorial disputes will be settled after the cessation of hostilities by a peace conference more fair-minded than the one of 1919-1920 had been.

At the strictly confidential sittings of the various peace preparatory committees, however, they were already discussing what of Stalin's demands might be acceptable. Adolf A. Berle's diary entry of May 2, 1942, reads: "He [Roosevelt] said that he would not particularly mind about the Russians taking quite a chunk of territory; they might have the Baltic republics, and eastern Poland, and even perhaps the Bukovina, as well as Bessarabia."[22] The leading members of the Advisory Committee, however, were not so obliging. At the May 30 sitting of the Political Subcommittee, both Pasvolsky and Anne O'Hare McCormick maintained that the Soviet Union will be satisfied with Lithuania and with Narvik being made a free port; there was no immediate threat to the other two Baltic states. Their confidence rested on their belief that Britain and the United States would be able to use the leverage the latter had gained through its Lend-Lease shipments to put effective economic and political pressure on the Soviet Union when the time came.[23] For this reason, Estonia and Lithuania were also included as potential members of the East European federation in the research staff summary of June 19, 1942.

For the moment, there was no talk of in Washington what was to become of the areas west of the Soviet Union's 1941 borders. In the second half of 1942 and in 1943, however, the Subcommittee did debate whether or not the planned Mid-European Union was compatible with the Soviet Union's real and putative interests. On the basis of the findings submitted by the research staff, by the end of 1942, it was generally agreed that the Soviet Union "is inclined to look upon this whole region of Central and Eastern Europe as properly within the Russian sphere of influence and to view with a certain suspicion the Polish-Czechoslovak Confederation," and plans for an East-European federation in general.[24]

Bowman and his associates analyzed in detail the pros and cons of such a union from the Soviet point of view. They pointed out that a confederation of this kind can come about only with the concurrence and support of the Soviet Union, and by no means against its will. They recommended that the union's originally envisioned defensive function vis-a-vis both its eastern and western neighbor must be modified to emphasize the German danger, and the need to ward it off. Moscow must be convinced that an economically prosperous and politically stable confederation is much preferable, from the point of view of its own security, to a subjugated or divided East-Central Europe. A confederation of this sort "can be established, if at all, only by the Western democracies in cooperation with Russia..."[25]

The shift in emphasis within the Department of State is most conspicuous in Sumner Welles's statements. The Undersecretary of State, who enjoyed Roosevelt's confidence, had initially, as we have seen, envisioned the Mid-European Union as a counterweight to Germany and the Soviet Union alike. By the summer of 1942, however, Welles was playing up a different aspect: "...The proposed union would not in any case be a menace to the Soviet Union. It would in fact act as a buffer between the Soviet Union and the Western powers, which would be helpful to the Soviets in case the international organization should at some time break down."[26] Arguments of this sort, of course, carried very little weight with the makers of Soviet policy. In a letter of June 7, 1943 to the British Government, Vyacheslav M. Molotov, People's Commissar for Foreign Affairs, left no doubt as to the Soviet stand: "As regards the question of the creation of a federation in Europe of Poland, Czechoslovakia, Yugoslavia and Greece including Hungary and Austria, the Soviet Government are unwilling to pledge themselves as regards the creation of such a federation, and also consider the inclusion of Hungary and Austria within it as unsuitable."[27]

When, in spite of this, Sir Anthony Eden suggested discussing the British federative solution at the October, 1943, meeting of foreign ministers in Moscow, the Soviets absolutely refused to place it on the agenda. The proposed federation, noted Molotov, smacked too much of the cordon sanitaire set up against the Soviet Union after World War I.[28] The message was repeated in Teheran in early December, when Stalin told Churchill he "did not want to see Austria reunited to Hungary or any other strong unit formed."[29] After the Soviet victory at Stalingrad and Kursk, while the Western allied offensive got bogged down in Italy, Soviet foreign policy objectives became more clear-cut, and Soviet insistence on them more self-assured.

By the end of 1943, United States diplomacy had more or less officially agreed to let Stalin have his way in Eastern Europe. In Teheran, Roosevelt agreed to have Poland "pushed" west, and agreed to the 1941 borders in the north and south as well. Somewhat earlier, Cordell Hull had told a fellow diplomat that he could, of course, go to Moscow to discuss the Baltic States and Poland's eastern borders, but in that case "he ought to take some of the United States Army and Navy with him."[30] An expedition of this kind, however, was something that neither Hull nor Roosevelt, nor any other American political force of consequence wanted to see. For though the United States had its own version of the postwar Eastern Europe that would be desirable, it was not in its interest to use military force to achieve it. This conviction was clearly reflected in all the statements made by the Joint Chiefs of Staff and the Department of Defense in 1943-44. Repeatedly, these communiqués emphasized that the United States was not to get involved "in the area of the Balkans, including Austria," and that "the Balkans and their troubles were beyond the sphere of proper United States action."[31]

In the course of the Moscow and Teheran conferences, it became an accepted fact that Central and Eastern Europe were particularly significant from the point of view of Soviet security, and that this gave Moscow certain privileges. The question, as of the end of 1943, therefore, was not whether or not Europe would be divided, but how divided it would be, and where the line of demarcation would lie. This latter set of questions, however, was the wellspring of much animated debate in Washington throughout 1944.

The controversy produced two camps, the "cooperationists" and the "confrontationists". Walter Lippman, like Armstrong a veteran of the Inquiry, and an influential political theorist though basically an outsider, was one leading spokesman of the cooperationists; Henry Wallace was another. As Lippman saw it, the time was past when the small states could feign independence, seesawing between sets of great powers all the while. The postwar world would consist of three, perhaps four, spheres of influence, and the small nations would have no choice but voluntarily submit to the directives of the dominant great power allotted them by geopolitics. In view of the fact that the Atlantic Charter nations had very little direct economic or strategic interest in Central and Eastern Europe, the countries of that region, much as they might deplore this on historical, cultural and psychological grounds, would have to accommodate to the Soviet Union.[32]

The confrontationist point of view, shared by Roosevelt's successor, Harry Truman, was formulated by Sumner Welles, who had resigned from government in the fall of 1943. Though Welles, too recognized the 1941 borders, and somewhat hypocritically assumed that "...the peoples of the Baltic States desire to form an integral part of the Union of Soviet Socialist Republics," he was determined to put a stop to further Soviet expansion. As late as 1944, Welles stood firm by the need for independent states in East Central Europe, joined together in some kind of federation.[33]

The Advisory Committee itself, specifically a new subcommittee headed by Armstrong dealing with the reorganization of Europe, finally took a good look at the new situation in February and March of 1944, and took a stand on the matter of the future of Eastern Europe. That the region east of Danzig (Gdansk)-Sudetenland-Trieste line would belong to the Soviet sphere of influence they took for granted. It was a *fait accompli*. American policy, they argued, would depend on how the Soviets interpreted the concept of sphere of influence. If they meant by it something akin to what the United States meant by the Monroe Doctrine, and, on the pattern of the Soviet-Czechoslovak agreement of 1943, made treaties of friendship and cooperation with the various countries, thus obliging them to an amicable foreign policy without interfering in their domestic governments or their trade relations with any other nation, then this was something the Americans could hardly take exception to. If, on the other hand, the Soviet aim was the "annexation" or "subjugation" of the states of Eastern Europe, this had to be thwarted as unacceptable. On the basis of testimony heard from Charles E. Bohlen, First Secretary at the Moscow embassy, and subsequently United States ambassador to Moscow, the subcommittee more or less assumed that the war will have exhausted the Soviet Union, especially its economy so thoroughly as to make it impossible for it to aim at more than a "minimal program" akin to that embodied in the Monroe Doctrine.[34]

Proceeding on this assumption, Armstrong's subcommittee still did not completely give up on the planned regional federation, or at least cooperation. It was clear, however, that this cooperation, if it came about at all, would be a far cry from what the Advisory Committee envisaged in the spring and summer of 1942. That official Washington had more and more reservations in connection with the original proposal is indicated also by the change in terminology. Instead of the terms "Mid-European Union," "confederation" or "federation," the 1944 documents, for the most part, contain the expression "regional groupings." A memo in connection with "a Democratic Danubian or East European Federation," dated January 22, 1944, notes: "At the present such regional units are viewed with disfavor in official quarters."[35]

3. *Hungary's Borders*

Both President Roosevelt and his Wilsonian Secretary of State believed that the most important guarantee of lasting peace in the postwar world was the creation of an international organization which, unlike the League of Nations, was strong enough, if it saw fit, to defend the *status quo* in the face of any aggression anywhere in the world. At the same time, they were only too aware of the fact that the only *status quo* that could be preserved in the long run was one which did away with the territorial injustices preserved, or created by the previous postwar settlement. A great deal of the Advisory Committee's efforts, therefore, were focused on identifying the various territorial disputes the world over, and coming up with proposals for their solution. It was specifically the job of the territorial Subcommittee to do so. The members of the Territorial Subcommittee did not aim at a radical revision of territorial boundaries. Though their chief goal was ethnic fairness, at the very first sessions they introduced the "Principle of Minimum Change," and this was to be the guideline in decisions involving both borders and population exchanges. In practice, this meant that they wanted to change the borders established in the wake of the World War I only to the extent absolutely necessary on ethnic, strategic, or economic grounds. Accordingly, they decided to look into not borders as such, but only the most disputed segments of each country's frontier.[36]

Besides the principles of ethnic fairness and of minimum change, the matter of which side the given country was on in the war also entered into the Territorial Subcommittee's deliberations. We must note, however, that the idea of "punishment" or "retribution" was never a dominant consideration, not even in the case of Germany or Japan. In the case of "satellite countries" such as Finland, Bulgaria, Romania, and Hungary, it was a very minor consideration indeed. Roosevelt and his Secretary of State, as is known, considered these countries "victims," not aggressors, and did not take seriously their declarations of war.

Most members of the Territorial Subcommittee shared their view. Thus, as we shall see in a moment, the Subcommittee not only strove for ethnic fairness in the case of two enemy countries, but, in the case of an allied and an enemy country, was capable of deciding in favor of the latter.[37] Of the over fifty areas of tension identified and examined by the Territorial Subcommittee, thirty-four were in Europe, and of these, twenty-four in Eastern Europe (*cf.* Map 1). Except for where Hungary bordered on Austria, every section of the Hungarian border, the Yugoslav-Hungarian, the Slovak-Hungarian, and the Romanian-Hungarian stretches of the frontier, was included among the areas in dispute. A fourth area of territorial tension with an impact on Hungary's future, and one separately listed and treated, was Ruthenia, a region that had belonged to Hungary until 1920, was part of Czechoslovakia between 1920 and 1939, and was reannexed to Hungary in 1939. The Soviet Union annexed it in 1944, and it has been part of the Ukraine ever since.

The Subcommittee first dealt with the Slovak-Hungarian border in the summer of 1942. By that time, Mosely and his research staff had prepared a number of background studies on the ethnic composition of the region, on Slovakia's development between 1919 and 1938, and on the findings of the American peace delegation of 1919-1920. Though their report included the relevant data of the Hungarian census of 1910, because of the alleged distortions in the Hungarian count, and because the Czech figures were more recent, they took the 1930 Czechoslovak census as the more reliable. On this basis, the ethnic Hungarian population of Slovakia without Ruthenia, was not 650,000 (as the more impartial figures of the 1921 Czechoslovak census also showed), but only 571,000.[38] Even so, it was clear that the Slovak-Hungarian border drawn in 1920 was considerably farther south than the ethnic frontier, and that it would be neither fair, nor expedient, unless one wanted to feed Hungarian irredentist feeling by restoring the 1920 demarcation line.

Since they were dealing with two enemy nations, Anne O'Hare McCormick suggested that they might leave the 1938-1939 borders well enough alone. The majority on the Subcommittee, however, rejected this proposal. In the course of the debate, Mosely pointed out that the First Vienna Award had been based on the Hungarian census of 1910, and was, thus, prejudicial to the Slovak population. He noted, moreover, that the 1939 reannexation of Ruthenia had absolutely nothing to do with the ethnic composition of the population. It had been strategic decision bolstered with historical arguments. Thus, rather than keeping the 1938-39 borders or restoring those imposed by the Treaty of Trianon, he recommended a compromise solution which, in effect, split the difference between the two boundary lines. The new border would involve no real hardship for Czechoslovakia's transportation system or economy, and was maximally fair from the ethnic point of view. The Czechoslovak census of 1930 had shown that Hungarians comprised the absolute majority of the population in ten border districts: six of them in the Žitný Ostrov (Csallóköz or Grosse Schuett), three in central Slovakia, and one in eastern Slovakia. It was this area of 2,355 square miles, with a population of 396,000, seventy-eight percent (309,000) of which was Hungarian, that Mosely wanted to see returned to Hungary. He also thought it desirable that the southern parts of the fifteen districts north of the border districts, areas of mixed population, with the Hungarians comprising the largest single group (for instance, the areas around Galánta and Érsekújvár), also belong, wholly or in part, to Hungary. On this proposal, the size of the pre-1938 Czechoslovak region, excluding Ruthenia, that would have remained in Hungarian hands was a minimum of 2,700 square miles, and a maximum of 4,500 square miles, with populations of 484,000 and 854,000, respectively. Redrawing the borders along the above lines would have decreased the ratio of ethnic Hungarians within Hungary's population to 64 percent in the first scenario, and to 59 percent on the second (*cf.* Map 2).

It was to improve these ratios somewhat that Mosely recommended that some measure of population exchange take place as well. The Territorial Subcommittee had Mosely's proposal on its agenda on five separate occasions. The main, and only serious, opposition to it came from Hamilton Fish Armstrong, who adduced every possible argument in the effort to leave Hungary with as little of the disputed territory as possible. He pointed out that Mosely's proposal was inconsistent with the Principle of Minimum Change, and did not take into account that Czechoslovakia was a victim of Nazi aggression, while Hungary was one of the aggressors. Armstrong went so far as to state that, because Czechoslovakia was so much more democratic than Hungary, "there never was any very articulate irredentist movement among the Magyars in Czechoslovakia," and that the cry "No, no, never!" had hardly ever had much of an echo north of the borders drawn at Trianon. The most Armstrong could envision was that the six southwestern districts that comprised the Csallóköz be recognized as belonging to Hungary.[40]

The vehemence of Armstrong's arguments was not something that other members of the Subcommittee could match, nor, probably, did they really want to. For while they did not agree with him on every detail, they did not really try to refute his arguments. The vote on September 4 rejected Mosely's proposal, and recommended that Hungary be allowed to keep only the above six southwestern districts, an area of 1,400 square miles, with a population of 275,000, 79 percent of which was ethnic Hungarian (*cf.* Map 2, Table 2). By way of a compromise, they left open the matter of where the three central and the one eastern district along the border would belong. The Subcommittee recommended that further research and discussion precede any decision on this issue.[41]

Transylvania, which had been part of Hungary prior to 1920, was part of Romania between 1920 and 1940, and was split between the two by the Second Vienna Award, i.e. between 1940 and 1944, was discussed by the Territorial Subcommittee on three consecutive occasions in February of 1943. The rapporteur was John C. Campbell, a thirty-two year old assistant professor of history, who, like Mosely, had graduated from Harvard and had also got his Ph.D. there in 1940. Campbell outlined four possible solutions, of which he deemed none to be particularly satisfactory. Restoration of the borders determined at Trianon was undesirable because even the 1930 Romanian census figures showed Trianon to have placed a million and a half ethnic Hungarians under Romanian rule. "It would," as Campbell put it, "perpetuate a difficult minority situation." Restoration of the pre-Trianon *status quo*, i.e. returning all of Transylvania to Hungary, was even worse: it would create a minority of three million Romanians, and was difficult to reconcile with the Principle of Minimum Change. The third possibility presented for consideration was to keep the borders drawn by the 1940 partition. Economic and infrastructure considerations argued against that solution, as well as the fact that the partition had annexed to Hungary not only the purely ethnic Hungarian easternmost region, the Székely region (Székelyföld) and the western regions with their predominantly ethnic Hungarian populations, but also the million Romanians living in the ethnically mixed regions. The fourth possibility was that of an independent Transylvania. "The idea of an autonomous Transylvania held certain attractions but it was hard to say how it would work since it would not be a satisfactory solution either to Hungary or to Rumania or to the local Magyar and Rumanian population."

Though Campbell conceded that there might indeed be such a thing as sense of Transylvanian identity, he thought it probable that both ethnic groups would rather see an independent Transylvania added to their own nation-state. Like Campbell, the members of the Subcommittee, too, found themselves in a quandary. Anne O'Hare McCormick ventured the opinion that independence was still likely to lead to less friction than "if the area were either under Rumanian or Hungarian sovereignty". Bowman and Armstrong, however, were both adamant on this score. Armstrong considered the idea of an independent Transylvania nothing short of "foolish and comic". He added that "the proposal for an autonomous Transylvania had been put forward by Otto of Habsburg as a way of detaching some territory from Rumania without creating too much of a row." Bowman, too, believed that independence would only make for a permanent state of undeclared war between Romanians and Hungarians for the possession of Transylvania. Alternative solutions, however, were not proposed.

On February 5, 1943, thus, the Territorial Subcommittee closed its first session on Transylvania without a resolution being passed. The only point they all agreed on was that Transylvania would have to come under the supervision of Allied or United Nations forces for the first few postwar years to word off the danger of armed conflict between its Hungarian and Romanian population. Deputy Secretary of State Berle, who had raised this possibility, expressed his hope that such a transitional period would provide time for tempers to cool, enough, perhaps, for the two ethnic groups to themselves agree on some kind of long-term solution, without interference from the great powers.[42]

The next session, on February 12, likewise closed without a resolution. Campbell and Mosely gave a detailed account of Transylvania's ethnic composition, with the conclusion that the matter of the Székely region had to be distinguished from that of the predominantly Hungarian strip along the border, and different solutions be found for each. To this, Adolf Berle made a quite unexpected counter-proposal:

> It might be a more fruitful approach to the Transylvanian problem to abandon all efforts to disentangle the population and to start from the theory of constructing a state. By that method one would concentrate on what would appear to be the most powerful element in the population, the one most likely to maintain itself as a group, and turn over to that group a territory included within the frontier most likely to lead to its stability. This would mean either enlarging Hungary as far as the Carpathians or the recreation of Versailles' Rumania.[43]

At the third session on Transylvania, the Subcommittee again reviewed all the possible approaches to the problem. Cavendish W. Cannon, head of the State Department's Southeastern European Department, advocated that they apt for an independent Transylvania, or rather, for a trialistic solution — loose federation of Romania, Transylvania and Hungary — reminiscent of an old idea of a former prime minister of Hungary, Count István Bethlen. Bowman, Mosely and Campbell were inclined to have the border strip go to Hungary, with the Székely region to enjoy autonomy within Romania. Armstrong continued to oppose the idea of an independent Transylvania, and wanted to see the whole go to Romania, except for a narrow border strip. Finally, John MacMurray, an adviser to Cordell Hull, took a stand for restoring the Trianon borders on the grounds that it was impossible to come to a fair decision in the matter of the Hungarian-Romanian territorial dispute. With no consensus forthcoming, Bowman adjourned the meeting, with hopes that those present would continue to study the matter and arrive at a resolution at the next session.[44]

Bowman's intentions notwithstanding, the Territorial Subcommittee never again returned to the question of Transylvania. What was taken to be its recommendation was the minutes of the March 2, 1943 meeting, which summarized the proposals that had been made in a way that gave preference to two of them. Most highly preferred was the idea that Transylvania should belong to Romania, with the Székely region enjoying wide-ranging autonomy, and the Romanian-Hungarian border revised to coincide with the linguistic border, or to lie just a little to the east of it. In second place was the notion of an independent state of Transylvania, which was to be a member of the proposed Mid-European Union, or a condominium of Romania and Hungary.[45]

An interesting feature of the Subcommittee debates on Transylvania was that the members of the Department of State frequently found themselves arguing for positions diametrically opposed to those of the experts. The latter tended to take ethnic composition as their point of departure, and offered solutions which differed from that worked out at Trianon only on points of detail. The former, particularly Berle and Cannon, were much more original and daring in their approach, and tended to support solutions favorable to Hungary.

That the State Department was inclined to favor Hungary and Transylvania's autonomy probably had a great deal to do with the Soviet Union's expected penetration of East Central Europe. In this scenario it seemed a wise move to try to prop up Hungary. Cannon, in fact, practically said as much at the third session, when he argued that separating Transylvania from Romania would make it harder for the Soviet Union to advance to the west, and in this sense, the proposal served Romania's interest as well.[46]

There is also some likelihood that in the two weeks between the first and the third of the Subcommittee's sessions on Transylvania, Otto von Habsburg, Tibor Eckhardt, János Pelényi, as well as some of the leading Hungarian democratic exiles, Oscar Jászi, Rusztem Vámbéry — working in concert or in a series of independent actions — had made good use of their contacts in the White House and in the Department of State.

It is well known that President Roosevelt, Sumner Welles and other members of the government met with Archduke Otto on quite a regular basis, and that the latter, in his own plans, always spoke of Transylvania as an independent member of the proposed federation. Eckhardt and Pelényi, too, were for Transylvanian autonomy, and they, as we have already had occasion to note, were on good terms with Deputy Secretary of State Berle. Though the acrimony between the conservative and the democratic groupings of Hungarian émigrés was, by that time, vituperative, and the two groups regularly denounced one another to their American contacts, it is highly probable that on the matter of Transylvania, they closed ranks. This is borne out by the series of articles in the Amerikai Magyar Népszava in the summer of 1943, in which Jászi and a number of his associates came out in favor of an autonomous Transylvania within a Danubian Confederation.[47]

There is also the letter Jászi wrote to Rusztem Vámbéry in 1942, in which Cavendish W. Cannon, who had proposed the notion of an autonomous Transylvania at the Territorial Subcommittee's third session, is referred to as "our mutual friend."[48] A final evidence of the activism of the Hungarian lobby during the Transylvania sessions is a report sent from Washington by a member of the Romanian secret service in February of 1943:

> Finally, Eckhardt has succeeded in convincing his friends in the United States that it is in the interest of the Anglo-Saxons to have a powerful Hungary, specially as a counter-balance to the Soviet Union. But in order to be powerful, Hungary needs Transylvania, which has many resources enabling Hungary to develop a big industry.[49]

This was practically a verbatim summary of the arguments Cannon used at the Subcommittee's third session on Transylvania. The stand taken by the "other side" was motivated primarily by considerations of ethnic fairness, and the Principle of Minimum Change. This, certainly was true of Mosely and Campbell, who were young enough to be impartial in the matter. In Bowman's case, loyalty to the "joint" decisions of 1919 probably played a part; in Armstrong's, his sympathy for Romania, and antipathy to Hungary.

The matter of the Yugoslav-Hungarian border was discussed on February 12, at the Subcommittee's second session on Transylvania. The rapporteur in this case was Cyril Edwin Black, an assistant professor at Princeton. One of the youngest members of the research staff, Black was not yet thirty years old, and, like Campbell and Mosely, was a Harvard graduate.

Based on his background research, Black distinguished five separate areas where the borders were open to dispute. Along the southwestern frontier established at Trianon, there were twenty-eight predominantly ethnic Hungarian communities in an area of Wend settlement; these he recommended that the postwar adjustment recognize as belonging to Hungary. The greater part of the Prekomurje, however, which was inhabited by Wends, and the predominantly Croatian Medjumurje, Hungarian territories since the spring of 1941, Black considered to be parts of Yugoslavia on ethnic grounds. Along the southern border, in Baranja, Baćka, and in the Banat, he recommended a compromise solution reminiscent of the American proposal of 1919, and one that followed linguistic borders to the extent possible.

The compromise would have left about as many Hungarians (150,000) under Yugoslav rule as there would have been Yugoslavs under Hungarian rule (174,000) if the recommended northern districts were returned to Hungary. This northern tract, an area of 2,476 square miles, had a population of 486,000, whose ethnic distribution, according to the 1921 Yugoslav census, was the following: ethnic Hungarians, forty-seven percent; South Slavs, thirty-six percent, and German speakers, sixteen percent (*cf.* Map 3).

Black's consistent attempt to implement the principle of ethnic fairness was, however, taken exception to in this case by Berle and Cannon, the very people who had been inclined to side with Hungary in the matter of its borders with Romania. Yugoslavia was an ally, and they took its side, more precisely, Serbia's side. Clearly there was no guarantee that the Yugoslav federation could be restored after the war. But Hungary, noted Berle "had broken its word and had behaved badly" in breaking its 1940 Treaty of Perpetual Friendship with Yugoslavia, and in having joined in Germany's 1941 aggression against it. Certainly, this was not the kind of conduct that they wanted to see rewarded at Yugoslavia's expense. The issue was decided by Pasvolsky. The head of the Advisory Committee found no reason for the United States to recommend changes to the pre-1941 Yugoslav-Hungarian border, and the Subcommittee voted unanimously for the *status quo ante bellum.*[50]

On Subcarpathian Ruthenia, the research staff completed its report in late October of 1943. Of the possible options, Harry N. Howard, a senior member of the team, and the one who took over for Mosely when the latter was absent, considered the reunification of Czechoslovakia and Subcarpathian Ruthenia "the best possible solution." He recommended neither the creation of an autonomous Carpatho-Ukraine nor the region's autonomy within either the Ukraine, or the Soviet Union, or Poland, or Hungary. He did, however, have his reservations about the proposed solution. "Simple restoration, however, might not solve the problem, since it might leave open the door for new revisionism on the part of Hungary, or possibly on the part of the Soviet Union." By way of a preventive measure, Howard thought that certain border adjustments might perhaps be made in favor of Hungary in the southwestern corner of the region, where even the Czechoslovak census of 1930 had put the ratio of Hungarians in excess of fifty percent. What argued against such change, on the other hand, was the layout of the transportation and communication network, particularly of the railway system. To leave with Hungary an area even approximating the one it had regained by the First Vienna Award, argued Howard, would cut the entire region off from Czechoslovakia, and would make communication between the various settlements of the region very difficult.[51]

Howard's report was distributed to the members of the Subcommittee on November 12, 1943, with the purpose of putting it on the agenda for debate in the near future. In fact, it never was put on the agenda. For the remainder of the year, the Subcommittee dealt exclusively with Asian affairs. Its last session was on December 17, 1943, since the Subcommittee as such was dissolved as part of the Advisory Committee's reorganization.

For, by summer of 1943, the Advisory Committee had accomplished a great deal of what it had been set up to do, while the series of Allied victories raised hopes that the war was rapidly drawing to a conclusion. It was this hope that led Secretary of State Hull to reorganize the peace preparatory committee. Though certain of its subcommittees, for instance, the Territorial Subcommittee, continued to sit for the rest of the year, the emphasis shifted from debate to summaries which, as Hull put it, "can serve as a basis of more specific considerations of policies and proposals." The task of recapitulating the debates and whatever proposals had emerged fell to the research staff, restructured as the Division of Political Studies already in January of 1943.[52]

The summaries dealing with Hungary were prepared by the research staff between the summer of 1943 and January of 1944. They presented a detailed account of the debates up to that time, including the Subcommittee's proposals. Still, reading them, one cannot help detecting small shifts of emphasis, and perhaps a selective grouping of arguments and counter-arguments. The purpose, one feels, is to make the original expert recommendations – based, as far as possible, on the principle of ethnic fairness – seem far more attractive than the Subcommittee's subsequent suggestions, motivated, without a doubt, by more partial considerations. We might, thus, with some exaggeration, see these documents as the circumspect "rebellion" of the disinterested young staff of experts against the political motives of the older generation, and the strategic considerations of the pragmatic career diplomats.

The summary dealing with the Slovak-Hungarian border, for instance, was prepared by Harry N. Howard in Mosely's absence who was away as consultant to the London-based European Advisory Committee. It offered as the first of the proposed solutions the Subcommittee's resolution that Hungary be allowed the six districts of the Csallóköz. Very fairly, it notes, further, that "the Territorial Subcommittee did not favor suggesting wider territorial concessions to Hungary." It goes on, however, to present as an equally possible alternate solution one that Mosely had held to be optimal, but which Armstrong had repudiated in the strongest terms: namely, that the ten southern districts where ethnic Hungarians formed an absolute majority, as well as the southern parts of the adjacent six northern districts, be ceded to Hungary. Altogether, this would have meant an area of 2,740 square miles, with a population of 484,000, sixty-four percent of which was ethnic Hungarian (*cf.* Map 2, Table 3). "This solution would eliminate from Czechoslovakia as large a Hungarian population as is possible without serious economic and strategic injury to Czechoslovakia," noted Howard. This option also involved Mosely's recommended exchange of the approximately equal numbers of Hungarian and Slovak populations left on the wrong sides of the new border, "thereby eliminating the ethnic basis for any further irredentism."[53]

We see much the same story repeated in the case of the Yugoslav-Hungarian border. Black briefly stated the Territorial Subcommittee's advice that the entire disputed border region be given to Yugoslavia on political grounds, and that there had been no support for carving up the area by ethnic groupings. He then went on to describe his own proposal, the one the Subcommittee had more or less rejected as a possible compromise. "This solution has not been discussed by any of the subcommittees," he noted, bending the truth somewhat, to put it mildly. The only change his "compromise proposal" contained over the one he had presented in February was that the line of demarcation to run through Bačka and the Banat had been refined. The population of the area he proposed to be granted to Hungary fell from 486,000 to 435,000, with the figures for the South Slavic minorities dropping from 174,000 to 148,000. The number of ethnic Hungarians left in Yugoslavia by the new variant, on the other hand, rose from 150,000 to 160,000.[54] (*cf.* Map 3, Tables 3 and 4, Adjusted line.)

The summary most closely reflecting the Territorial Subcommittee's stand was the one dealing with Transylvania. The Subcommittee, as will be recalled, in the absence of a consensus, had postponed making a clear-cut recommendation for a later session never in fact held. Campbell's summary followed Berle and the Subcommittee's expressed hope in assuming that at the end of the war, Transylvania would, for a while, be occupied by Allied or United Nations troops. As to where Transylvania's temporary administrative borders were to be drawn, along the pre-Trianon line, the Trianon line, the 1940 line, or along a new line to be determined by the Allies arbitrarily or through plebiscite, the summary was undecided. Of the possible solutions, the two most preferred by the Subcommittee were recommended: border adjustments in Hungary's favor and an autonomous Székely region within Romania; or alternately, the "creation of an Autonomous or Independent Transylvania within a Federation or Union of East European or Danubian States." Neither the pre-Trianon nor the post-Trianon *status quo*, nor the validation of the Second Vienna Award, nor an autonomous Transylvania outside some federation was recommended.

As compared to the earlier documents treating of Transylvania's future, Campbell's August 1943 summary was a forward step in that it specified the size of the strip of land along the western border to be returned to Hungary: an area of 3,475 square miles, shown by the 1930 Romanian statistics to have a population of 591,000, fifty percent of which was ethnic Hungarian. The alternative recommendation, less closely based on ethnic boundaries, involved leaving Hungary in possession of 5,600 square miles of post-Trianon Romanian territory, with a population of 1,980,000, only thirty-six percent of which was ethnic Hungarian (*cf.* Map 4, the two top tables). For his part, Campbell unequivocally supported this latter solution. The first of his two reasons was that the Arad-Nagyvárad (Oradea, Grosswardein) railway would, in that case, run all the way on Hungarian soil, instead of criss-crossing the border at several points. The second was that, not counting the Székely region, this latter solution would leave roughly equal numbers, about half a million each, of Romanians and ethnic Hungarians under foreign rule, and the exchange of these populations, as Campbell saw it, would be relatively easy to effect.[55]

The abstract dealing with Subcarpathian Ruthenia differed from the Subcommittee presentation of late 1943 primarily in being much more constructive. For one thing, Howard specified the possible forms that the southwestern strip to be ceded to Hungary might take. He presented three options: recognition of the borders established in 1938 by the First Vienna Award; the purely token gesture of returning 125 square miles of the area to Hungary; and a "compromise solution" between the two extremes, which would leave Hungary with 535 square miles of the 731 square miles reannexed in 1938. Of the population of 90,000 involved, the 1930 Czechoslovak census specified fifty-nine percent as ethnic Hungarian, as compared to the 1910 Hungarian census figures also given by Howard, which put their ratio at eighty-eight percent (*cf.* Map 5). Howard's chief argument in support of the compromise solution was the consideration of ethnic fairness; the communications problem it would involve he deemed to be quite secondary, and one that could be remedied with the building of new railways.[56]

At the end of 1943, the research staff also reviewed the matter of the Austro-Hungarian border. Since their absolutely correct information was that Hungary was laying no "serious" claim to the Burgenland, more than seventy percent of which was German-speaking, the matter was not considered particularly problematic. It was taken for granted that after the war, the region would continue to belong to a once again independent Austria. This was the gist of the report submitted on November 8 by Mary Bradshaw, a new member of the research staff.[57]

The above-outlined summaries prepared by the research staff became the basis of "more specific considerations of policies and proposals," even as Hull had intended them to be. The groups that were to "consider" them were the Inter-Divisional Country and Area Committees set up in late summer of 1943, which set to work immediately, and continued to study the reports all of the first half of 1944. These Committees consisted of members of the research staff, and the officials of the Department of State involved with the countries and areas in question. Bowman, Armstrong, and other prestigious members of the Subcommittees, though called in for consultation, were not involved directly in this work either.[58]

The first of the Inter-Divisional Country and Area Committees to be set up, on August 12, 1943, was the Inter-Divisional Balkan and Danube Region Committee. Harry N. Howard was appointed chairman. By the spring of 1944, the Committee had submitted its recommendations regarding Hungary's borders in reports of a page or a little more. As compared to the research staff's summaries of 1943, these were both more concrete and more unambiguous, containing, for the most part, only the recommended solutions. For all that, they did leave room for some flexibility.

In the case of the Slovak-Hungarian border, for instance, the Committee recommended the cession to Hungary of only the six districts of the Csallóköz, on the grounds that Czechoslovakia's postwar government would not be willing to agree to more. It did not, however, rule out the possibility of supporting "a more just solution on a purely ethnic basis, "...i.e. the cession of ten entire districts, and parts of another six, if later circumstances should be favorable to its adoption."

In view of the military situation, and of the Soviet Union's expansionist plans, the Committee suggested alternative solutions in the case of Subcarpathian Ruthenia as well. If the post-war settlement was such that the region was returned to Czechoslovakia — the alternative the Committee preferred — they wanted to see the borders revised in a way "which would leave predominantly Magyar districts in Hungary" without, however, disrupting railway communications toward Slovakia. Should Subcarpathian Ruthenia end up as part of the Soviet Union, however, they wanted to see the borders redrawn to coincide with ethnic boundaries, independently of any other consideration.[59]

For the Yugoslav-Hungarian border, the Committee supported Black's compromise proposal. This meant that, as opposed to the

Territorial Subcommittee's stand, this higher-ranking Committee was for Hungary's keeping the northern part of the Baranja-Bačka-Banat region.[60]

No pithy recommendation was ever made concerning Transylvania, due, perhaps, to the significance of the matter, or perhaps to its basic insolvability. The Committee accepted the research staff's 1943 summary; the only change it made was to mark some of the solutions as "recommended" solutions. As a temporary measure in the immediate postwar period, it suggested keeping the 1940 borders, i.e. the ones established by the Second Vienna Award. As a long-term solution, it recommended that the strip stretching from Arad to Szatmár, an area of 5,600 square miles, with a population of 1,098,000, be ceded to Hungary, with the Székely region to enjoy autonomy within Romania. The idea of an independent Transylvania, until this phase a preferred solution, was listed as one of the possible, but not recommended solutions in this document of April 20, 1944.

The reason for this is probably that the idea of an East European federation of which an independent Transylvania was to be a part was coming to appear more and more chimerical in the light of the Soviet Union's ever more evident expansionist plans, especially given the advances being made by the Soviet army.[61] We shall see in what follows how far the Committee's plans in connection with Hungary's borders were influenced by this very real political consideration.

No new report was drafted concerning the Burgenland either. The Inter-Divisional Balkan – Danube Region Committee's report of April 17, 1944, was a verbatim copy of Bradshaw's summary of November 8, 1943.[62] The Committee's recommendations with regard to Hungary, the borders, the need for a new form of government, the armistice, and so on, were outlined in a fourteen page document, dated May 1, 1944, and headed: "The Treatment of Enemy States: Hungary." The paragraphs on the Czechoslovak-Hungarian, Yugoslav-Hungarian, and Austro-Hungarian borders were verbatim transcripts of the respective April précis on the subject.

The paragraphs treating Transylvania, however, were very different. There was no reference to an intermediate, postwar phase, nor to a United Nations peace keeping contingent. There was no talk of autonomy for the Székely region within Romania. Of all the recommendations made to redress Romanian-Hungarian territorial grievances, all that remained was the suggestion that the "small strip" between Arad and Szatmár be ceded to Hungary. The idea of an independent Transylvania, on the other hand, cropped up again, as something which, despite the problems it involved, "should not be excluded from consideration."[63]

The recommendations of the Country and Area Committees were presented to a high-level select committee set up by the Department of State in early 1944; the Committee on Post-War Programs. Its chairman was Cordell Hull, and its deputy chairman the new Undersecretary of State, Edward R. Stettinius; members included the Deputy Secretaries of State, department heads, Pasvolsky, who had headed the 1942-43 Advisory Committee, the chairmen of the various Subcommittees, for instance Bowman, as well as the leading members of the research staff, such as Notter, Mosely, and Howard.

The fourteen page proposal on Hungary was discussed and accepted at the May 26 session. In his commentary, Mosely emphasized that the most difficult of the territorial problems, and one that was hardly likely to receive a satisfactory solution, was the issue of Transylvania, or rather, the matter of the Székelys of the Székely region. His comment, however, was received in silence. The little debate there was, centered on the tone of the proposal: since they were dealing with an enemy state, someone suggested, the text ought to have a harsher tone. Berle and others rejected this, saying that Hungary was but a "satellite state," and as such was not to be equated with Germany.[64]

The only subsequent change in the position adopted on May 26 was that, in July of 1944, it was condensed to four pages, and in September of 1944, to a page and a half. The recommendations for how to deal with the various disputed areas along Hungary's borders were reduced first to a paragraph, and finally to a sentence or so. Gone was the "provisional" nature of the proposed Slovak-Hungarian settlement: the six districts of the Csallóköz were all that was suggested for cession to Hungary. Subcarpathian Ruthenia and the Yugoslav-Hungarian border region were mentioned without their territorial limits being specified, while all that was left of the Transylvanian problem was the "narrow strip" to be returned to Hungary between Arad and Szatmár.[65] These were the modifications contained in the briefing prepared for President Roosevelt in September of 1944, which the President took with him to the second conference at Quebec.[66]

Like the idea of a Mid-European Union, the real value of all this painstaking study of Hungary's disputed border regions depended on how far these recommendations would be put into practice. Initially, the members of the Advisory Committee were optimistic on this score. Their optimism was based on "assuming a complete victory for the United States and a free hand in reconstruction." A corollary of this assumption was Bowman's belief that "larger countries like the United States could exert influence without any direct intervention."[67]

Besides their exaggerated notion of the position of strength in which the United States would find itself after the war, the Department of State was encouraged also by the fact that the emigré politicians of the countries concerned did not reject offhand the idea of a settlement that was perhaps less advantageous from their own point of view, but was, on the other hand, more fair. As Beneš, the ex-president of the Czechoslovak Republic, declared in July of 1940:

> Nothing that has been imposed upon us since Munich do we consider to be valid in law... This does not mean that we desire as our war aim a mere return to the *status quo* of September, 1938... We wish to agree on our frontiers with our neighbours in a friendly fashion... Changes in detail are possible....[68]

A 1942 article of his contained much the same message.[69] Similar statements were made by other members of the Czechoslovak government-in-exile as well. For instance Finance Minister Ladislav Feierabend, in his speech to several members of the Advisory Committee on April 12, 1943, and Foreign Minister Jan Masaryk, in an interview conducted by Ferenc Göndör on November 13, 1943, and in an other statement on April 4, 1944.[70]

The Yugoslav government-in-exile made no such promises. Its communique of May 20, 1942, stated no more than the determination to restore the pre-1941 Yugoslavia.[71] Since, however, neither the American nor the British government would guarantee this any more than they would the Czechoslovak borders drawn at Trianon, in 1942-1943 it was still quite conceivable that the matter of the Yugoslav-Hungarian border would be decided by bilateral negotiations. The American experts working on the peace proposals thought this all the more likely as they had no very clear-cut notion of Yugoslavia's future. While, with small adjustments of its borders, they supported the restoration of pre-1938 Czechoslovakia, repudiating the idea of both an independent Slovakia and of an independent Subcarpathian Ruthenia, they were not at all convinced of the expediency of restoring pre-1941 Yugoslavia.

President Roosevelt was as uncertain on this score as anyone else. Twice in 1943, in the course of his discussions with leading members of the Advisory Committee, he spoke of Yugoslavia's restoration as improbable, and of an independent Serbia and an autonomous Croatia as possibilities.[72] As late as September of 1944, Otto von Habsburg recalls him saying that "Yugoslavia is, in his view, an unnatural state. It should be transformed into a federation."[73]

The United States had no easy task justifying its support for the territorial claims of an enemy state against those of an ally, and a member of the United Nations. For all that, the Department of State never wavered in distinguishing between Germany and its allies. While in drawing the tentative borders of Germany the ethnic principle played practically no part at all, in the case of the small satellite states, it remained the fundamental consideration.

Thus, when the principles of territorial adjustment were rethought one more time in the summer of 1944, we find the following line of reasoning in the report of June 21, 1944, classifying territorial disputes by types:

> In the interest of a stable and lasting settlement in the Balkan-Danubian region, it may be desirable to consider on their merits certain claims of Hungary and Bulgaria against members of the United Nations... If these two states, which after the last war had to accept rather severe terms not entirely consistent with principle of national self-determination and for that reason not supported by the United States at that time, are denied even a hearing, the struggle between satisfied and revisionist states in this area will continue and may be exploited again by Germany or by some other power. European security and the long-term interest of the United States in peace and stability in Europe would be better served by a territorial settlement calculated to promote friendly and stable relations among all the nations of central and southeastern Europe than by a policy of exclusive reliance on one or another grouping of states within that region.[74]

Still, though there was no change in the principles, the method envisioned for their implementation in 1944 differed from what had been thought feasible in 1942. Agreement reached through bilateral negotiations was the only recommended way for a loser state to settle its territorial dispute with a victor state. In practical terms, this would mean restoring the prewar borders as the first step, and then the two sides, perhaps with the mediation of the great powers, reaching some peaceful consensus on the ultimate borders. In the case of territorial disputes involving two loser nations, plebiscite remained the recommended solution, or arbitration by the great powers.

The "third party" with an immediate interest in Hungary's borders was the Soviet Union. In the first phase of the war, as is common knowledge, Moscow repeatedly reassured Budapest that the Soviet Union had no territorial claims against Hungary, and that the Soviet leadership considered Hungary's claim against Romania to be well founded, and one that would enjoy Soviet support when it came up at the postwar peace conference.[75]

After the summer of 1941, however, when Hungary joined in Germany's attack on the Soviet Union, the Soviet stand changed. Thenceforward, the Soviet Union called into question the legitimacy of Hungary's revised borders with Czechoslovakia and Yugoslavia alike, as well as of the Second Vienna Award. The first indications to this effect reached Washington in early 1942. Ambassador John C. Winant reported from London that Sir Anthony Eden had information that Stalin meant to compensate Romania for the loss of Bessarabia with "territory now occupied by Hungary," i.e. with Transylvania.[76] The information was confirmed by Molotov's memorandum of June 1943, which, among other things, noted that the Soviet Union did not "consider as fully justified the so-called arbitration award carried out at the dictate of Germany in Vienna on 30th August 1940 which gave Northern Transylvania to Hungary."[77]

It was at this point, as we have noted, that the members of the Advisory Committee recognized the contingent nature of all their planning, and shifted from comprehensive reorganization proposals toward a solution as far as possible in keeping with the Principle of Minimum Change. For all that, they continued to strongly oppose the en bloc restoration of the 1920 borders.

The United States first came up against the Soviet Union's alternate plans fort Transylvania directly in the spring of 1944, at the time that the Romanian armistice was negotiated. The Department of State wanted to see the settlement of territorial disputes postponed until the peace conference, and wanted an armistice agreement that contained absolutely no reference at all to borders. The Soviet Union, however, wanted an armistice agreement to contain guarantees that it would get back Bessarabia, which had been annexed to Romania near the end of World War I, and was, thus, willing to include in it the compensatory condition that after the war, "Transylvania or the greater part thereof" would be returned to Romania. The conflict was finally settled in a compromise. At Churchill's insistence, the American side agreed to the Soviet formula against its better judgement; while the Soviet Union, for its part, agreed to have appended to the sentence on Transylvania a qualifying clause: "subject to confirmation at the peace settlemen "[78]

Washington had no real way of knowing the Soviet stand on Subcarpathian Ruthenia. On June 9, 1942, Molotov had written to Beneš in London saying that the Soviet Union regarded the decisions of the Munich Conference – and the border revisions it effected – as null and void. In his speech of November 12, published also by the *Izvestia*, Beneš understood this to mean that Stalin supported Subcarpathian Ruthenia's reannexation to the postwar Czechoslovak state. At other times, the Soviet press spoke of Subcarpathian Ruthenia as a part of the Ukraine, i.e. as "trans-Carpathian Ukraine."[79] The Advisory Committee's reports, thus, took account of both possibilities. Though the preferred solution was to have the region returned to Czechoslovakia, they were prepared to see Subcarpathian Ruthenia become part of the Soviet Union.

4. *Views on Hungary's Postwar Government*

Interwar American opinion on Hungary was typically divided. There were scores of diplomatic reports, travelogues, press reports and memoirs that spoke of the 1920 Treaty of Trianon as an outrage, and pointed with approval at the modernization the country had achieved in spite of the crippling blow the treaty had dealt the Hungarian economy.

On the alternative, no less schematic view, the postwar disintegration was no more and no less than the inevitable catching up with multinational Hungary: the country's difficulties were rooted not in the terms of the peace settlement, but in the selfish and narrow-minded policies of the still ruling "feudal" aristocracy, which clung to the system of great estates, had suspended the secret ballot, in short, lorded it over a county that enjoyed not even a modicum of social and political democracy. Which of these two pictures someone presented depended as much on his or her political predilections and prejudices, as on who had been his or her guide to discovering Hungary.

Classic examples of how far this was true are the two United States ambassadors to Hungary in the 1930's: Nicholas Roosevelt, who served from 1930 to 1933, and John F. Montgomery whose tenure lasted from 1933 to 1941. Reading their memoranda, one has the feeling that they are speaking of two different countries. As Roosevelt saw it, the "survival of feudalism" was the country's salient feature. "Most of the Hungarian peasants were living under conditions but little removed from those of the serfs in Russia of the nineteenth century."[80] In Montgomery's view, on the other hand, the "stories about feudal Hungary" were stories and no more, told "in order to calm the world's conscience, which was a little troubled by the fact that in the name of national self-determination, more than three million Magyars had been put under Czech, Rumanian and Serbian rule." In reality, Hungary was well on the way to modernization, and though the conditions of the agricultural workers fell somewhat short, the condition of the industrial working class was on a par with that of American workers.[81]

Each one of the two pictures had its appeal to certain groups within the American business, political and scholarly communities. Among "official" Hungary's known supporters were a number of prominent Americans. This included Professor Archibald Coolidge, the founder of *Foreign Affairs*, whose sympathy for the "Hungarian cause" dated back to his 1919 travels in Central Europe. At that time, he had been a decided opponent of the new border arrangements being planned for Hungary.[82] Another was General Harry H. Bandholtz, the American member of the Allied mission to Budapest in 1919-1920, the man who had protected the Hungarian National Museum's collection from the plundering Romanian armies, and who was on friendly terms with Count Albert Apponyi, among others.[83] Jeremiah Smith, the Boston lawyer was stationed in Budapest between 1924 and 1927 as the commercial representative of the League of Nations. Senator William E. Borah, Wilson's opponent and chairman of the Foreign Affairs Committee to 1940, was perhaps the most influential of all the Americans urging the revision of the Treaty of Trianon.[84]

There is some indication that President Roosevelt, too, was pro-Hungarian in sentiment. His personal sympathy was said to be based partly on his having bicycled through certain parts of the Monarchy during his student years, Transylvania being one of these parts. The experience, so the story goes, had a positive and lasting impact on him. The second impression was just as personal, and dated back to his years in the navy during the First World War. While in Rome on one occasion, he found that the Italians spoke with great admiration of a "daring" Hungarian admiral of the Austro-Hungarian navy, Miklós Horthy, the man who was elected Regent of Hungary in 1920. That this episode was something Roosevelt was fond of recalling is indicated by the message he had Montgomery convey to Horthy in 1937, which made reference to their shared naval past. In September of 1943, the President is reputed to have told Zita, Otto von Habsburg's mother, that "he liked Hungary... more than any other country in Europe," and that "he wanted to save the country."[85]

Be that as it may, Roosevelt's sympathy was certainly not unconditional, and did not keep him from being critical of many aspects of Hungarian policy. For instance, he believed the system of land tenure to be quite obsolete, and we know from a letter of Montgomery's that when they spoke in the summer of 1937, he "expressed considerable interest in the subject of dividing up estates in Hungary."[86]

The other picture, that of a deplorably feudal Hungary, was most effectively kept in the limelight by Hamilton Fish Armstrong. While recognizing the superior moral qualities of conservatives like Counts Bethlen and Teleki, Armstrong essentially subscribed to the views of Mihály Károlyi, Oscar Jászi, Rusztem Vámbéry and Robert W. Seton-Watson, and criticized Hungary's interwar political *status quo* from their democratic point of view.[87] Like Armstrong and Nicholas Roosevelt, Sumner Welles, too, was highly critical of the Hungarian domestic political scene, relying over and above the official sources, primarily on Beneš for his information.

> In Hungary, the regent and the Hungarian governments attempted the impossible task of trying to solve Hungary's basic problems through a policy that retained the essentials of medieval feudalism. It is true that concessions were made to the twentieth century in the form of a thin veneer of political reform. But of concessions to the demands of modern economy there were none. None of the real social or economic ills of the country were squarely faced. The great estates of the Hungarian landlords were left precisely as they had been for many centuries. The system of taxation (...) was not reformed in any fundamental way. No effective effort was made to further industrialization. In short, the economy of the country remained largely static.

Armstrong and Welles, however, differed on one essential point when it came to Hungary. Armstrong considered the Trianon borders to be basically acceptable, and thought the problem to lie only in the successor states' ungenerous treatment of the minority nationalities; Welles, on the other hand, believed that readjustment of Hungary's borders was a *sine qua non* of a just peace in the Danube region, and wanted particularly to find a satisfactory solution to the problem of Transylvania.[88]

Though Eastern Europe, let alone Hungary in itself, can hardly be said to have been a major focus of American diplomatic interest in the interwar years, still there were occasions when these two diametrically opposing interpretations collided directly. One such occurred in the early 1920's, when Armstrong's journal published an unusually harsh critique of Hungarian affairs by Oscar Jászi. Bowing to the protests made by the Hungarian ambassador, by William R. Castle of the Department of State, and especially by Professor Coolidge, not much later Armstrong published an indirect refutation written by István Bethlen, which was, in fact, an apology for the newly consolidated system.[89]

Much the same sequence of events took place in the early 1940's, except in reverse order. At President Roosevelt's request, the *Foreign Affairs* published Otto von Habsburg's article on the "reconstruction" of the Danube Basin. By way of counterweight, Armstrong also simultaneously published an article by Beneš, as well as one expressly written by Rusztem Vámbéry at Armstrong's request.[90]

The Advisory Committee, as well as the numbers of the research staff dealing with the future of postwar Hungary, Mosely, Howard, Power and Bradshaw, were as critical of interwar Hungary as Armstrong and Welles. Textual analysis as well as personal contacts point to the influence of Rusztem Vámbéry on their thinking. It followed that they saw absolutely no chance of the Horthy regime's surviving the war, and expected that defeat would bring in its wake Hungary's radical democratization.

Land reform was the issue that they gave most attention to. In late 1943 and early 1944, thoroughgoing studies examined the state of Hungarian agriculture, and the history of post-1918 reform legislation.[91] Two further studies in the spring of 1944 contained concrete proposals for postwar land reform. The radical redistribution of holdings was specified in both documents as "a prerequisite for the establishment of a more democratic Hungary." Thoroughgoing land reform, argued the author, probably Power, basing his reasoning on Vámbéry's 1942 *Foreign Affairs* article,

> ...would open the way for peaceful development of social and political democracy and would eliminate the control of a reactionary minority which has monopolized political power at home and threatened the peace and security of the Danubian region through its cooperation with an aggressive Germany.

For all that, though he did not rule out the possibility of an indiscriminate and wholesale land grab, the social discontent among the peasantry being as pervasive as it was, this was not something that he would have liked to see. What he would have preferred was "a rationally planned reform" of the kind contained in the People's Law promulgated during the democratic revolution of 1918-19, and reiterated by Mihály Károlyi and Arnold Dániel in the program they submitted in 1942. It was land reform "under the guidance of competent agronomists and with proper physical and financial implementation." In concrete terms, this would have meant nationalizing estates of over fifty-eight acres (a hundred *holds*), and parcelling them out as farms of between eight to fifty acres in size. The five thousand landowners thus deprived of their lands were to receive no compensation, but would have been given some form of financial aid to help them set up a new livelihood. Those who wanted to stay in agriculture would have been allowed to keep "peasant-sized farms." The entire process was envisioned as requiring about ten years.[92]

The other problem studied in depth was the matter of the postwar political system, and the desirable composition of the future government. The studies prepared in early 1944 distinguished and reviewed the possibilities of five different kinds of political organization: authoritarian, soviet, centralized democratic republican and decentralized democratic republican (the distinction is Vámbéry's), as well as the constitutional monarchic system. The preferred possibility was "a democratic government in either a monarchical or republican form." The studies expressed strong reservations in connection with both the authoritarian and the soviet systems, and thought it highly unlikely that the Hungarian people would opt for either of these.[93]

For the leaders of any democratic government, they looked to a popular-front-type coalition of Social Democrats, Smallholders and Liberals, to Károlyi and the democratic emigres he headed, as well as to certain intellectual groupings within Hungary. Of the latter, specific reference was made to the populist writers, as well as the younger generation grouped around journals such as the bourgeois radical *Századunk*, the Catholic *Jelenkor*, and the *Ország Útja*.[94]

The research staff thought it impossible for the political elite of the Horthy government to remain in power, and particularly for the Regent himself to do so. "The Russians have expressed their objection to the retention of the Regency and of the regime of the landlords. "What was more, the old guard's remaining in power" would mean the continuation of an authoritarian regime. In all probability Hungary would again be a factor of instability in the Balkan-Danubian region." Their objection went beyond the person of Horthy himself, and extended, naturally enough, to the far rightist Arrow Cross Party and the government party, and even to "conservative-liberal" opposition figures such as István Bethlen, and to "pseudo-Smallholders" of the likes of Tibor Eckhardt, who spent the last years of the war in the United States.

The research team noted that "Count Bethlen...is considered in some English and American circles as a Hungarian of great possibilities, despite his somewhat advanced age," and conceded that in the 1920s, "he restored order and to a certain extent economic stability in

Hungary." But they agreed with the leftist critics of the Horthy regime in considering his dyed-in-the-wool anti-democratic stand as a consideration of even greater weight, to say nothing of his restrictions of the franchise, and his having been the one to obstruct any real land reform. Thus, he was not someone they wanted to count on in the future.[95]

As regards Eckhardt, they knew that he favored land reform, but also that he opposed completely doing away with the latifundia and the medium-sized estates. This, his anti-Semitic past and his ties to Horthy made him suspect in the eyes of the research staff, who wrote of him as follows:

> There is a good evidence to believe that Eckhardt has been sent abroad by Horthy to establish a Free Hungarian movement so that Hungary will have a foot in each camp at the conclusion of the war. Eckhardt is an opportunist and no leadership can be expected from him for a far reaching land reform program.[96]

The most that the Department of State could envision for the anti-German elements of the old ruling elite was a role in the immediate postwar period of transition. But even this they considered a less than desirable solution. In the transition period already, the Inter-Divisional Balkan and Danube Region Committee would have preferred a popular front government, one including the liberal democrat Károly Rassay, the radical nationalist, Endre Bajcsy-Zsilinszky, the Social Democrat Károly Peyer, the Smallholder Zoltán Tildy, and the historian Gyula Szekfű. In the event that Hungary did not turn against the Germans, and the Allies had to take it by military force, they counted on a temporary postwar period of martial law.[97]

The research staff did not rule out the possibility that the new democratic Hungary would be a monarchy. This, however, was by no means tantamount to their supporting Otto von Habsburg's claim to power. There is no denying, of course, that Otto's name came up frequently in their discussions. But only as a possible option, never as the solution recommended, or desirable from the American point of view. This was so in spite of the fact that Otto had confidentially reassured the Department of State that he would assume the Hungarian throne only subsequent to being confirmed in his claim by a plebiscite.[98]

In general, there were two weighty reasons given against Otto's kingship. One was that there was no trace in his writings of his favoring land reform, and that his ties to the aristocracy were too strong. In short, he was not enough of a democrat. The other reason was that the putative postwar leaders of the neighboring successor states would not have him. In the light of this, on January 27, 1944, the Inter-Divisional Balkan and Danube Region Committee, like the preliminary studies and committees, rejected the notion of "the restoration of the Habsburgs to the throne of Hungary."[99]

The conclusions of the research staff and of the Committee, thus, were completely in keeping with how the Department of State saw matters. How far this was so is indicated by the fact that when in early April, 1944, Archduke Otto asked President Roosevelt to endorse the creation of a Hungarian Resistance Committee, Cordell Hull was adamant against it. His reasoning coincided with that of the Foreign Office, namely, that "the future of Hungary is primarily in the hands of the Hungarians within Hungary," and that emigre groups were not to be used to foment resistance. Hull was opposed to Otto's brother's activities in Lisbon as well, and did all what he could to frustrate it. His memorandum to Roosevelt of May 25, 1944, sums up his stand very well:

> I think you will agree that the involvement of this Government in questions concerned with the Archduke Otto's political aspirations is something very carefully to be avoided because of the political implications, both in this country and abroad.[100]

To the end of 1943, while he was still a member of the government, Sumner Welles, too, warned Roosevelt to avoid giving the impression that he supported a Habsburg restoration.[101] Finally, we might quote Adolf A. Berle's diary entry for late December of 1942:

> My understanding is that the policy of the United States is very definitely opposed to any Habsburg restoration.... There may be difference in some quarters as to why the war is being fought. But there is no difference on the proposition that it is not being fought to restore the Habsburg monarchy....[102]

Emil Csonka, Archduke Otto's biographer, might, nevertheless be perfectly right in stating that Roosevelt not only sympathized with Otto's claim to the Hungarian throne, but also considered it "the most constitutional solution."[103] There was, however, not much that the President could do in the face of opposition from the Allies (England), his Secretary of State and most of his advisers, to say nothing of American public opinion. Consequently, unlike Beneš, the Polish government-in-exile, and other Eastern European emigre politicians, Otto never got the kind of support, either as a Hungarian or as an

Austrian, which would have enabled him to play a leading role in postwar developments in either of his two countries.[104]

The above set of recommendations for Hungary's political reorganization were incorporated in "The Treatment of Enemy States: Hungary" summary of May 1, 1944, which the Committee on Post-War Programs passed, without significant modifications, on May 26. The only points at all disputed had to do with the degree of support to be given the democratic forces within the country, and the degree to which the Habsburg restoration should be opposed. The resolution approved in the second matter reads as follows: "The United States should not look with favor on the restoration of the Habsburgs to the throne of Hungary." Some members would have preferred the more categorical "should oppose" wording, but the suggestion was rejected on the grounds that that "would commit us to positive resistance and might lead to difficulties." To save time, they left it to Mosely to come up with a term stronger than "should not look with favor" and weaker than "should oppose." Mosely's solution was "should disapprove," and that is the term found in all subsequent references to the Habsburg restoration.[105]

Unlike the Advisory Committee's suggestions for a Mid-European Union and for border readjustments, the above program for Hungary's postwar political reform appeared to be realistic even in the last phases of the war. This, in spite of the growing fears in the course of 1943-44 that the Soviet Union would not be content to interpret the notion of sphere of influence in the limited sense of the Monroe Doctrine, but would aim at the Sovietization of East Central Europe. The "Declaration on Liberated Europe," however, signed at the Yalta Conference, which reiterated the right of all peoples to free and democratic self-determination, laid these concerns to rest.

The only cause for anxiety subsequently was Roosevelt's compromise, probably made in the interest of having the Soviet Union join in the war on Japan. This did not insist on a high-level four-power commission, whose job it would have been to make sure that the terms of the Yalta Declaration were observed. Significantly, the Department of State had ascribed as much importance to such a commission as to the Declaration itself.106 Those who, like Charles E. Bohlen, knew something of the Soviet mentality, saw this as an omen. He opined that "the Soviet leaders attached less weight to general principles than did the leaders of the western powers"[107] In 1945, however, they formed a minority. The rest of those in the Department of State thought with their own heads, and naively believed that people were bound by their written and spoken word.

5. *The Game is Up*

The idealistic plans formulated between 1942 and 1944 behind the padded doors of the Department of State disintegrated during the last year of the war, and in the course of 1946-1947. That they did so was due not to some conceptual void in American diplomacy, as some have suggested, nor to Roosevelt's illness, but to the Soviets establishing their dominance in the region, and to the Americans having no material interest in challenging this predominance.

Basically, Washington had no objections to the new Hungarian regime that took shape in 1944-45. While it was obvious that both the interim government and the National Assembly came into being under Soviet tutelage, the Department of State acknowledged that Béla Dálnoki Miklós's cabinet was "a well-balanced group representing the significant pro-Allied political forces," and that "it is a group of responsible personalities."[108] As opposed to the governments of Poland, Romania and Bulgaria, which it justly considered Soviet "puppet governments," Washington accepted the Hungarian leadership as representative, and made no demand for its reorganization. Consequently, Hungary's internal affairs were not among the controversial issues at either Yalta or Potsdam, and the Hungarian government was the first of all the East European governments to be recognized by the United States, as early as September 1945, prior even to the election of the National Assembly. This decision, made by James F. Byrnes, Secretary of State in the new American cabinet formed after the death of President Roosevelt in 1945, was meant to underline that the United States would encourage democracies, and reject communist dictatorships.[109]

In these early days, there were two crucial points on which Soviet-American discord focused in the matter of Hungary: the amount of reparation the country was to pay, and the make-up and operation of the Allied Control Commission. The Soviet Union demanded 400 million US dollars from Hungary, payable within five years, of which 80 million dollars were to go to Czechoslovakia and Yugoslavia. The Americans thought this was too much, and, along with the British, wanted the amount reduced. The compromise was 300 million dollars, payable in six years, with the Soviet Union to receive 200 million dollars.[110]

The debate over the make-up and operational procedures of the Allied Control Commission also ended in compromise. Accepting that the Soviets would chair the Commission, Washington was able to insist that the representatives of all three great powers be given equal rights, that the missions receive their orders from their respective governments, and that the Commission, as such, not be subordinated to the Soviet High Command.[111] "The United States Government recognizes that the Soviet Union's interest in Hungary is more direct than are ours... We do not, however, consider that the Soviet Union has any special privileges or dominant position in Hungary."[112]

During the year and a half following the election of the National Assembly in November of 1945, Washington took exception to two significant events on the Hungarian domestic scene: nationalization – particularly the nationalization of the oil industry, in which American investment reached 59 million US dollars, and the gradual elimination of political pluralism and of political liberty, a dictatorial tendency subsequently referred to as "salami-tactics" (i.e. the gradual whittling away of political and personal freedoms). The White House and the Department of State voiced their objections regularly at the meetings of the Committee, as well as at other bilateral and international forums. Still, as long as the Smallholders' Party held the majority of the seats in parliament, and Ferenc Nagy was the head of the coalition government, they considered the regime democratic and representative, and did not relinquish their support. There was, however, a permanent qualifier attached to this support. In the jargon of the Department of State, it was "limited encouragement." This meant that unlike the Mediterranean and other economically or strategically important regions, Hungary was a place where Washington was determined to confine itself strictly to economic and political measures to maintain its influence in the country.[113]

That the United States would not go beyond "limited encouragement" was amply manifest in its loans and economic aid to Hungary between 1945 and 1947,[114] as well as in the discussions preliminary to, and during the negotiations at, the 1946 Paris Peace Conference. American support for Hungary's foreign policy objectives against Romania and the Soviet Union in the matter of Transylvania was strong, but, contrary to what one might have expected in the light of the work done by the Advisory Committee, was much weaker against Czechoslovakia and Yugoslavia.

The Potsdam Conference of July, 1945, was the last time that American foreign policy objectives included an ethnically-based solution to the Czechoslovak-Hungarian and Yugoslav-Hungarian border disputes.[115] By the time the Allied foreign ministers met in London in September, the issue had received a new formulation. There, and from there on, the Allies were in agreement that "the frontier with Hungary should be, in general, the frontier existing in 1938," and that the only subject still in dispute was Transylvania, and the Romanian-Hungarian border.[116]

Several factors contributed to the Americans' abandoning the principle of ethnic fairness, which they had considered so important at the time of the peace preparations. The most significant was that contrary to Washington's expectations, the governments in Belgrade and Prague were most adamant against any kind of frontier adjustment. The same politicians who, in 1942-43, and even in early 1944, had considered the redrawing of the Hungarian-Slovak border a distinct possibility, believed, from the summer of 1944, that the only way to resolve the border dispute between the countries was to remove the Hungarian population from Czechoslovakia. The Czechoslovak government-in-exile first expressed this view to the American government on November 23, 1944, and then reiterated its position from time to time after its return to Prague, at which time it also registered its claim on five Hungarian villages in the Bratislava (Pozsony) area.[117]

Similar tendencies could be observed in Yugoslavia as well. The government in Belgrade asked for Allied permission to "exchange" forty thousand ethnic Hungarians, over and above those who had already fled to escape retaliation at the hands of the Yugoslav partisans; it registered an official claim to a fifty square mile area of the Austro-Hungarian border region north of the river Drava; and emphasized in its propaganda the legitimacy of annexing other border-region Hungarian territories (mainly in the province of Baranja), and the necessity of preserving the "South Slav character" of northeastern Yugoslavia.[118]

It is due primarily to the firmness of the United States Government that the Yugoslav claims were not satisfied, and the Czechoslovak demands were only partially met. The Department of State took exception to unilateral mass relocations even in the case of the German population. As far as the Hungarian and other East European populations were concerned, Washington strongly objected to solving territorial differences by punishing entire ethnic groups for the sufferings of the war. It took a particularly firm stand against the government in Prague, which, nevertheless, managed to get three of the five villages it had asked for, in exchange for giving up its notion of unilaterally relocating 200,000 ethnic Hungarians.[119]

The Truman administration, however, would not go so far as to follow the recommendations of the Advisory Committee in order to eliminate the possibility of future territorial disputes between Hungary and its neighbors. The fact that these issues did not even come up at the various rounds of the peace talks had very little, to do with the roles played by these various countries in the course of the war. In the case of the Italian-Yugoslav dispute over Istria, for instance, Washington was quite capable on the grounds of ethnic fairness of siding with the ex-enemy, Italy, thereby moderating somewhat the excessive Yugoslav-Soviet demands.

It is probable that if Hungary had been more important strategically and if Washington had had a military presence at hand to give weight to its proposals, as indeed it did in the case of Istria, the Advisory Committee's recommendations would not have been so soon forgotten. There is yet another reason why the matter of the Czechoslovak-Hungarian and Yugoslav-Hungarian borders never came up in the course of the postwar negotiations: Britain's attitude. The British government had decided to support the restoration of the 1938 borders even before the Potsdam Conference.[120] All the above being as it was, it would have been a Quixotic gesture indeed for the United States to insist on trying to implement the Advisory Committee's suggestions.

Unlike the Csallóköz and the Baranja-Bačka-Banat issues, the status of Transylvania remained uncertain until May of 1946, with the *status quo ante bellum* being finalized only in August. Washington had been irked by the Soviet-approved restoration of Romanian local government in northern Transylvania on March 9, 1945, and questioned the government's legitimacy. Accordingly, the American delegation in Potsdam recommended that

> the three principal Allies proceed in the near future with preliminary talks concerning the establishment of a definite boundary between Hungary and Rumania, and that favorable consideration be given to revision of the pre-war frontier in favor of Hungary on ethnic grounds.[121]

When the preliminary talks were held at the September, 1945 meeting of the Council of Foreign Ministers, the Soviet delegation made no secret of the fact that it wanted to see "the whole of Transylvania" go to Romania. The joint British-American stand, however, was for "examining the respective claims of the two States." Secretary of State Byrnes noted in the course of the debate that "the change which he had in mind would not affect more than 3,000 square miles." This was about five hundred square miles less than the minimum area recommended by the Advisory Committee in 1943-44, and there is no knowing how exactly Byrnes arrived at the figure. It is possible that he simply rounded down the original figure of 3,457 square miles. No decision was taken on the matter at the London session, and the Council agreed to adjourn the debate.[122]

The next time Transylvania was discussed was at the April, 1946 meeting of the deputy foreign ministers, likewise held in London. The Soviet government — which a few days earlier had had the high-level Hungarian delegation visiting Moscow believed that Hungary's raising the matter of its territorial claims against Romania was something the Soviets considered to be justified[123] — insisted in London that the Trianon borders be restored. With Britain and France refusing to support it, the United States was not in a position to press its own revisionist plans, but did suggest that "provision be made to leave the way open for direct negotiations between the Governments of Rumania and Hungary with a view to adjusting the frontier so as to reduce the number of persons living under alien rule." The Russians, however, refused to agree to even this watered down wording.[124]

With no consensus forthcoming, the deputy foreign ministers submitted a Soviet, and an American recommendation to the May session of the Council of Foreign Ministers. Had he had British and French support, and Roosevelt to back him, it is possible that Byrnes would have insisted on at least a token compromise. Alone as he was, however, he judged the matter to be a lost cause, and did not want to further test Soviet-American relations, which were strained enough as it was, with insistence on having his way in a "third-rate" issue of this sort. In return for a trivial Soviet concession, he thus withdrew the American motion, and accepted the Soviet plan.[125] Subsequently, John C. Campbell, secretary to the peace delegation, justified Byrnes's move as follows: "With so many clauses in the four treaties in dispute between the United States and the Soviet Union, this one did not seem worth arguing about any longer."[126] In 1946, when Ferenc Nagy was in Washington, Byrnes felt a need to exonerate himself: "We were reluctantly forced to the view that the population in Transylvania was so intermingled that without an exchange of populations no adjustment of the frontier would provide a solution to the ethnic problem."[127]

Byrnes came in for a great deal of criticism for his permissiveness not only in this, but in other matters as well. Sumner Welles, a number of the senior members of the Department of State, and later even President Truman expressed dissatisfaction with his conduct of affairs. This gave some credibility to the American efforts to reassure the dejected Smallholder Government, which had been misled in Moscow and now felt itself abandoned by Washington. The Hungarians were told that the game was not yet up, that what the Americans had agreed on was only a draft of the peace treaty, and that the conference itself would be the place to effect changes in it. This was the gist of what Philip Mosely told the Hungarian delegates to Paris on May 17, 1946, and this was the assumption that guided the activities of Arthur Schoenfeld, the American ambassador to Budapest.[128]

Byrnes himself was more honest and more realistic. All he would promise Prime Minister Ferenc Nagy was that if the Soviet Union undertook to raise the question again, the United States would gladly support Hungary's claims.[129] To anyone who knew the Soviet Union's stand on the matter, this meant that Washington had closed the Transylvania file; the borders between Hungary and Romania would be the same as the ones set at Trianon.

Trusting that Mosely and Schoenfeld would turn out to be right, at the August 14 session of the peace conference the Hungarian foreign minister, János Gyöngyösi, asked that Romania surrender to Hungary an area of 22,000 square kilometers, and a population of two million people. A few days later, on American advice, he modified his demand to 4,000 square kilometers, with a population of less than half a million.[130]

The American support he had counted on, however, was not forthcoming. At the September 5 session of the Romanian territorial and political committee, where Hungary's demand was reviewed again for the last time, the United States delegate, William Averell Harriman, made the following statement about the draft peace treaty: "The United States had not been a strong supporter of the proposed text but wished to make it clear that he would vote for it since it had been agreed by the Council."[131] With this, the issue of Transylvania, which Sumner Welles had called one of Europe's most pressing problems in his book published in 1945, was taken off the agenda, much to the dismay of the circle of American experts. They realized that ignoring the problem would by no means make it disappear. "How can it be imagined," asked Welles, "that the cession of this entire region ... to either Rumania or Hungary can ever result in anything but new conflicts, new complaints, new oppressions and a festering sore in the body politic of Europe?"[132]

John C. Campbell, secretary to the American delegation, and the Advisory Committee's Transylvanian expert, concluded his article on the territorial settlement agreed at the peace conference by noting that the compromises born "did not conform to American hopes and American principles." This being so, "it should be possible for the world's statesmen to look again at the map of Europe and to make changes which are called for by the interests of the European peoples themselves."[133]

The defeat suffered by American diplomacy at the hands of the Soviets had its repercussions in Hungary, where, in June of 1947, Ferenc Nagy was forced to leave the country, and the systematic liquidation of the Smallholder Party got under way. The United States was outraged by the Hungarian Prime Minister's exile. President Truman called it a disgrace, and the Department of State spoke of it as a coup d'état. Once again, however, Washington's vehemence was soon spent. Some junior members of the Department of State did suggest that the Nagy case be brought before the United Nations, but the idea was rejected by the head of the European Department, H. Freeman Matthews, who did not want the matter to distract the Security Council's attention from the problem of Greece.[134] As Americans saw it, in the summer of 1947, Hungary became one of the communist states of Eastern Europe. The country's short-lived democracy was commemorated by John F. Montgomery in a book published in 1947, probably with the State Department's approval. "For a second time within a decade, a small European country, Hungary, is being turned into a satellite of an overwhelmingly strong neighbor."[135]

Interestingly enough, American diplomacy never quite gave up on Hungary, nor on the rest of Eastern Europe. For over forty years, with but slight shifts of emphasis, it had on its agenda a goal first formulated in 1948: "The gradual retraction of undue Russian power and influence from the present satellite area and the emergence of the respective eastern-European countries as independent factors on the international scene."[136]

Far from being up, perhaps the game is just starting.

NOTES

1. For the Inquiry in general, see: Lawrence E. Gelfand, *The Inquiry. American Preparations for Peace*, 1917-1919 (New Haven, 1963). For its activities as they touched on Hungary, see Peter Pastor, *Hungary between Wilson and Lenin: The Hungarian Revolution of 1918-1919 and the Big Three* (New York, 1976), and Sandor Taraszovics, "American Peace Plans and the Shaping of Hungary's Post-World War I Borders," in *Essays on World War I: Total War and Peacemaking. A Case Study on Trianon.* Ed. by Béla K. Király, Peter Pastor and Ivan Sanders (New York, 1982), 227-254.

2. Harley Notter, *Postwar Foreign Policy Preparation 1939-1945* (Washington, 1949), 3-82; and *Post World War II Foreign Policy Planning. State Department Records of Harley A. Notter*, 1939-1945. Ed. by Eduard Mark (Congressional Information Service, 1987), IX-XII.

3. These and later biographical data are based on various encyclopedias.

4. Hamilton Fish Armstrong, *Peace and Counterpeace. From Wilson to Hitler. Memoirs of Hamilton Fish Armstrong* (New York, 1971).

5. Franklin D. Roosevelt Library, Hyde Park. Adolf A. Berle Papers. Box 45, 80, and especially 211 and 214, particularly the Diary entries for April 25,

1940, May 6, 1942, Oct. 3, 1942, and Dec. 15, 1942; see also National Archives, Washington (hereafter: NA), RG 226. Office of Strategic Services, Foreign Nationalities Branch (hereafter: OSS, FNB) INT-15 HU-54, 223 and 523.

6. Harley Notter, *op. cit.*, 119-159, and 520-525.

7. Arthur J. May, "The Mid-European Union," in *The Immigrants' Influence on Wilson's Peace Policies*. Ed. by Joseph P. O'Grady (Lexington, 1967), 250-271.

8. Robert H. Ferrel, "The United States and East Central Europe before 1941," in *The Fate of East Central Europe. Hopes and Failures of American Foreign Policy*. Ed. by Stephen D. Kertész (University of Notre Dame, 1956), 48-49; Zsuzsa L. Nagy, "The United States and the Danubian Basin 1919-1939," in *Etudes historiques hongroises* (Budapest, 1975), 353-382; Sterling Memorial Library, Yale University, New Haven, Montgomery Papers. No. 353. Box 2. The Messersmith and Montgomery correspondence of 1937-1938.

9. John F. Montgomery, *Hungary, the Unwilling Satellite* (New York, 1947), 215; and Emil Csonka, *Habsburg Ottó. Egy különös sors története* (München, 1972), 356.

10. For an analysis of these and other proposals not presented here, see NA RG 59. Notter File, Box 56. P-46. Proposals for the political reorganization of Eastern Europe, August 19, 1942. For Otto's and Beneš's programs, see Otto of Austria, "Danubian Reconstruction," and Eduard Beneš, "The Organisation of Postwar Europe," *Foreign Affairs*, (January 1942), 226-252; *cf.* Joachim Kühl, *Föderationspläne im Donauraum und in Ostmittel-Europa* (München, 1958), 108-110.

11. In the case of documents included in the volume, reference will be to location within the volume. Part I, 1.

12. Sumner Welles, *The Time for Decision* (New York, 1944), 255-256.

13. Part I, 1.

14. *Idem.*

15. *Idem.*

16. Part I, 2.

17. NA RG 59. Notter File, Box 55. P Minutes-12., May 23, 1942.

18. *Loc. cit.*, Box 57. P-Doc. 204. The feasibility of an East European Union, February 10, 1943.

19. *Loc. cit.*, Box 54. P-Doc. 214. Tentative Views of the Subcommittee on Political Problems, March 12, 1943.

20 *cf.* Geir Lundestad, *The American Non-Policy Towards Eastern Europe, 1943-1947* (New York, 1975), 349-351.

21. NA RG 59. Office of European Affairs. M 1244/17. Negotiations with regards to "Treaties of a Political Character" which have taken place between the Soviet and British Governments since the outbreak of the German-Soviet war. *cf.* Elisabeth Barker, *British Policy in South-East Europe in the Second World War* (London, 1976), 129; and Stephen Kertész, *The Last European Peace Conference: Paris 1946 — Conflict of Values* (Lanham, 1985), 5-6.

22. Franklin D. Roosevelt Library, Hyde Park. Adolf A. Berle Papers. Box 214. May 2, 1942.

23. NA RG 59. Notter File Box 55. P Minutes-13, May 30, 1942, and Box 59. T Minutes, October 9, 1942.

24. *Loc. cit.*, Box 56. P-Doc. 135. Official Russian Views on Post-War Settlements, November 11, 1942.

25. *Loc. cit.*, Box 61. T-Doc. 222. Russia and an East European Federation, October 26, 1942.

26. *Loc. cit.*, Box 55. P Minutes-13, May 30, 1942.

27. NA RG 59. M 1244/17. Records of the Office of European Affairs, 1934-1947.

28. Kertész, *op. cit.*, 7-8.

29. United States Department of State, *Papers Relating to the Foreign Relations of the United States* (hereafter: *FRUS*): *The Conference at Cairo and Teheran 1943* (Washington, 1961), 879-880.

30. Eduard Mark, "American Policy toward Eastern Europe and the Origins of the Cold War, 1941-1946. An Alternative Interpretation," *The Journal of American History*, Vol. 68. No. 2 (Sept. 1981), 317-320.

31. Philip E. Mosely, "Hopes and Failures: American Policy Toward East Central Europe, 1941-1947," in Kertész, ed., *op. cit.* 62-63.

32. Walter Lippman, *U.S. War Aims* (London, 1944). 48-53.

33. Welles, *op. cit.*, 254-255, and 332.

34. NA RG 59. Notter File, Box 84. R Minutes-12, 13, 14, February 4 and 18, and March, 3, 1944.

35. Part III, 1.

36. NA RG 59. Notter File, Box 54. P-Doc. 151-c. Tentative Views of the Territorial Subcommittee. December 7, 1942, and Box 59. T Minutes-15 and 16, August 14 and 16, 1942.

37. Franklin D. Roosevelt Library, Hyde Park. Official File, Box 1. Folder 226. Roosevelt to Congress on June 2, 1942; and *The Memoirs of Cordell Hull* (New York, 1948), Vol. II, 1114 and 1576.

38. For the Czechoslovak census of especially 1930, its methods and distortions, see Gyula Popély, "Az 1930. évi csehszlovák népszámlálás végrehajtása," in *Magyarságkutatás 1988*. Eds., Gyula Juhász and Csaba Gy. Kiss, (Budapest, 1988), 145-176.

39. Part II, Chapter I, 1, and Chapter II, 1, 2, 3.

40. Part II, Chapter I, 2, 3 and 4; Chapter II, 4 and 6.

41. Part II, Chapter I, 5.

42. Part II, Chapter I, 6.

43. *Idem*, 7.

44. *Idem*, 8.

45. Part II, Chapter II, 9.

46. Part II, Chapter I, 8.

47. NA RG 226. OSS. FNB. INT-15HU-352 and 353.

48. *Loc. cit.*, INT-15HU-80.

49. *Loc. cit.*, INT-15HU-677. The Romanian secret service report found its way into Mihail Antonescu's files; a copy was returned to Washington in December of 1944.

50. Part II, Chapter I, 7, and Chapter II, 7.

51. Part II, Chapter II, 11. and NA RG 59. Notter File, Box 65. T-Doc. 387. The Problem of Subcarpathian Ruthenia: Basic factors, October 28, 1943.

52. Eduard Mark, *op. cit.*, (1987) XI.

53. Part II, Chapter III, 1.

54. *Idem*, 2.

55. *Idem*, 3.

56. *Idem*, 5.

57. *Idem*, 4.

58. Notter, *op. cit.*, 177.

59. NA RG 59. Notter File, Box 152. H-32a. Supplement. April 20, 1944.

60. *Loc. cit.*, H-26. Supplement. April 19, 1944.

61. *Loc. cit.*, Box 153. H-43a. Transylvania, April 20, 1944.

62. *Loc. cit.*, H-86. Burgenland, April 17, 1944.

63. Part IV, 1.

64. NA RG 59. Notter File, Box 140. Minutes, May 26, 1944.

65. Part IV, 2 and 3.

66. Part IV, 4.

67. NA RG 59. Notter File, Box 59. T Minutes, June 6, 1942, and August 14, 1942.

68. *Loc. cit.*, Box 58. P-256. Official Policies and Views Regarding the Post-War Settlement, May 25, 1944.

69. Beneš, *op. cit.*, 237-238.

70. See note 68, as well as Box 63. T-Doc. 327. Summary of Czechoslovak Peace Aims, May 5, 1943, and NA RG 226. OSS. FNB. INT-15HU-456.

71. NA RG 59. Notter File, Box 58. P-Doc. 256, May 25, 1944.

72. *Loc. cit.*, Box 54. Talks with F. D. Roosevelt, 1942-1944. *cf.* Box 59. T Minutes, October 9, 1942.

73. *FRUS. The Conference at Quebec.* Washington, 1972, 369.

74. NA RG 59. Notter File, Box 67. T-Doc. 49ld. Policy toward the Settlement of Territorial Disputes in Europe. June 21, 1944.

75. Gyula Juhász, "A második bécsi döntés," *Külpolitika*, (1987/5), 152; *cf.* Andor Gellért, "Magyar diplomaták Moszkvában, 1934-1941," *Új Látóhatár*, (1975/1), 17-35.

76. NA RG 59. Office of European Affairs. M 12444/17. Negotiations with Regard....

77. Ibid.

78. NA RG 59. Notter File, Box 109. CAC-82. Prel. Rumania. February 21, 1944, and *FRUS. Diplomatic Papers 1944.* Vol. II. (Washington, 1966), 148-152, 170-180, and 200, as well as Vol. V, (Washington, 1967), 526.

79. NA RG 59. Notter File, Box 70. T-Doc. 200a. Soviet War Aims..., September 14, 1943.

80. Nicholas Roosevelt, *A Front Row Seat* (Norman, 1953), 189-190.

81. John F. Montgomery, *op. cit.*, 22 and 28.

82. Francis Deák, *Hungary at the Paris Peace Conference* (New York, 1942), 15-21, and Peter Pastor, *op. cit.*, 101-102.

83. Harry Hill Bandholtz, *An Undiplomatic Diary* (New York, 1933).

84. Marian McKenna, Borah (University of Michigan, 1961), 275; and Mark Imre Major, *American-Hungarian Relations*, 1918-1944 (Astor, Fla., 1974), 84-92.

85. Csonka, *op. cit.*, 293, 235; and John F. Montgomery, *op. cit.*, 45.

86. Sterling Memorial Library, Yale University, New Haven, Montgomery Papers, No. 353. Box. 2. Montgomery to Louis G. Michelmey, November 17, 1937.

87. Armstrong, *op. cit.*, 171-174.

88. Sumner Welles, *Where Are We Heading?* (New York, 1946), 128-130.

89. Oscar Jászi, "Dismembered Hungary and Peace in Central Europe," *Foreign Affairs*, (Dec. 1923), 270-281; and Count Stephen Bethlen, "Hungary in the New Europe," *Foreign Affairs*, (April 1925), 445-458. *Cf.* Armstrong, *op. cit.*, 279.

90. Otto of Austria, *op. cit.*; Eduard Beneš, *op. cit.*, and Rustem Vámbéry, "The Tragedy of the Magyars. Revisionism and Nazism," *Foreign Affairs*, (April 1942), 477-488; *cf.* Csonka, *op. cit.*, 345.

91. NA RG 59. Notter File, Box 65. T-Doc. 430 and 431. Hungarian Land Reform since 1918, and Hungarian Agriculture.

92. *Loc. cit.*, Box 66. T-Doc. 465. A Suggested Basis for Land Reform in Hungary. March 11, 1944, and Box 153. H-87-a. Hungary, Land Reform. May 2, 1944; *cf.* Vámbéry, *op. cit.*, and Paul Tabori, "The Problem of Hungary," *The Contemporary Review*, (September 1942), 159-164.

93. *Loc. cit.*, Box 71. TS-58. Hungary IV. Permanent Government, February 9, 1944, and Box 153. H-104. January 27, 1944.

94. *Idem*, and Box 66. T-Doc. 465. March 11, 1944; *cf.* RG 226. OSS. Box 177. No. 27158.

95. Part III, 3.

96. NA RG 59. Notter File, Box 66. T-Doc. 465. March 11, 1944.

97. Part III, 3.

98. NA RG 59. Notter File, Box 68. T-Doc. 553. The political position of the Archduke Otto von Habsburg. December 5, 1944.

99. *Loc. cit.*, Box 153. H-104. January 27, 1944; and Part III, 1.

100. *FRUS. Diplomatic Papers 1944*. Vol. III. (Washington, 1965), 860-876.

101. Franklin D. Roosevelt Library, Hyde Park, President's Secretary's File. Box 77. Welles's letters of March 31, 1942 and Aug. 30 to Roosevelt.

102. *Loc. cit.*, Adolf A. Berle Papers. Box 214. Diary, December 8, 1942.

103. Csonka, *op. cit.*, 363-364.

104. For details, see Péter Sipos and István Vida, "Az Egyesült Államok és Magyarország a második világháború végén," *Valóság*, (1980/2), 72-74.

105. NA RG 59. Notter File, Box 140. Minutes, May 26, 1944, and Part IV, 1.

106. Philip E. Mosely, *op. cit.*, 76.

107. NA RG 59. Notter File, Box 84. R Minutes 14, March 3, 1944.

108. *Loc. cit.*, Records of the European Affairs, 1934-1947. M 1244/17. Matthews's memo of December 28, 1944.

109. Stanley M. Max, *The United States, Great Britain and the Sovietization of Hungary, 1945-1948* (New York, 1985), 25-32.

110. *Idem*, 13-14.

111. Sipos and Vida, *op. cit.*, 82-85.

112. *FRUS. The Conference at Malta and Yalta. 1945* (Washington, 1955), 245.

113. Max, *op. cit.*, 63-92.

114. For details, see Péter Várkonyi, *Magyar-amerikai kapcsolatok 1945-1948*, (Budapest, 1971), 171-198.

115. Potsdam Conference Documents 1945. Reel 1. The Berlin Conference. Territorial Studies. July 6, 1945. University Publications of America (Microfilm).

116. *FRUS. Diplomatic Papers 1945.* Vol. II. (Washington, 1967), 279; *cf.* Bennet Kovrig, "Peacemaking after World War II: The End of the Myth of National Self-Determination," in *The Hungarians: A Divided Nation.* Ed. by Stephen Borsody (New Haven, 1988), 69-88.

117. NA RG 59. Notter File, Box 116. CAC-328. December 15, 1944; FRUS 1946. Vol. II. *Council of Foreign Ministers.* (Washington, 1970), 418; *cf.* Sándor Balogh, "Az 1946. február 27-i magyar-csehszlovák lakosságcsere egyezmény," *Történelmi Szemle*, (1979/1), 59-66.

118. Potsdam Conference Documents 1945. Reel 1; Enikő A. Sajti, *Nemzettudat, jugoszlávizmus, magyarság* (Szeged, 1991), 123-131.

119. NA RG 59. Notter File, Box 154. H-165, and Box 116. CAC-328; *FRUS. Diplomatic Papers.* 1945. Vol. IV. (Washington, 1968), 928-929; and *FRUS. 1946.* Vol. III. *Paris Peace Conference: Proceedings* (Washington, 1970).

120. Mihály Fülöp, "A berlini (potsdami) értekezlet és az európai béke," *Külpolitika*, (1987/5), 170.

121. Potsdam Conference Documents 1945. Reel 1, and No. 407; *cf. FRUS. Diplomatic Papers 1945.* Vol. V. 509-510, 524-527.

122. *FRUS. Diplomatic Papers 1945.* Vol. II. (Washington, 1967), 147-150, 184, 227-228, 275-283, 311; *cf.* Sándor Balogh, "Erdély és a második világháború utáni békerendezés," *Külpolitika*, (1987/5), 188-189; Bennet Kovrig, *op. cit.*, 77.

123. Kertész, *op. cit.*, 115-127; *cf.* FRUS. 1946. Vol. VI. (Washington, 1969), 280-282; Ferenc Nagy, *Küzdelem a vasfüggöny mögött* (Budapest, 1990), I, 277-278.

124. *FRUS. 1946.* Vol. II. *Council of Foreign Ministers.* (Washington, 1970), 259-260.

125. *Ibid.*

126. John C. Campbell, "The European Territorial Settlement," *Foreign Affairs*, (October 1947), 212.

127. *FRUS. 1946.* Vol. VI. (Washington, 1969), 306-308.

128. *Loc. cit.*, 302-304; Vol. II. *Council of Foreign Ministers.* (Washington, 1970), 441-442.

129. Nagy, *op. cit.*, 301.

130. *FRUS. 1946.* Vol. III. *Paris Peace Conference: Proceedings* (Washington, 1970), 210-221, 249-282; *cf.* Balogh, *op. cit.*, 197-198.

131. *Idem*, 375-376.

132. Welles, *Where Are We Heading*, 128-129.

133. Campbell, *op. cit.*, 218.

134. Max, *op. cit.*, 105-110.

135. Montgomery, *op. cit.*, "Dedication."

136. Max, *op. cit.*, 125-126.

DOCUMENTS

Part One:

Plan of an East European Union and Hungary

§ Document 1 §

Minutes of the Subcommittee on Political Problems, May 9, 1942

Strictly Confidential Minutes P - 10

Meeting of May 9, 1942.

Present:
Mr. Welles, presiding
Mr. Hamilton Fish Armstrong
Mr. Ray Atherton
Mr. Isaiah Bowman
Mr. Benjamin V. Cohen
Mr. Norman H. Davis
Mrs. Anne O'Hare McCormick
Mr. Leo Pasvolsky
Mr. Paul Daniels
Mr. Paul B. Taylor, secretary

Mr. Welles, in opening the meeting at 11:10 a.m., stated that, as agreed upon at the last meeting, the discussion would deal with a potential Danubian federation and with its component parts.

He then asked Mr. Pasvolsky to explain a map, prepared by the Office of the Geographer in collaboration with the Division of Special Research, of the territories of the Austro-Hungarian Empire, the boundaries of the post-war Succession States being superimposed. Mr. Pasvolsky pointed out on the map the changes in political status which took place in respect of each part of the Dual Monarchy. Mr. Welles said that this explanation gave a very clear picture of the area.

He suggested that in approaching the problem of the morning, we might leave Poland out of consideration and attack the problem principally from the political point of view, with its economic aspects also considered, of the utility of a Danubian federation per se. We might then consider the enlargement of the arrangement to include

Poland and possibly Austria. He supposed that the initial problem is to determine whether there is anything of value in the conception of the reconstitution of Austria-Hungary. He then asked Mr. Armstrong for a statement of his views on this subject.

Mr. Armstrong asked whether the question referred solely to a Habsburg restoration or whether any type of government of the area might be considered. He himself did not believe in the practicability of a Habsburg restoration. He admitted that such a régime might be imposed, but he thought this would be going back to something which it had been necessary to destroy at the end of the last war – it would be a re-creation of a principal factor in creating the last war. He would not necessarily favor a veto of the restoration of a Habsburg (presumably Otto) in one of his own countries, but he would point out that such a veto would not necessarily come from us but rather from within the countries in which the restoration was to take place. The sine qua non of a restoration would be social reforms in Hungary (i.e. land reform) and political reforms along democratic lines in both Hungary and Austria.

Mr. Welles then inquired the opinion of the other members concerning the general nature of a possible Danubian federation. Was it conceived as purely economic, or as also political in nature? Mr. Davis expressed his feeling that such a federation ought at the beginning to be purely economic. Such a union would help a broader kind of political unity to develop without its being forced. It would give time and incentive to work on the development of more complete union. Mrs. McCormick inquired whether the union should not also be political: Even the possession of purely economic powers would force the federation to assume political functions. Mr. Davis agreed that if the Danubian countries were tied together economically, they would surely have to stand together politically. He thought that they might have to have some close political union, but he questioned whether one should try to go so far at first. He thought it more feasible to think of a confederation than of a federation.

Mr. Armstrong pointed out that here, as in the discussion on Germany, the question arises whether any historical precedents exist for federation in which the countries devolve from unity to federation – in which a united country becomes a member of or is broken up into a federation. Here, of course, one could not speak of, a direct transition from a unitary state to a federation. Rather, this development would take place with a twenty-year period in between. Mr. Welles said he could think of no such precedent and asked whether Mr. Bowman had any in mind. Mr. Bowman replied that while there were a few cases chiefly in Latin America, some of these existed chiefly on paper, were of short duration, and were in any case not applicable to the present problem. Mrs. McCormick added that there probably have been a few modern examples, but that they have been short. She pointed out, however, that strong support for a Danubian federation has existed for some time in the Danubian area itself, and that a number of specific proposals for such a federation have been made. Mr. Welles suggested that the Central American Union would be a case in point. The parallel was, however, not exact, and he could think of none in Europe. Mr. Armstrong pointed out that most federations were agglomerations of individual states, but that here the process would be reversed: a devolution from unity to a looser organization.

Mr. Davis said that Dr. Beneš was the main factor in keeping the Danubian countries from getting together at the end of the last war. Each of the Succession States followed a highly protectionist and competitive policy toward the others. Hungary, for example, succeeded in establishing an industry in competition with that of Czechoslovakia, and then granted it high tariff protection. All of the leaders in that area realized that they should get together politically, but they found themselves unable to do it economically. Mr. Armstrong queried whether Mr. Davis' statement concerning Dr. Benes applied to the period immediately after the Peace Conference. He himself thought that the chief problem was that the leaders in all these countries felt themselves on the skids and were unable to act. Mr. Davis recalled that in 1930 and 1931, there was a strong feeling in the Danubian area that a union was necessary, and that they were even talking about having someone come in as a director. Each leader, however, was afraid to tackle it himself. Mrs. McCormick pointed out that the Little Entente was the chief factor in preventing the creation of such a union.

Mr. Atherton said that Lord Lothian had been one of the strongest advocates of a federation in Central Europe, and that he based his idea upon the British Empire scheme. Mr. Welles agreed, and then referred to the plans of Prime Minister Sikorski and of Mr. Tibor Eckhardt. Sikorski's idea, he said, is one of complete economic federation and of incipient political federation among the Baltic states, Poland, Czechoslovakia, Hungary, Rumania, and Yugoslavia. The Eckhardt plan was similar but purely economic, as was categorically stated by Eckhardt. His plan, however, embraced two federations: the first to consist of Poland and the Baltic countries including Finland; the second group to include the Danubian states, that is, Czechoslovakia, Hungary, and Rumania. While there might be links between these two federations, each was envisaged as an independent state.

Mrs. McCormick said that mention might also be made of the Hodza plan, which confines itself to the Danubian area. Mr. Hodza, she pointed out, being a peasant is chiefly concerned with the agricultural problem. His plan expresses the aspirations of the "Green International".*

Mr. Davis thought that the big powers — France, Germany, and Italy — have always been an obstacle to the creation of a Danubian union. He himself had always had the feeling that a settlement of the Danubian area could be the key to peace and security. In his view, the most fatal mistake made at the end of the last war was the failure to create unity in Central Europe. While Wilson's Fourteen Points had called for the lowering of trade barriers, in actuality no practicable scheme for accomplishing this was found.** Mrs. McCormick agreed, pointing out in particular that if we could get a plan for the Danubian region, it would help considerably in dealing with the German problem. Mr. Davis, referring to the difficulty of establishing a federation, said that it is a terrible problem to get local government into operation. He thought that a proposed plan should not interfere with local government but should work from it. He did not like the idea of setting up a broad framework first that would lead to dictation of all matters of local government.

Mr. Atherton queried whether it would not be wiser to proceed in the reverse direction. He said that in establishing a federation we would naturally interfere as little as possible with local governments. If, however, we could get a broad framework of a federation, it would then be possible for the local people to adopt policies which would contribute to it. If, however, no such framework were created, the local government bodies would exhaust themselves in the kind of rivalry and unconstructive effort which had gone on in the past.

---

* "Green International" was the international association of the European peasant parties between the two world wars. It was established in Prague, in 1922; between 1928 and 1930, the number of participating national peasant parties was 18. Its ideology was a typically Eastern European democracy of the peasantry. [The notes of the editor are identified by asterisks.]

** Wilson's Fourteen Points was a presidential program for world peace, delivered to the United States Congress on January 8, 1918. The removal of trade barriers was covered by Point III: "The removal, so far as possible, of all economic barriers, and the establishment of an equality of trade conditions among all the nations consenting to the peace and associating themselves for its maintenance." In, Richard B. Morris, ed., *Basic Documents in American History* (New York, 1956), 154-155.

Mr. Cohen was asked whether he would have something to say on this question. He replied that, in his view, economic functions cannot be separated from political functions. The performance of economic functions can take place only in a political framework, but we should try to have the federal administration as small as possible so that each group will feel that the rules are being administered by the states. He thought this form would provide the best basis for later evolution. He pointed to the early American experience and observed that to have the states administer the rules tends to increase their power. This gradual process toward unity would be best adapted to the Danubian situation. Moreover, the economic functions of the modern state embrace much more than the problem of tariffs. The control of such matters must in some way be linked back to the states. Mr. Davis conceded that if an economic unit is created, it must have what amounts to political authority. He thought, however, that we should not try to force any exact form of government upon the countries concerned. Mr. Cohen agreed that he did not favor strong centralization.

Mr. Armstrong, referring to the Sikorski and Eckhardt plans, inquired whether these two men have definite ideas as to the arrangements which should be made for the rest of the territory. He pointed out that Bulgaria, Yugoslavia, and Greece are not included in the Eckhardt plan. Each plan, he said, leaves Austria out temporarily for strategic reasons. He understood that a certain pressure exists in London and in other capitals for the Anschluss or Austria and Germany. Eckhardt, he said, is working closely with Otto, who is interested in Austria and not in Hungary. The Sikorski plan, he thought, was a little less self-seeking in a nationalistic sense than that of Eckhardt. It must be remembered that Poland would be a relatively powerful state. The larger the group, the less power Poland would necessarily have. Thus, Sikorski's plan was not a mere scheme for establishing Polish hegemony. However, the motive of the Eckhardt proposals seemed to be that of trying to restore as much of Austria-Hungary (especially Hungary) as possible. Transylvania, for example, was included. Mr. Welles said that the Eckhardt plan leaves the political organization out. Its basic idea is that of two relatively self-sufficient economic units. Yugoslavia, Greece, and Bulgaria are not included in it. The Balkan states, he said, see less economic possibilities in such schemes and are less interested in them than are the states further north.

Mr. Atherton raised the question whether the two groups envisaged by the Eckhardt plan were too small to compete with Russia. Mr. Davis said that there is no particular intercourse between the Baltic and Danubian groups. Mr. Atherton, referring to the northern of these two envisaged units, said that it would merely repeat the type of structure established after the last war — a unit with no outlet except through the Baltic. This must, he thought, be another outlet — to the south. This brings us back again to the Polish plan.

Mr. Welles then asked Mr. Bowman whether, in his view, the Eckhardt plan provides for two relatively self-sufficient economic units. Mr. Bowman doubted that it did, saying however that the practical question involved consideration of what would happen up to the time of the establishment of a federation. The time factor would have to be kept into consideration, as it actually overshadowed the question of federation. The height of power of the United Nations will be the end of the fighting. At that time the moral and military power of the United Nations could instantly re-arrange the territorial situation. Later this would become increasingly difficult. It must be kept in mind that immediately after the fighting, some shifting could be done which was not based entirely upon what had existed before. These shifts, he said, could be stable insofar as they were rational and took into account practical political considerations. He pointed out, too, that the countries in this area are in general unstable, politically inexperienced, and nationalistic. Economic matters are so confused with political motives that the meaning of the maneuvers of these countries is often obscure. We would also want to take Russia and Germany into account in deciding this question. Furthermore, how far can we ourselves go politically in making any arrangements stick? He quoted Oppenheim's statement that in 1920 the world had been "shocked at its own boldness." The peoples of the world, and particularly the American people, had in 1920 rapidly retired from the bold conceptions of the Peace Conference period. He asked whether we will experience that again. Is it not true that all of the suggestions which we would make rest on the assumption that we are not going later to be frightened by our own boldness? Otherwise, what we do here is purely "paper stuff." He wondered whether the political leaders will not soon have to undertake the task of mobilizing support in public opinion. In other words, we have a second assumption in addition to our first assumption of a complete victory by the United Nations: We assume that we are not going to be afraid of our shadow afterward. He would emphasize, therefore, that we should not limit ourselves to considering what has been done, but that we should consider what is possible with a rational set-up.

He questioned whether economic associations that do not carry with them political associations — the type which we had been discussing — are feasible. What is it, ha asked, that draws out loyalty? Nothing, he answered, only (1) "the dream that experience destroyed" (i.e. the League of Nations) and (2) nationalism. This latter, he said, rests on human nature, on the ties to the land, the family, the neighborhood, etc. Therefore, if we say "unite," public opinion will oppose the suggestion; but if we urge union for the common interest with a limitation of sovereignty, in which account is taken of these local ties and in which, purely on grounds of common interest, these local units join together, public opinion may accept it. In his opinion, a league of nations that will allow regional autonomy seems best. That was his feeling also in relation to the German question. He suggested that in considering the Danubian federation, we ask two questions: First, how did it work when free to do so? We can't ignore the fact that Germany has a preponderant interest in the Balkans. He referred to an article written by Mr. Armstrong in *Foreign Affairs* in 1932,* in which the high proportion of German trade with this region and the small proportion of trade of Great Britain and France with it was stressed. On the other hand, Germany accounted for about eighteen percent of this trade, a figure which has been greatly increased since. Mr. Armstrong pointed out that 1932 was about the last year in which the situation in the area was normal. The Tardieu Danubian plan of that year was really the last plan of this sort which received any consideration. He noted that this plan was strongly favored by Herbert Butler in a book which Mr. Welles had recently recommended: *The Lost Peace.*** ask, namely that of seeing what it is that is to be changed. He suggested that much research work had been done concerning the actual economic structure and functioning of these countries, and that this material would be very useful. He doubted whether Eckhardt and Sikorski, for example, had done much on this task. The question he then defined as being: What boundaries shall we put around what area?

Mr. Davis concurred in Mr. Bowman's suggestion that the economic group of the League of Nations could be very helpful in a study of this sort. He referred especially to Mr. Loveday and said that Mr. Loveday and his group had done more on these questions than anyone else. Mr. Bowman said that he had one thing more to add. His earlier statements had not implied any disbelief in economic regions. These regions must, however, be worked out very carefully, and perimeters can be drawn only on the basis of close study.

---

* Hamilton Fish Armstrong, "Versailles. Retrospect," *Foreign Affairs*, (October 1932), 173-189.

** Harold Beresfold Butler, *The Lost Peace. A Personal Impression* (New York, 1942).

Mr. Armstrong presented the view that it is of importance to organize these areas in the strongest possible way. This, he said, is a fundamental part of the establishment of peace in Europe. He pointed out that in earlier times there was a buffer state between Russia and Germany. When this was taken away during the last war, Germany tried to organize the entire area. Later on, after the war, we tried, and the entities which we created were not strong enough. He pointed out that several regional groups have so far been envisaged. The aim must be to make these groups strong. He himself would hate to plump for a plan that would make any other regional plans unlikely. If were are to impose political sacrifices such as the loss of sovereignty and social and economic sacrifices such as the breakdown of the land-owning class in Hungary, it will be necessary for us to make these sacrifices general and not limited to some one country or class. He pointed out also that a larger grouping offers less chance for the play of political motives than does a smaller one. In the Eckhardt plan for example, one sees these old ambitions again. Summarizing his views, Mr. Armstrong said that the most hopeful course in the long run is that of making the area of the fedaration as large as possible; of securing it by an international organization; of forcing all concerned to accept the federation. This includes not only the Danubian countries; Germany and Italy must not ask preferential treatment, and we and Great Britain must not ask for most-favored-nation treatment. In that way he would try to emphasize economic factors rather political factors, but to make an area large enough. He thought that there was a chance that if this were done, the federation would constitute a limit upon Germany and upon a resurgence of the old Slav-German struggle, which is a danger for the future.

Mr. Welles, concurring, said that a requisite of any plan is the recognition of nationality. What must be done is rather to avoid its becoming pernicious. He thought as large an area should be included as is possible from a practical standpoint. Whether the organization later becomes political or not, we can start in this way. If such an organization can be established, it would be a counterpoise to both Russia and Germany. Mrs. McCormick agreed that the federation would have to be large. Mr. Davis said that the Danubian countries have always put politics ahead of economics. If we should reverse this, creating solid economic conditions, the opportunity will be provided for a healthy political development. Mr. Armstrong pointed out that there is less chance that outside great powers will control a large unit than a small unit.

Mr. Atherton, returning to the question raised by Mr. Bowman, questioned how much interest American public opinion would have in

Europe after the war. The average person is interested in little beyond local matter and cannot be counted on for a sustained interest in international affairs. Accordingly, it is likely to be our general policy to interfere as little as possible in most European situations. We may, however, lay down certain areas in which this country can be expected to have an interest.

One of these would be a dismembered Germany, another France and England, and a third a general economic grouping of Eastern Europe as a counterweight to Russia and Germany. Mr. Atherton further voiced his opinion that American post-war interest will lie more in the Far East than in Europe. Mr. Welles disagreed with this, stating that in his view the American people will demand a determining voice in the European settlement as well as in the Far East. Mr. Atherton, disagreeing, said that we will be drawn more into the Far East than into Europe. Mr. Welles, conceding that certainly we would be involved in Far Eastern affairs, did not believe that this would affect our participation in European affairs. Mr. Atherton observed that it possibly would not do more than to dissipate our strength. Mr. Davis and Mrs. McCormick agreed that the American public would certainly feel that it does not want another world war to start in Europe.

At that point Mr. Welles asked Mr. Pasvolsky for his views on the question of the morning. Mr. Pasvolsky began by saying that he was embarrassed on two scores: first, that he disagreed with much that had been said as to the value of a Danubian federation, and second, that he considered the political questions involved in this more important than the economic ones. He believed he could best present his views by describing the course of thought pursued in writing his book of the Economic Nationalism of the Danubian States some years ago.* He had started, he said, in an effort to prove that the dismemberment of Austria Hungary was a crime. He found, however, that his studies led him to the opposite conclusion. He had started with the proposition that Austro-Hungary had been an economic unit as opposed to the fragmented post-war Danubian world, and that therefore it was necessary to get back to the Dual Monarchy. He had limited himself to the economic aspects of the question because he saw no reason to believe that even a start could be made on the political aspects. He found that Austria-Hungary before the last war consisted of two politically autonomous units — a true federation under the Crown. The two parts were united

---

* Leo Pasvolsky, *Economic Nationalism of the Danubian States* (New York, 1928).

in a customs union and for certain other purposes. He discovered, however, that even with this organization, Austria and Hungary nearly broke apart whenever they had to revise the tariff. Concentration of agriculture and industry in different parts brought about disagreement. He found also that every ten years, in connection with the renewal of the Austro-Hungarian Bank, there was sharp strife. These difficulties were always reconciled but generally along the lines of Austrian desires. In his opinion, the reason for this was that political reasons governed all these actions, and that Austria was the dominant factor politically. Mr. Welles asked whether Austria was not also financially dominant. Agreeing that it was, Mr. Pasvolsky made a second observation about pre-war Austro-Hungarian economic functioning. Hungary succeeded, he said, in building a textile industry and in competing with the industry of Czechoslovakia. How was this possible? First, Hungary had enough banking resources; second, the Hungarian Government used its power to buy uniforms in order to further home industries; third, the Hungarian state railway administration imposed different freight rates, and these tactics were paralleled in other fields by measures which are generally called administrative or indirect protectionism. In summary, pre-war Austria-Hungary solved its economic problem only through forced industrialization with the use of foreign capital and through the exportation of 200.000 men per year. After making this study, Mr. Pasvolsky had gone to the five Succession countries. He had pointed out that if they were to have a union, its tariff would have to be established by diplomatic negotiations as opposed to the method of majority vote in Congress in this country. Admitting, he said, that it would be possible to adjust internal differences among the states, "Who will determine the unified tariff?" It was clear that this would need to be done by negotiation. The uniform answer which he received on this, however, was, "We will think about that when we come to it." Only once, he said, had this question really been faced. That was in the project for a customs union between Austria and Germany in 1931.* He noted, however, that even in that proposal, they had omitted the unified tariff and had recourse instead to the mere grant of reciprocal tariff preferences between the two countries. The entire plan, he pointed out, was only a preliminary project for a customs union and not a customs union itself. Continuing, he said that a primary problem of an economic federation

* The plan for a customs union between Germany and Austria was presented by Austria's Minister for Foreign Affairs, Johann Schober, on March 20, 1931. It fell through, due to the leading European nations', primarily of France's, Great Britain's and Italy's, opposition.

is its relations with the outside world. A second problem is whether the territory is really self-sufficient. He stated that in his view, the Danubian territory is not at all self-sufficient. Even if, he said, Czechoslovakia and Austria were willing to give up their agricultural tariff protection, this would afford to the other Danubian countries only a small additional market. Similarly, if the agricultural countries of that area were to give up industrial production, this step would increase by very little markets of the industrial states of the area. The result is that all of the Danubian states are forced to deal chiefly with non-Danubian states and are therefore thrown back on their need for relations with the outside world. This means, he added, political decision.

In concluding, he said that in thinking of economic matters, one must distinguish nation, region, and world. The relation of a nation to the world is, he said, difficult enough. To throw in, however, a second element, the functioning of a nation in a regional group which would in turn have relations to the world, would introduce a new factor of strain in international relations. No regional area, he said, is better off by itself than in a well-functioning world. No region is really big enough to be self-sufficient. The evolution of the Danubian question was, he said, characterized by what followed the Tardieu plan,* the last regional plan which received serious consideration. Meeting at Stresa in 1932 in an attempt to alleviate the plight of agriculture, the representatives of Eastern European states turned away from strictly regional arrangements and embraced the idea that states outside the area concerned should grant preferential tariffs on their agricultural products. This illustrated the fact that the essential economic problems of the Danubian countries cannot be solved solely by those countries, but by arrangements which take account also of relations with outside countries.

Mr. Welles observed that this had been a very interesting analysis. Mr. Davis said that in the past Germany and France, not being really dependent upon the products of the Danubian states, had had the "drop" on them. Some South European states, however, such as Yugoslavia, were really dependent upon the Danubian area. Mr. Pasvolsky then

* The Tardieu plan proposed closer economic cooperation, in the form of reciprocal customs concessions, between the six Danubian states: Austria, Czechoslovakia, Hungary, Yugoslavia, Romania and Bulgaria. The plan was named after French Prime Minister André Tardieu, who presented it on March 2, 1932. It failed to materialize because of the conflicts between the concerned nations, and because of counter-measures instituted by Germany and Italy.

distributed copies of some foreign trade statistics for the Danubian countries which revealed the small volume of trade between the Danubian countries themselves and, on the other hand, the large amount of trade which each Danubian country had with non-Danubian countries. Mr. Davis then asked whether, if these states constituted an economic unit, they would not be in a better position to negotiate as a unit. Rumania, Yugoslavia, and Hungary, he said, are so competitive that they are not so susceptible to German power as are the other states. Mr. Pasvolsky indicated that he was particularly opposed to the Eckhardt plan on the ground that if a regional federation were to be established at all, it should be made within as self-sufficient an area as possible. He observed that gains might be made if competitive countries would get together and organize as sellers. This would be similar to certain recent Pan-American arrangements. Such an arrangement would, however, presuppose an organization somewhat different from a federation. It would be an arrangement set up by treaty for dealing with other countries as buyers.

Mr. Welles then interjected that we might take the matter on that basis for the sake of argument. We might consider arrangements of this sort embracing Poland, Czechoslovakia, the Baltic countries, Hungary, Rumania, Yugoslavia, and Austria. It would be assumed that these countries would agree on a unified tariff. The great bulk of this economic area would be agricultural with only a small industry, which would mean there would be no really balanced economy. Turning to Mr. Cohen, he then asked what the latter's opinions on this matter were in the light of the experience of this country.

Mr. Cohen repeated his view that politics and economics could not be separated because politics plays a part in the determination of the economic. However large and rich a country may be, he said, it cannot be self-sufficient, and the attempt to make it so is not desirable. It does not follow, however, that some internal arrangements are not necessary. In this country, the large area of relatively free trade is an important factor in its prosperity. In Mr. Cohen's view, merely voluntary arrangements as to tariffs and the like by the Danubian countries would not work. It would be necessary to "institutionalize" these arrangements on some way. He was using the word "institutionalize" deliberately as he meant to leave his conception definitely flexible. He agreed with everything Mr. Pasvolsky had said except his conclusions.

In any case, proposals for regional arrangements would require very careful thought. As an additional possibility, he suggested that there be free trade as between the countries but not a unified tariff upon products from outside. Mr. Atherton pointed out that this would involve a central political organization of some sort. Mr. Cohen agreed, but thought its powers would be limited. Continuing, he raised the question whether we cannot create institutions that will assist in the construction of a stable order in the area. There would of course be a larger regional unit for restricted purposes; within that, smaller entities constituting more complete unions. He thought we might consider enlarging the geographical scope of the projected area to go as far south as Greece.

Mr. Welles said the point was well taken. Continuing, he asked whether it is not true that some sort of economic union would be the only manner of bringing about a rise in the standard of living. Mr. Pasvolsky observed that this was precisely what he questioned. He did not deny that it would bring about some rise in the standard of living, but did not appear to think that this rise would be comparatively important. He had no objection, he said, to the establishment of a Danubian union of some sort if the countries involved wished this. Mr. Welles replied that these countries cannot be expected to establish such an arrangement by themselves: They need, he thought, to be told how to do it.

Mr. Armstrong then asked whether some substitute of an international nature could not be found for the regional arrangement under discussion. Can't we, he asked, as relatively disinterested powers who will determine the peace, make that contribution? Such action, he said, would need to take place immediately at the end of the war. We should also, he thought, give economic direction to the efforts of these countries. All of their political decisions, he thought, must be centralized. If this is so difficult to organize in a region, he asked, shouldn't we find some international substitute for it? Mr. Pasvolsky observed that to create a world system that would enable these countries to trade, would lend them really substantial help. Mr. Cohen agreed, but stated that the problem is rather this: What is the best way to work toward a satisfactory long-range solution? Mr. Pasvolsky agreed, but indicated that, in his opinion, the best way would be to secure agreement by the powerful nations first. If this were done, he said, the smaller and weaker countries will be forced to accept the scheme. Mrs. McCormick stated that we must take for granted that the great powers will reform to some extent. She pointed out that the responsibility for past conditions in the Balkans rests largely upon the great powers. Mr. Welles thought that there was always a possibility of our being misled, as Dr. Pasvolsky was being misled, into feeling that just because the great powers reform, human nature can't wreck the gains they had made. Some regional organization, he thought, may furnish a balance.

By joining together, they can speed up their industrial organization and make themselves a more potent factor in Europe. Mrs. McCormick pointed out that up to now each Danubian country has been the rival of the others. If they could be brought to realize that their survival depends upon common action, they will accept the necessary arrangements. Mr. Welles thought there was a great deal in this point. Mr. Bowman said that these countries had once trusted the great powers and had been let down. Mrs. McCormick said that Prime Minister Sikorski and others realize that their nations must unite in order to exist.

Mr. Cohen then asked Mr. Pasvolsky whether, in the latter's opinion, if this country were divided into four states, we would have made more rapid progress with trade treaties than has been the case. Mr. Pasvolsky stated that less progress would have been made. Mr. Cohen, concurring, said that our experience showed that where central organization is weak, special influences are strong locally. This was, he said, an answer to Mr. Pasvolsky's question as to the proper approach to make. Mr. Pasvolsky answered that the problem would be somewhat simplified if we could have larger states. Mr. Cohen observed that we cannot create unitary states in the Danubian area. This fact does not, however, mean that an intermediate stage of organization cannot be found. Mr. Davis summed up Mr. Pasvolsky's view by saying that he believed that regional arrangements would be of some assistance provided the international organization was not neglected.

Mr. Welles then said that we must explore carefully the questions that had been raised. He thought it was time for this subcommittee to come into closer contact with the territorial subcommittee. For the next meeting we must have something much more definite to shoot at. It would, he said, be necessary to have a map which would show a potential economic federation with the territorial scope described by Mr. Cohen, including Greece and the other Balkan States, Austria, Czechoslovakia, Poland, and the Baltic states, excluding Finland. Finland would be considered rather as a member of the Scandinavian group. He suggested that the committee try to see whether such a unit would be economically conceivable, as he was beginning to think it was. That would be the fundamental question. If this could be done, what national regrouping in that area would be necessary to make the arrangement work, assuming that the units will have complete autonomy and sovereignty? The aim would be to get cohesive national groups. To that end, where should the frontiers be drawn? In answer to the question whether frontier adjustments could be considered, Mr. Welles pointed out that minority problems might make this expedient.

Mrs. McCormick suggested that this might mean the establishment of smaller national areas in the groupings and asked whether, for example, Czechoslovakia would be envisaged as being restored with its pre-war frontiers. Mr. Welles said he would envisage as big a Czechoslovakia, as before with the possible exception of the Sudetenland, but that he had had the Hungarian minorities chiefly in mind.

Mr. Armstrong then asked whether the task was not big enough to postpone the consideration of frontiers until later and to think for the present of pre-war frontiers. Mr. Welles agreed. Mr. Bowman stated that the territorial subcommittee could take up this question in the afternoon.

The chairman closed the meeting at 12:45 p.m.

Paul B. Taylor, secretary
Box 55

****

§ Document 2 §

AN EAST EUROPEAN UNION

(as considered to June 19, 1942)

Secret P Document 24

Basic Assumptions

The regional organization should have the form not of a federation but of a union of independent and sovereign states, cooperating for limited objectives through common non-legislative institutions, loosely rather than tightly organized. Provisionally the union is considered as including all states of Central and Eastern Europe between Russia and Germany from and including Estonia on the North to Austria on the West and Greece on the South.

The union should be imposed, if necessary, and should be guided for an indeterminate time, by the United Nations.

Its main object should be security, but economic incentives and advantages should be developed. Over-all international security would be guaranteed by the United Nations and the world organization, and the security organization of the union should be integrated with the world security organization within which should function.

The United Nations should promote the formation and stability of the union by making all necessary boundary adjustments in the region as rapidly as possible after the war.

Summary of Functions of Regional Organization

(1) Security relations with the outside world and with international organization;
(2) Intra-regional security and order by means of a regional constabulary or gendarmerie;
(3) Foreign relations of the union as such, and cognizance of external relations of component states;
(4) Intra-regional economic relations; and
(5) Economic relations with the outside world.

Constitution

The regional constitution, in the form of articles of union, would include written guaranties of certain individual and group rights—certain civil rights such as freedom of speech and religion, free elections, and rights of ethnic minorities. The union organization would have clearly defined and limited powers at the beginning, with the possibility of growth provided.

Executive

An executive would be chosen by majority vote of the political council (or presidium) and empowered to carry out delegated duties in regard to security. He would be subject to removal by, and special instructions from the political council.

Political Council

(a) *Composition.* The political council should consist of two members from each component state. One of the representatives from each state should be the Prime Minister or his plenipotentiary; the order should be a representative of the national parliament or his alternate.

(b) *Functions.* At the outset at least the functions of the political council would deliberately be limited.

Its sole executive function would be the maintenance of intra-regional security, effected through control of the regional gendarmerie. It would establish and exact the regional quota of forces required of the component states for the maintenance of the gendarmerie of the union. And it would be responsible for filling the regional quota required for the police force of the international security organization. Discharge of the security function would be lodged in the executive described above.

Its political functions would include the foreign policy of the union in its relations with the rest of the world, and the taking of cognizance of any national relations of component states with outside nations or groups which were in violation of the undertakings of the union. The council would seek to prevent disputes between component states or to undertake their settlement so far as possible. And it would decide the contribution of the component states for the necessary expenses of the union.

Its administrative functions would be the maintenance of a regional administration including a central secretariat. Whether this council would have responsibility for collection and apportionment of customs duties remains under discussion.

The members of the council would be responsible for the action by their individual governments to secure national approval and enforcement of decisions.

Economic Council

(a) *General Nature.* The economic council would be separate from the political council. It would be an advisory body except in certain contingencies not yet agreed upon. Its recommendations would be referred to the governments of the component states for approval. It would represent the region as a whole, and not merely the interests of individual states; accordingly the council might be called "Council for the Economic Development of the East European Union." This council might be the medium through which international plans for economic development of the region were handled.

(b) *Functions.* This council would be charged with making recommendations of the governments of the component states on economic interests of concern to the region, and it would have powers as broad as possible to initiate recommendations on general economic policies. Remaining under discussion are (a) whether it should be responsible for union administration of economic arrangements approved by the component states, and (b) whether it should be charged with enumerated functions relating to such matters as freedom of transit, communications, etc., in the union as a whole.

(c) *Composition.* Each state should be represented in the economic council by not more than five experts. Each state would select any number of experts up to the maximum. Such experts would be selected by the government in each state, from the Central Bank, industry, labor, agriculture, and the professional classes. The terms of reference to the governments regarding the selection of representatives should stress that the delegates should know what they were to consider and should be competent as experts in those subjects. The experts would be assisted by staffs.

(d) *Tenure of office of the members.* The length of terms of the members would not be fixed.

(e) *Voting.* The delegation from each state in the economic council would vote as a unit. The question of voting in the council as to recommendations remains for discussion after receipt of a report on the economic council requested from the subcommittee on economic problems; the proposed possible solutions are: (a) no percentage specified and minority views circulated with the recommendations; and (b) a fixed percentage of two-thirds or three-fourths; and possibly unanimity in certain matters. As to approval by the states of the recommendations, tentative conclusion of views is also deferred until the requested report is received; proposed possibilities are that two-thirds or three-fourths of the component states should approve measures to become effective for the entire union, but possible unanimity should be stipulated in certain matters. While a "double majority" of the same percentage, – e.g., two-thirds of the council and of the states, – might be a satisfactory solution, it might be feasible to require only a simple (or two-thirds) majority in the council if the required number of state approvals were set at a higher majority of two-thirds (or three-fourths).

Any number of states could voluntarily undertake common measures they might desire provided not contrary to the articles of union.

(f) *Foreign Advisers.* Three economic advisers would be appointed by the United Nations to represent them in the economic council. These advisers would serve for three-year terms but initially so scaled that one might come up for appointment or re-appointment after one year, the second after two years, and the third after three years. No one of the three should come from Europe (including Russia).

These advisers would have a voice in the council but have no vote or veto power. Their practical power would reside in the denial or grant of economic benefits by the United Nations. They should advise the whole council, not the component delegations. They should be competent on economic problems in general. They would be assisted by staffs. They should have the widest possible power of initiative with respect to recommendations on economic problems of the region.

The advisers should be closely linked to appropriate world organization committees which would be established, (possibly similar to the Economic and Financial Committee of the League of Nations); these committees might appoint the advisers or they might be selected by some type of United Nations' body, perhaps set up for the purpose, representing the United Nations' authority. These matters were deferred for discussion in connection with problems of world organization.

Judicial Organization

A regional judicial system would be created, to include a regional court with provision for appeals to a court of international justice in cases important to the union or its members. Appeals are envisaged in the following:

(1) disputes or differences between component states;

(2) any cases arising from an allegation that any state had not performed its duties under the Articles of Union;

(3) any allegation by an individual that the Bill of Rights had not been carried out in respect of him and that he had no redress.

The Component States of the Union: Rights and Duties

Each state of the union could maintain the diplomatic relations customary to independent and sovereign states. Each state would be responsible for contributing to the international security force such quota as the political council agreed each state should provide. Contributions of men from state would be in accordance with the population. The state quotas of men in the regional gendarmerie are neither envisaged to be situated in the states from whence they came, nor in the event of need to use union security forces to maintain peace in the union would the state quotas be used in their own states if avoidable. No state would have national military forces; municipal police forces only would be permitted in the states.

States would retain the power to approve or disapprove the recommendations from the economic council, and they would be free voluntarily to make economic arrangements among each other that were not in violation of the articles of union. Remaining under discussion is the percentage of state approvals of recommendations which would be required for adoption as binding in the union.

In the event of a regional approach to international organization, the delegates of each state to the international political organization might be its two representatives in the political council of the union, voting by states rather than together as a region, but this remains for consideration in connection with world organization.

Relations with the United Nations and International Organization: Summary of Tentative Views

(a) *Gendarmerie.* The United Nations would vest control of the regional gendarmerie in the political council after making the essential decisions concerning military forces in the region. The commanding officers would at the outset be selected by the United Nations, which would also determine the size of the force for a stated period.

(b) *Security.* The general security organization would require of the union the regional quota or contribution necessary for the international police force. Regional security arrangements would be integrated with the general security system.

(c) *Political Relations.* The union as such might not be represented in the international political organization; this remains for later consideration.

(d) *Economic Relations.* The United Nations would give advice to the union on economic questions through three advisers.

(e) *Judicial Relations.* Provision for appeal from the judicial organization or tribunal of the union to an international judicial organization would be made.

Box 56

****

§ Document 3 §

Minutes of the Subcommittee on Political Problems

(excerpt)

Strictly Confidential Minutes P - 17

Meeting of June 27, 1942

Present:
Mr. Welles, presiding
Mr. Hamilton Fish Armstrong
Mr. Adolf A. Berle
Mr. Isaiah Bowman
Mr. Benjamin V. Cohen
Mr. Green H. Hackworth
Mr. John V. A. MacMurray
Mrs. Anne O'Hare McCormick
Mr. Leo Pasvolsky
Mr. James T. Shotwell
Mr. Myron C. Taylor
Mr. Paul C. Daniels
Mr. Harley Notter, research secretary
Mr. Paul B. Taylor, secretary

(...) The more he had thought over the question, particularly during the past week, the more difficult it seemed to have a complete East European Union covering the entire area we had thought of. He wondered if success would not be more likely if were to have a Northern East European Group and a Balkan Group. Our whole objective was the inducement of peace by removing the possibility of war or exploitation by big powers, such as Germany, Russia, and Great Britain, against the small states of the region; and by making the people of the region as prosperous and contented as possible. We had thought the best way to achieve this was by creating a buffer, not subservient to Germany, the Soviet Union, or to Great Britain. The question thus arose whether a division of the area into two parts would diminish the possibility of accomplishing that objective.

Mrs. McCormick thought it would be necessary to define the boundaries of the two groups and to determine what liaison there should be between them. It would, she thought, be extremely hard to get the antagonistic peoples together at the beginning. She thought Austria offered a possibility as a sort of liaison country — a meeting ground. Turning to Mr. Welles, she said that she did not know what conversations he and other officials had had on such questions. Mr. Welles said that so far as he could determine, it would be an appallingly difficult job. The bitter feeling of Yugoslavia and Greece toward Bulgaria — the justifiably bitter feeling — was one which he, personally, had rarely seen equaled. Mrs. McCormick referred also to the bitterness between Hungary and Rumania. Mr. Welles added the hatred of Czechoslovakia and Hungary; and of Yugoslavia and Hungary. There would be question whether the danger would diminish by having all of these countries together. Mr. Pasvolsky asked whether we could draw a line between the groups which would minimize the effects of these antagonisms. Mr. Welles said that one group would be Lithuania, Poland, and Czechoslovakia (and Austria?). The Balkan Group would consist of Greece, Bulgaria, Yugoslavia, and Rumania.

Mr. Armstrong raised the question as to what power would try to exploit the area and under what conditions it could succeed. Mrs. McCormick thought that Russia would be likely to dominate the Northern Group while Germany would dominate the Southern. Mr. Welles said, "Or *vice versa*." Mr. Armstrong thought it would be more likely to be vice versa. The question would arise as to the social policy maintained by Soviet Russia after the war. This could, he pointed out, over-ride all other considerations. He felt that the appeal of Pan-Slavism was the strongest in Yugoslavia and Bulgaria. He thought there was some possibility of improvement of the relations between Bulgaria and Yugoslavia if there were very radical Bulgarian and Yugoslav régimes. This possibility had been indicated by the Stambulsky régime* in Bulgaria; if, however, the Bulgarian dynasty** were to hold, he thought there Bulgarian-Greek antagonism was worse than the Bulgarian-Yugoslav. Mr. Armstrong thought, however, that even this might be better in a successful organization.

Mrs. McCormick said there had been a movement at one time toward a *rapprochement* between Venizelos and a Bulgarian leader whose name she had forgotten (Stambulsky?). Mr. Armstrong concurred that there had been such a movement between the two countries in

---

* I.e., Alexandur Stambolisky, who was prime minister of Bulgaria between 1919 and 1923. He created a dictatorship of the peasantry against the urban and well-to-do population, the like of which was unprecedented in Europe at the time. He was shot "while trying to escape" during the rightist takeover in 1923.

** From 1886, Bulgaria's sovereigns were descendants of the Saxe-Coburg ducal family: from 1887 to 1918 Ferdinand I, from 1918 to 1943, Boris III.

1925 and 1926. The Bulgarian Dynasty had been the chief obstacle to it, while the Greek Church had been a great assistance.

Mr. Shotwell said that it had been very surprising in 1912 when the two countries had got together in an alliance.* They could do things. He thought that if they were to get rid of the nationalists, the peasants would not cherish hatreds as in the past. The secretary of Stambulisky, who had worked for him, had been convinced that the peasants were kept from friendly relations with the Greeks by their nationalist leaders. Mr. Armstrong said that they were kept from it by being killed.

Mr. Armstrong, continuing the earlier discussion, said that half of the area would be very likely to come under Russian influence.

Mr. Bowman said that in studying this question, we would have to ask what were the minimum conditions of success. What were natural affiliations? On top of that, explorations would be made in the direction of Mr. Berle's five points. It would be necessary to investigate what natural affiliations had taken place in the past; in what directions they had been capable of extension of others had seen the need of it. He asked whether that would be a good direction in which to go. He asked whether the economic experts could not give us in a short paragraph a statement of these natural developments during the past twenty or twenty-five years.

Mr. Welles said it was clear that an association of Lithuania, Poland, Czechoslovakia, and Austria would have historical background to it, provided that the "bogy" of a Habsburg restoration were removed. He would assume that in a new world situation, some old objections would be in part removed. Then we would have the problem of Hungary. From every standpoint of expediency, Hungary would have to be part of the Northern Union. If we took the historical background, Yugoslavia would form part of this group; but if we were to go further back, Yugoslavia should be a member of the Balkan Group in case there were to be two groups. So far as he was concerned, he was not "wedded to the view that just because Slovenia and Croatia had been part of Serbia in the past, they should always be."

Mr. Armstrong said he wished to refer again to Hungary — the character of the régime, to the need for changes of agricultural tenure, and to the feudal set-up which existed in Hungary. These had been of extreme importance in Hungary's politics. Count Apponyi had, he

---

* The reference is to the First Balkan War of 1912, when Bulgaria joined forces with the armies of Greece, Montenegro and Serbia against Turkey.

recalled, made the claim to the Crown of Bohemia through Archduke Otto in 1926. Mr. Welles asked whether this claim had been made at the League of Nations. Mr. Armstrong said that Count Apponyi always went to the League of Nations; at the same time, making such individual arrangements with state as he could.* In that atmosphere it had been no use to ask Masaryk to talk about frontier adjustments in Slovakia. He thought, therefore, that the character of the régimes in Hungary, Poland, and Bulgaria – these three, he thought, were the most backward socially, especially Hungary in the matter of land tenure – was a factor of great importance.

Mr. Berle said it appeared that there were really only two possibilities as to the division between the North and South Group. The question concerned only whether Austria and Hungary were to go with the Northern Group or with the Southern Group. He wished to suggest, as a new possibility for consideration, that we turn them south. The east-west line might be at the southern Czechoslovak boundary, running from there to the northern part of the Black Sea.

Mr. Welles asked Mr. Berle whether he meant that the Northern Group would consist of Lithuania, Poland, and Czechoslovakia. Mr. Berle said that was what he had meant. Mr. Cohen said unless one did that, there would not be a cohesive force to hold the Balkan Group together. Mr. Berle said that had been the reason for his suggestion.

Mr. Cohen said one reason that had induced us before, to limit the functions of the union was that of making possible the inclusion of all the states of the region. He wondered, accordingly, whether if we were envisaging smaller unions, more powers might not be given to such unions. Moreover, the territorial division suggested by Mr. Berle enabled us to use the Northern Group to help hold the Southern Group together while leaving also the possibility that Austria and Hungary could go either way.

Mr. Welles thought that, from the standpoint of our objectives, it was clear that the larger group was the better of the solutions. However, having in mind the point which Dr. Bowman had made as to insurance against difficulties, he was puzzled as to whether the disruptive forces of such a union would not be so great as to defeat our purposes.

---

* We have no knowledge of Count Albert Apponyi's ever having made any demand at the League of Nations for the Crown of Bohemia, either in his own name, or on behalf of Archduke Otto. Apponyi was Hungary's representative to the League of Nations from 1923 to 1933. His activities as such focused on protecting the rights of the Hungarian minorities in the neighboring countries.

Mr. Shotwell said that at the last Peace Conference maps like those presented to the committee, representing a possible East European Federation, had been prepared and presented by Masaryk. It had turned out, however, that Masaryk could not even overcome the nationalism in his own country. It had been a great tragedy. He thought there was a danger of our deluding ourselves as to the realities. The intellectual leaders of the area in the nineteenth century had become the nationalist leaders of the twentieth. Until recently there had been few political contacts and only limited social ones. The peasants were not, he thought, nationalists, but their intellectual leaders had adhered to the disruptive forces. This was the most difficult problem of federation. There was no place where people understood the American principle of federation. For example, the fact that Count Apponyi's estates had been in Slovakia had dominated his thinking. He did not think we could place our hopes too high unless the movement were not to be dominated by the intellectuals of the past generation.

He thought something could be done along these economic lines. He was glad that Mr. Berle had mentioned communications first. He could remember the time when it took three days to travel from Skoplje to Monastir. That time had later been out from breakfast to tea. He wished that he knew more about what the Germans had done to smash these old ideas. He thought, however, that the strongest pull which there could be toward union would be something outside the region — some international influence or activity.

Mr. Welles asked Mr. MacMurray for his opinions. Mr. MacMurray said he was completely puzzled. He had to contend with the idea that the easiest way would be the largest organization. However, this would involve so many disparates and irreconcilables that he was afraid that we were proposing something too big to be put together. Accordingly, not on any definite grounds, but merely on an instinctive feeling, he thought that there should be at least two of these groups. In this case, he thought that Turkey should be included in the Southern Group. It had, in recent years, been a most useful factor in the Balkan meetings. It had no territorial ambitions and had been a very useful means of communication between the other governments. Mr. Welles said that this was a very interesting suggestion.

Mrs. McCormick referred to another difficulty which had been faced in the post-war period and which was embodied by Count Apponyi. Apponyi and others had maintained a policy of grievances. Their whole feeling had been dominated by their grievances. She thought that this time we should not think too much of victors and vanquished. She recalled an experience she had had when visiting the American College at Sofia. The students had just discussed the death of John Buchan.[*] It was a very international meeting. At the end, the President of the college had asked them to sing. They had then broken immediately out into their "Dobrudja" song. There was, she said, an amazing underlying feeling for Dobrudja in Bulgaria,[**] Mr. Welles said that this was very interesting.

Mr. Armstrong said that there were two factors; first, the Bulgarian claim to Dobrudja; and second, the Apponyi attitude —"something natural plus". At one time when he was visiting Count Apponyi at his home, the latter had said, "I don't need to talk to you about the Rumanian problem. You have a negro problem in your own country and so you understand it." He said that both of these things existed in different countries.[***]

Mrs. McCormick said that the Bulgarians had always felt that the Balkan Entente was aimed against them. Mr. Shotwell said that even in their own meetings of the Bulgarian Entente, the old Macedonian question[****] had come to the fore. He thought that mediation by a present-day of Turkey would be very useful.

Mr. Welles agreed that this was a very interesting suggestion indeed. He wondered whether the inclusion of Turkey would not mean the very determined opposition of Russia. Mr. Armstrong asked whether Mr. Welles meant the opposition of Turkey's "own ally."

Mr. Welles: "Their ally?" He said that the position in this respect had materially changed. This would raise, moreover, the old question of the straits again.

Mr. Shotwell said that the adoption of the Stalin or Curzon Line the boundary of Poland might affect the problem.[*****] Mr. Bowman

---

[*] American novelist John Buchan was born in 1875, and died in 1940.

[**] The reference is to Southern Dobrudja which Bulgaria, in accordance with the terms of the 1913 Peace Treaty of Bucharest, ending the Second Balkan War, had to cede to Romania.

[***] Armstrong visited Apponyi in Budapest in 1922. For Armstrong's report on the visit and on the topics of the meeting, see: Peace and Counterpeace. Memoirs of Hamilton Fish Armstrong (New York, London, 1971), 173.

[****] The so-called "Balkan Entente" was established on February 9, 1934, by Turkey, Greece, Romania, and Yugoslavia. The regional security organization was formed to maintain the status quo in the Balkans, and to discourage Bulgarian revisionist attempts at the annexation of the Macedonian-inhabited territories belonging to Greece and Yugoslavia.

[*****] The "Curzon Line" was the Polish-Russian frontier, or rather, the demarcation line proposed by the 1919 Paris Peace Conference. It was named after George Nathaniel Curzon of Kedleston, the United Kingdom's Foreign Secretary from 1914 to 1924. In the Polish-Russian war of 1920, Poland

said that the territorial committee would give the committee "an earful" on the Curzon Line two weeks hence.

Mr. Welles said he wished to go back to what Mr. Bowman had suggested in regard to the terms of reference to the economic subcommittee. Taking the entire area as now indicated, where should the line be drawn? He asked whether the members agreed to Mr. Berle's suggestion that Austria and Hungary be included in the Southern Group. There was, in addition, a third possibility —that Austria remain outside. Mr. Armstrong thought there were great disadvantages of "leaving Austria hanging." It would make a sort of football out of Austria.

Mr. Bowman thought there was a partial answer to the Polish dynamite which Mr. Shotwell had referred to. His own mind ran back over to what mathematicians would call an "inescapable series," the difficulties mentioned by Dr. Shotwell and further difficulties. We could then say that we saw no hope. We would then have individual states, at least eight. We could wipe the slate clean and start again. If we should do this, what combination could be indicated? What loose arrangements of states could we envisage? This empirical, ad hoc method was realistic, "but never had a solution in it." When he got through his own thinking, he still felt that somewhere, even in the distance, there was a goal. He was forced back to some more generalized picture of the East European problem. He would place great emphasis on the identification of mutual advantages and working arrangements of the last twenty years; what advantages had they? What could have been done? That seemed fundamentally a job for an economic specialist to go into — a history of the attempts which had been made. He thought we would be aided if we knew factually what the experience had been. He asked whether anyone was prepared to bring forward experience on this.

Mr. Shotwell said it should not be forgotten that the Habsburg Monarchy had rested on prestige —the prestige of its army, the church, and the intellectual cooperation of the United Nations? In the League of Nations, Austria had asked that the intellectual cooperation work be centered there. This had been refused. Could there be something of this alongside the economic factor?

Mr. Bowman said that Dr. Shotwell's colleague, John Dewey, had written an article in the first volume of *Foreign Affairs* on "Ethics and

---

established a border much farther to the east (*cf.* Map 1). The Soviet-Polish border drawn after World War II more or less coincides with the 1919 Curzon Line.

International Relations".* It had dealt with the terrible problem which confronts a world in a time of territorial fragmentation and confusion in developing common bases of ethics. Each nation favored its own ethic, sought to aggrandize it and looked at everything in terms of it. The thought of the writer had run forward to the point that the greatest consideration was flexibility. His only concrete suggestion was the outlawry of war. (Mr. Shotwell noted that the outlawry of war had been taken as an example of flexibility). Continuing, Mr. Bowman said that these conclusions had left him flat. This was, he said, nearly always true of writings on international affairs. It was also true of the discussions of this committee.

Mr. Welles said he wished to go back and insist on claiming for this Government a "guaranteed position."

He was still worried (although physically and for other reasons it seemed most reasonable) about the approach to our Southern Union through the inclusion in it of Austria and Hungary. Mr. Berle said he was not sure of this himself; he had merely thought it worth consideration. Mr. Welles thought that Austria, finding herself in that position, would assume a certain prestige. This would be entirely justified, as we all knew, that from the standpoint of culture Austria would assume a leadership. Mr. Shotwell said that it would naturally assume a leadership in economic matters as well.

Mr. Welles then said we should then make our terms of reference to the economic committee *on that line*, with an alternative to include Austria (and Hungary?) in the Northern Group.

Mr. Taylor observed that our approach now seemed to be that of "diving up the trouble between the Northern an Southern Groups and of segregating most of the trouble in the Southern." He wondered whether we could handle the matter better in that way. Mr. Welles said his own feeling was that the better solution was the whole union, but he wondered whether we could still achieve our major objectives and lessen the objections if we had two groups.

The question was asked whether Mr. Welles and Mr. Berle had talked with representatives of these countries on this matter. Mr. Berle said that no one of that group had the concept of a single union. Mr. Welles said he had never found one who had the conception of one union, most favoring three unions; some, two. Mr. Berle said that the

---

* John Dewey, "Ethics and International Relations," *Foreign Affairs*, (March 1923), 85-89.

Czechs were the only ones who had offered any support for a single union.

Mr. Pasvolsky said that the new Russian frontier on the map (pointing to Map V) was most significant. It put the Russians next to Czechoslovakia. He thought that a balance of power in the region was of great importance.

Mr. Welles asked whether Mr. Pasvolsky had meant an *internal* balance of power. He agreed that this was of great importance. Mr. Pasvolsky said it might be useful to have a memorandum on the political history of the region.

As to the internal balance in the union as a whole, taking the three possibilities: (1) in the north, a reduced Poland would be about equal to Czechoslovakia. Czechoslovakia would have much friendlier relations with Russia. The Poles wanted to bring Hungary into the group as an offset to Czechoslovakia. Poland plus Hungary would be difficult for Czechoslovakia to handle even with Rumanian influence; (2) in the Southern Group the line of development would be in the direction of close relationship between Yugoslavia and Bulgaria. That would be the dominant factor. It was not clear what the Russian policy would be. He thought that Russia was not nearly so close to these countries as to Czechoslovakia.

Mr. Welles said that if the lines were to exist as shown on that map, there would be a fairly good balance. Russian influence would be preponderant in Czechoslovakia, Bulgaria and Yugoslavia while anti-Russian influence would be preponderant in Hungary, Poland, Austria, and Rumania. He thought this would make a fairly equal balance. If the region were divided into two groups, and the Northern were left intact. Poland, Lithuania and Czechoslovakia would have a balance; in the South there would also be an internal balance in sentiment regarding Russia.

Someone asked whether Rumania was anti-Russian. Mr. Welles said that if anything could bring Rumania and Hungary together, it would be hatred of Russia. Mr. Armstrong thought, on the contrary, that Rumania might conceivably be in good terms with Russia. Mrs. McCormick said that Davila, who was working closely with the Czechs, was certainly not on good terms with the Russians. Mr. Armstrong said that Maniu had not been particularly anti-Russian. Mr. Welles said, however, that when one considered the Bessarabian massacres and a whole series of other incidents,* one saw that all of these would have the effect of creating hatreds between the Russians and Rumanians. Mrs. McCormick mentioned the problem of Transylvania. Mr. Pasvolsky referred to the antagonism between Carol and Antonescu.**

Mr. Armstrong said that in some countries the idea of not bringing Austria and Hungary into the Southern Union would be very agreeable. Since the last war they had tried to break the old ties; for example, in trade and banking.

Mr. Welles said that he had asked the committee to take so much time for the discussion of this matter — and the discussion had confirmed him in his own judgment — because all the views tended, in case there were to be a separation, to show that there would have to be a three-way division and not a two-way. Mr. Armstrong asked what the third division would be. Mr. Welles answered that it would be Austria, either with one or two other states or alone.

Mr. Armstrong asked whether the economic subcommittee was working on projects of actual help regarding the Balkan area. Such projects would, he said, constitute the bait which we could offer. Mr. Welles said that we had crystallized just this.

Mr. Taylor said that the first problem was to discover the needs of the area and the particular economic facts; and that when this was done, we might pass on to the question of the means of assistance.

Mr. Welles said that he was clear in his own mind that if we could reach a decision as to what was politically desirable, then the economic subcommittee should see what it could do to carry out this decision — to bolster up the system envisaged.

One thing similar to what Mr. Armstrong had referred to, which we had done in this hemisphere, might be mentioned. It was the so-called development corporations. We might make the same kind of gift to the East European Group. It gave a great leverage power to us. Mrs. McCormick thought the most important thing was to try to convince the people of the area of the advantages of a union. Mr. Taylor asked whether these groups had to do with the operations of business. Mr.

---

* The reference is to the mass murders and atrocities committed in Bessarabia and in other Russian territories by the Romanian armies of occupation.

** On September 6, 1940, immediately after the Second Vienna Award dividing Transylvania, the Romanian extreme right, headed by General Ion Antonescu, declared King Carol II weak and impotent, and forced him to abdicate and leave the country. He was succeeded by the 19 year old Michael I, who, until 1944, did little but assist as Marshal Antonescu, calling himself *Conducator* (leader of the nation), established a fascist dictatorship.

Welles said that the projects went on ostensibly under the guise of local operation and control; ostensibly with American consultants and advisers. Really, he said, these American advisers "run the show".

Mr. Shotwell said that another alternative would be American interest in the Balkans through the period of relief into the period of reconstruction. This raised the question whether the Department of Agriculture would help on problems of soil erosion and the like. Theoretically, we could stimulate an interest in the common peasant in this way which might over-ride nationalism. Mr. Welles said that was really the idea he had had in mind.

Mrs. McCormick said we might consider again the problem of the three groupings. We could, she said, easily see two. The question then concerned the disposition of Austria and Hungary. The other two seemed fairly logical. Mr. Cohen said that in regard to Austria and Hungary, he felt somewhat as Mr. Armstrong had. He would rather view it as having the possibility of going either North or South than as being a third group. It seemed cut off from markets. Mr. Armstrong said that Austria and Hungary cut the Northern Group off from the Southern. Mr. Berle said that we must pre-suppose that Austria would have Trieste. This would canalize the German trade in that direction and would also absorb a lot of that which went through Czechoslovakia. Mr. Armstrong said that if joined, the Czechs could use it too. Mrs. McCormick thought that Austria and Hungary should be with the Northern Group.

Mr. Welles again said that the entire union was a desirable objective. However, from the standpoint of economic arrangements, we would consider two units as a possible alternative; whether Austria and Hungary should go North or South to be determined by the economic advantages which the economic subcommittee would show us. This was, he said, the reference to the economic subcommittee. This reference would, in turn, be broken up into the six or seven points stated earlier in the meeting.

Mr. Cohen said that, in this connection, the three alternatives might be considered.

Mr. Taylor asked whether when the report on the entire group were revised, it should be distributed to the members of this committee for their consideration. Mr. Welles said we would need this as soon as available. We would, however, return in two weeks to the Germanic problem, especially as regards East Prussia, and other problems affecting the Polish frontier.

Mr. Armstrong referred to certain questions connected with this problem which had been referred to the Council group. Studies of the

Eastern and Western industrial regions had been worked out in terms of alternatives and would be supplied to Mr. Pasvolsky before the next meeting. One study dealt with territorial problems while one dealt with financial and economic ones.

Mr. Welles said he gathered that the Council on Foreign Relations had done a considerable amount of work which would be of value to us. Mr. Armstrong said the Council had not done anything specifically on an East European union. Mr. Welles said that he had meant that they had worked on economic aspects of these problems.

Mr. Pasvolsky noted that there might also be a report from the security subcommittee on the military aspects of partition.

Mr. Welles said he wished to say one more thing before the meeting adjourned. In order to save time, it seemed to him that some helpful preliminary work could be done on a problem which would come to this committee in time — that was the problem of an international organization which had been made the last point in the chart. At the rate at which the committee was now moving, a long time would elapse before this matter could be considered. He thought it might be desirable for a subcommittee of this committee to consider this question and to draft something in concrete terms for the full committee. If agreeable, he would ask a small subcommittee to sit on that question during coming weeks. Mr. Pasvolsky said that that subcommittee might offer projects for research on this problem. Mrs. McCormick said it would be more important to have ideas than research. Mr. Welles stressed that what was desired was something definite and concrete for the whole committee to work on. Mrs. McCormick said that she had constantly felt it necessary in our discussions of particular questions to have some definite ideas of the over-all organization. Mr. Welles said that if it was agreeable, he would ask a small subcommittee to work with him on that and perhaps to get one or two outside consultants. He said that the committee would meet again two weeks from today.

The meeting was adjourned at 12:45 p.m.

Paul B. Taylor, secretary

Box 55

Part Two:

Frontiers of Hungary

Chapter I

Minutes of the Subcommittee on Territorial Problems

§ Document 1 §

(Excerpt)

Secret T Minutes 15

July 31, 1942

Present:
Mr. Isaiah Bowman, presiding
Mr. Hamilton Fish Armstrong
Mr. John V. A. MacMurray
Mrs. Anne O'Hare McCormick
Mr. Leo Pasvolsky
Mr. Philip Mosely
Mr. Easton Rothwell

(...) Slovak-Hungarian Frontier

Mr. Mosely introduced the discussion of the Slovak-Hungarian frontier by commenting upon the following documents made available to the committee:

1. Alternative Territorial Solutions. Secret
2. Historical Outline, 1918-1939.
3. The American Position on the Northern Boundary of Hungary in 1919.
4. The American Position on the Northern Boundary of Hungary in 1920. Secret
5. Hungarian Census of 1910.
6. Analysis of Czechoslovak Census of 1930.

7. Tentative Maps: Population by Native Language, 1910; Population by Nationality, 1930.*

(Mr. Bowman requested that a copy of these documents be made available to Mr. Berle, who was not present.)

Mr. Mosely referred to the map showing the disputed frontier area, and commented upon the boundary established by the Vienna Award of November 2, 1938, by which Hungary received approximately 12,000 square kilometers and a population of 1,027,000, including many non-Magyars. He also discussed the boundary established by the Hungarian-Slovak Protocol of April 3, 1939, under which Hungary annexed part of Eastern Slovakia, in addition to obtaining certain rectifications of the Vienna line and annexing Ruthenia. The ethnic line would, he said, run somewhere between the 1937 and 1939 boundaries. Beginning at the west, the *Grosse Schuett* was preponderantly Magyar, although a bridgehead was left to Slovakia. Farther to the east the Slovakia were to be found south of the 1939 frontier in relatively large numbers. According to the figures of the 1930 Czech census, the cities of Losonc, Rimaszombat, Rozsnyó, Kassa, Ungvár, and Munkács would all return to Slovakia for ethnic reasons.

If the frontier were drawn on ethnic lines, leaving roughly equal numbers on either side of the frontier the result would be to improve slightly Hungarian transportation facilities, without seriously interfering with those of Czechoslovakia. From the standpoint of security, Czechoslovakia and Hungary would be deprived of any substantial advantages of terrain.

Mr. Bowman said that Mr. Mosely's summary had clearly outlined the problem and that the first item to be discussed was the general question of whether a substantial number of people could be transferred from one state to another. Mr. Armstrong believed that this question should be considered in the light of Point Two of the Atlantic Declaration, stating that, "They desire to see no territorial changes that do not accord with the freely expressed wishes of the peoples concerned."** He thought it was necessary to clarify how Point Two would affect changes of territory, either on the side of the allies or that of the enemy.

---

*All significant statements of the listed documents are contained in Part II, Chapter II, 1-2, and 4-5 of this volume.

**Dénes Halmosy, *Nemzetközi szerződések 1918-1945* (Budapest, 1983), 526-527.

Did it mean a resort to plebiscites or some other means for expressing self-determination?

Self-Determination

The discussion continued on the subject of self-determination. Mr. Pasvolsky said that it would be necessary to translate Point Two into machinery for its fulfillment, and this would constitute one of the real problems of the territorial subcommittee. Mr. Bowman said that if the implementation of Point Two were not subject to discussion in the territorial subcommittee, the committee had better disband. The Atlantic Declaration was described by Mr. Armstrong as, in a sense, a reply to territorial changes forced upon Europe by the Axis. Mr. Bowman agreed, adding that it was necessarily general in statement. Mr. Pasvolsky said that the specific meaning of the postulates set forth in the Atlantic Declaration were left to others, including this committee, to decide.

Commitments

Mr. Armstrong said that promises or commitments more specific than those of the Atlantic Charter had presumably been made by the United States and its allies to various peoples. These commitments should be analyzed, he thought, as a means of knowing what territorial adjustments would be compatible with promises already made. Mr. Pasvolsky explained that promises already made. Mr. Pasvolsky explained that a careful compilation of commitments had been made by the research staff, and that all those pertaining to each problem should be brought together when that area was being studied. He went on to say that the official position of the United States has been to make no commitments with respect to frontiers and to accept none made by other nations. Mr. Mosely commented that, in recognizing the Czechoslovak Government-in-Exile, the American Government had specifically refrained from recognizing the pre-Munich frontiers of that state. (...)

x x x

SLOVAK-HUNGARIAN FRONTIER

Preliminary discussion was invited upon the problem of the Slovak-Hungarian frontier. The boundaries established by the Vienna Award of November 2, 1938 and by the subsequent Hungarian-Slovak protocol of April 3, 1939 were shown to have included within Hungary all of Ruthenia, a portion of eastern Slovakia, and extensive areas in south-portion of eastern Slovakia, and extensive areas in southern Slovakia, whose populations included many non-Magyars. The ethnic line would run somewhere between the 1937 and 1939 boundaries. If the frontier were drawn on an ethnic basis, Hungarian transportation facilities would be slightly improved, without seriously dislocating those of Czechoslovakia. From the standpoint of security, neither Czechoslovakia nor Hungary would gain any substantial advantages of terrain.

A minimum of 600,000 Magyars was said to reside within the contested area, according to the 1930 census.

Nevertheless, the preponderantly Slovak areas could be served out without preventing the transfer to Hungary of approximately 400,000 Magyars.

Principles and Procedures of Territorial Adjustment

Point Two of the Atlantic Declaration, stating the right of territorial self-determination, was thought to impose broad restrictions upon extensive boundary adjustments, although the specific application of this and other policies of the Declaration was regarded as subject to inquiry and deliberation.

Commitments made to the various states were regarded as placing another possible limit upon boundary adjustment. It was explained, however, that the official policy of the United States has been to make no commitments with respect to boundaries and to recognize none made elsewhere.

Box 59

****

§ Document 2 §

(Excerpt)

Secret T Minutes 16

August 14, 1942

Present:
Mr. Isaiah Bowman, presiding
Mr. Hamilton Fish Armstrong
Mr. Adolf A. Berle
Mr. John V. A. MacMurray
Mrs. Anne O'Hare McCormick
Mr. Philip Mosely
Mr. Easton Rothwell

The chairman convened the meeting at 5:15 p.m., and asked if the committee wished to proceed with the discussion of the Danzig problem and the Slovak-Hungarian frontier problem as planned. (...)

There were no immediate comments upon the Danzig proposal and the chairman therefore re-stated a conversation held before the meeting between him and Mr. Armstrong on the general problem of boundary change. Briefly, they had agreed on the desirability of changing boundaries as little as possible, and of placing the burden of proof upon those who suggested any change. Any decision in principle that boundaries should be redrawn to fit ethnic requirements would reopen the whole problem with its manifold possible difficulties.

On the other hand, to leave boundaries unchanged would be to leave the international sore spots unhealed, and would provide critics the opportunity to claim that the committee's conceptions were fixed in the pre-war groove. Mr. Armstrong had said that for these reasons it would be desirable not to apply the general principle of minimum change to the exclusion of necessary adjustments here and there. The *Grosse Schuett*, other areas of Slovakia, and Danzig, as well, afforded pointed illustrations of needed change, Danzig was a particularly significant area since it did not directly contravene the principles of minimum change. While the area was German in composition, it had not been under German sovereignty. Moreover, Germany had made a treaty with respect to the status of Danzig and had later violated it.

Mr. Armstrong added that it would be generally desirable to return to the boundaries of the last twenty years for the special purpose of not opening up territorial questions between our allies and their enemies.

The necessity to proceed cautiously with boundary change was increased by the interpretation likely to be placed upon the Atlantic Declaration. Many persons would probably believe, regardless of what the Declaration actually says, that we are obligated to restore the former frontiers of re-established nations. If we change frontiers in certain countries, we may then be accused of having "sold out", either to the enemy or to certain of our allies. As a means of averting this, it would be desirable to avoid calling entire frontiers into question. Instead, attention should be concentrated upon specific problem areas, such as the *Grosse Schuett.* There the case for adjustment is quite clear, since the population is predominantly Magyar, the Czechs have shown some willingness to make concessions to Hungarian claims, and the American position has been clear from the beginning. Instead of referring to adjustment of a frontier, it would be desirable to talk of settling a specific dispute in a given district. To facilitate adjustment in the case of the *Grosse Schuett* we could promise to assist in building the roads required by the Slovakia. At all events, it would be important to work out something quickly between the Czechs and the Hungarians soon after the close of hostilities.

Mr. Bowman commented favorably upon Mr. Armstrong's suggestion of concentrating upon minor areas and adjusting specific problems. Our efforts should, in the first instance, be directed toward furthering negotiations between parties concerned in any specific dispute rather than towards laying down the basis of settlement, he thought. Mr. Berle believed that the latter suggestion, while excellent, implied a profound change in the method of boundary settlement. Mr. Bowman, however, referred to the boundary dispute between Peru and Ecuador as affording an example of such procedure.* When those two states threatened to go to war over a boundary that had presumably been settled, outside parties intervened to see that the disputants reached an agreement without resort to war. The role of the United States was especially interesting, since this nation had abstained from pressure and permitted Argentina and Brazil to take the lead. Adjustment had been easier because Ecuador had found greater advantage in American aid and subsidies for the building of a large air field than in proceeding with war against our will. The President of Ecuador had been able to make the necessary concessions because he could say to the country and to the legislature that the country was pressed on all sides and therefore

*The 1941 dispute over boundaries between Peru and Ecuador was settled by the 1942 Rio de Janeiro Agreement, when Ecuador "voluntarily" relinquished its claim, and yielded most of the disputed territory to Peru.

had to accede. Mrs. McCormick thought that the procedures used in the Peruvian-Ecuadorean dispute were especially suggestive.

Mr. Bowman referred to another of Mr. Armstrong's suggestions, namely, that it would be desirable to ascertain the minimum of necessary rectification in any problem area. As applied in the disputed zone between Slovakia and Hungary, this would mean ascertaining those specific areas where adjustment could be considered inescapable. From the standpoint of essential change, Danzig offered an unique problem. The Free City had been created after the last war to meet a specific need, yet the experiment had failed. Today it is desirable to eliminate this problem area in Europe. The immediate obstacle to any solution is the German population resident there. This obstacle might be overcome by dividing the territory, as projected earlier in the meeting, and facilitating the migration of the remaining Germans.[1] The Danzig area could be regarded as manageable from this standpoint whereas the larger area of East Prussia could not be. It might of course be said that the cession of territory to East Prussia would be a case of rewarding the aggressor. This was not necessarily so, since it had already been decided that Germany should not gain by aggression. Even if the territory were added to East Prussia, the future disposition of East Prussia remained uncertain.

Mrs. McCormick observed that we could not anticipate getting all the solutions we want after this war, but we should nevertheless concentrate upon obtaining these solutions most apt to prove stable and durable. Mr. Bowman added that we must, under no consideration, arrive at the peace table without specific proposals for particular problems. This had been a weakness of the American Delegation at Paris in 1919. While its position had been essentially idealistic and it had performed a useful function from that standpoint, the American Group was always in a position of having to comment upon proposals already made by other delegations. This time, by virtue of our greater prestige and military strength, our proposals must be more specific.

Mrs. McCormick stated that Europe would probably be so much worse off after the present war that the victor powers would almost be in a position to impose their own peace terms. She had recently been

---

1 At meetings of the subcommittee on July 10 and July 17, it was tentatively concluded that: Danzig should be transferred outright to Poland. (Port and transit facilities possibly to be provided for Germany. Emigration of German population to be facilitated, and to be under international supervision for two years.)

told by an informed Frenchman that the United States must go to the peace table with a precise and definite program. This program would very likely prevail, regardless of what other peoples or nations might wish. Mr. Armstrong thought that this view was perhaps too sanguine, but Mrs. McCormick and Mr. Bowman pointed out that for some months during 1918 and 1919 the United States had enjoyed just such a position. Mr. Armstrong stated, however, that this time we are proposing changes in the *status quo* to which the peoples affected will probably object. Mrs. McCormick thought that the chaos throughout Europe will nevertheless compel acceptance of American proposals. Mr. Bowman was inclined to agree, and said that territorial adjustments must be arrived at speedily, and must be carried out from the very first moment.

Mr. Berle reverted to the proposal Mr. Armstrong had made for a settlement of minor boundary disputes. He thought it was necessary to consider methods of action. First, the boundaries drawn should become the administrative boundaries for the occupying forces. Second, at the moment they are established, there should be set up "under the guns of the peace conference" a territorial council or bureau (possibly to become part of the permanent international machinery) to settle disputed points. The disputants should be expected to consult and arrive at an adjustment. The United Nations should see that the parties negotiated on even terms (enemy nations excepted) and that justice and common sense prevailed in the settlement. Third, in the event that the disputants failed to reach a solution, the solution laid down by the occupying forces should continue. Mr. Berle said that he had omitted the enemies because any obligation with respect to them was not yet clear. On the other hand, it was necessary to consider what kind of a mandate with respect to boundary adjustments between friendly states would be given to a bureau or commission of the United Nations or to any similar authority.

It was generally thought that Mr. Berle's suggestion was a good one. Mrs. McCormick said that the important objective would be to get the parties to a dispute to reach agreement upon it by themselves. Mr. Bowman stated that for such a purpose larger countries like the United States could exert influence without any direct intervention. Smaller countries are not in a position today to fight one another in terms of modern warfare. At the same time, they are often unable to reach solutions through negotiation, especially when one of the assistance and the moral pressure afforded by larger countries.

Mr. Berle explained that the committee on economic reconstruction had tentatively agreed on the desirability of a United Nations Bank and a United Nations Transport Authority. The United Nations Bank would perform functions that had not been performed by the Bank of International Settlements. Together with the United Nations Transport Authority, it would be placed in operation "under the guns of the United Nations" and would tend to prevent any single nation from establishing an overwhelming financial position. He thought that it would be useful for the territorial subcommittee to try its hand at elaborating the implications of such international authorities for the settlement of disputes involving territory and questions of sovereignty.

Mr. MacMurray thought that the proposals advanced by Mr. Berle resembled the actual situation surrounding the Chinese-Japanese negotiations regarding Shantung.* To begin with, the negotiators were themselves uneven in strength, and the Chinese knew that their countrymen stood ready to repudiate them if they made a single concession. The arrangements which provided for British and American observers during part of these negotiations had been useful, if only because they provided opportunity for both sides to talk and thereby to ease the tension and reach preliminary agreement. The outside observers themselves said little or nothing. It was their presence alone which exerted influence.

Mr. Armstrong thought that the illustration was apt, and said that in boundary disputes we or the United Nations might use our "good offices" to obtain some form of *quid pro quo* for the side which had to give up most. Mrs. McCormick believed that the Shantung situation was very different from that which will prevail after the present war when the disputant nations will likely be weak, disarmed, and chaotic. Mr. Armstrong and Mr. MacMurray were inclined to believe that Mrs. McCormick underestimated the probabilites of conflict and the possibility that the smaller nations may obtain arms from one source or another before the victory is complete. Mrs. McCormick maintained, however, that nations would be exhausted after the present struggle, and Mr. Berle believed that they would not be able to provide the elaborate installations necessary for carrying on modern war. Mr. Armstrong thought it conceivable that a dispute between Czechoslovakia and Hungary over the boundary problem might even go so far that we would be called upon the employ force against the Czechs in favor of the Hungarians, a situation which would, of course, be impossible.

---

*With the signing of the Shantung Agreement in accordance with the decision reached at the 1921-1922 Washington Conference, Japan was forced to restore to China the province of Shantung given to it by the Treaty of Versailles, and also to evacuate the coastal regions of Eastern Siberia.

Mr. Mosely felt that any consideration of specific boundary disputes should take into consideration the general problem of an East European Union. If one aim was to establish lasting cooperation among the peoples of this area, some concessions would necessarily be made to certain countries. On the other hand, if no regional organization emerged from the post-war settlement, it would probably be necessary to strengthen some nations, territorially and strategically, as against others. It would also be necessary to know whether Soviet Russia and Great Britain would have predominant influence in the East European area.

Asked as to the British position on the problem of boundary settlements in Central and Eastern Europe, Mr. Berle stated that he would not be surprised if the British had made certain commitments in this respect. They may, however, be retreating from a position taken earlier. They may have agreed to relinquish to Russia the arbitration of disputes in the East European area. This may, however, only have been a pseudo-commitment and may not have been taken seriously. Mr. Berle explained that no more information was available concerning the agreement between Czechoslovakia and Soviet Russia, to which he had referred at an earlier meeting.* Mr. Armstrong stated that M. Ninčić of Yugoslavia was inclined to believe that no such agreement had been made. Ninčić had spoken to President Beneš in connection with the recent negotiations between Russia and Yugoslavia, and President Beneš had not given much credence to the report of a Russo-Czech agreement. Ninčić had felt that there was no reason why President Beneš would refuse to disclose it, but Mr. Berle thought this assumption was open to question. This phase of the discussion was concluded by Mr. Armstrong's observation that the desire of the British to prevent the Czechs from reaching an agreement with the Russians now might reflect a desire on the part of Great Britain to keep the territorial problem open. (...)

The chairman asked whether the committee was prepared to support the suggested change in the Slovak-Hungarian boundary. Mr. Armstrong replied in the affirmative, provided the problem was stated in terms of specific changes for definite problem areas. This met with Mr. Bowman's approval. Mr. Mosely then referred the committee to the map on the Slovak-Hungarian frontier problem (Czechoslovak Series II). He explained that the dotted red line showed the area returned to

---

*The agreement on assistance and postwar cooperation between the Czechoslovak government-in-exile and the Soviet Union was signed only on December 12, 1943, following the Allied conference in Teheran.

Hungary in 1938 on the basis of the 1910 census, a basis that was unfair because the Hungarian method of taking the census gave every possible advantage to the Magyar element and because taking 1910 as a baseline ignored the movements of population which had occurred in the last thirty years. The heavy red line indicated the additional territory seized by Hungary in 1939 upon the basis of Machtpolitik. Between 1910 and 1938 certain areas, such as the *Grosse Schuett* and the Little Hungarian Plain, had remained overwhelmingly Hungarian in population. Areas to the east, on the other hand, showed a much stronger Slovak population in 1930 than in 1910; this was due in part to the disparity in rate of natural increase as between Slovaks and Hungarians, in part to the removal of Hungarian pressure after 1918. At the present time, the towns of Levice, Lučenec, Rimavská Sobota, Rožňava, and Košice are in predominantly Slovak territory, and on grounds of ethnic justice should be transferred to Slovakia. On the other hand, on ethnic grounds, the area of the *Grosse Schuett* (except for a small strip adjacent to Bratislava) should go to Hungary, together with the towns and surrounding areas of Galánta and Érsekújvár. A narrow southern strip in the district of Levice, Lučenec, Sobota Rimavská and Rožňava could also be transferred to Hungary; this shift would bring the line of territorial demarcation into fairly close concordance with the facts of ethnic distribution, without injuring the transportation system in Slovakia. In the Košice district, on the other hand, no concession could be made to Hungary without injuring the Slovakian railway system. Under the line of demarcation as suggested minorities approximately equal in size would remain on opposite sides of the frontier.

Mr. Armstrong requested that a map be made to show by lines rather than by dots the predominantly Hungarian and the predominantly Slovakian areas in the disputed zone. In other words, each specific problem area should be outlined. Mr. Bowman added that it would be desirable to segregate those areas within the disputed zone in which the case for transfer to Hungary is strongest. The committee should be specifically informed as to the problems in each case, whether of railways, administrative divisions, overlapping jurisdictions, or any other. It would be desirable to present this information orally to the committee at its meeting August 21, and see whether a memorandum would be desirable.

Mr. Bowman went on to remind the committee that it has the responsibility if determining whether it wishes to take a broad position on the boundary problems of this and other areas, or whether it wishes to take a position in terms of the specific history of people living there for the last twenty-five years. He recalled that when the problems of Hungary were discussed at the Paris Peace Conference, decisions had been made with respect to every other country before Hungary's claims were considered. The Americans, whose position on Hungary was more equitable than the actual decision, had lost out because they had not viewed Hungary's problems in relation to those of neighboring states. They had always been dealing with "friendly" states, with the result that the enemy state received only what was left.(...)

x x x

PRINCIPLES AND PROCEDURES OF BOUNDARY CHANGE

The meeting was mainly devoted to a discussion of principles and procedures of boundary change.

Principle of Minimum Change

The advisability of changing pre-war boundaries as little as possible and of placing the burden of proof on those seeking change was reaffirmed. It was said that any attempted major boundary adjustment for ethnic or other reasons would likely create manifold difficulties by reopening the problem of boundaries everywhere.

Certain specific boundary adjustments were nevertheless regarded as unavoidable, both for the alleviation of former international frictions, and to correct manifest injustices or striking violations of the ethnic principle. Hence it was suggested that the desirable approach to boundary adjustment would be to concentrate upon settlements within specific disputed areas than to call entire frontiers into question. It would, therefore, be desirable to ascertain the specific disputed areas along controversial frontiers, and the minimum of necessary rectification in each area.

Slovak-Hungarian Frontier

The application of these procedures was recommended as a basis for consideration of the disputed frontier zone between Slovakia and Hungary. An analysis was requested of those areas within the disputed zone in which the case for transfer to Hungary might be strongest, together with a statement of the specific problems of each area. The boundary might be brought into fairly close concordance with the facts of ethnic distribution, without injury to the Slovak transportation system, if the *Grosse Schuett* and a narrow southern strip were recognized as preponderantly Hungarian. It was thought that the *Grosse Schuett* offered an appropriate example of a specific area definitely requiring adjustment. (...)

Adjustments by the Disputants Themselves

It was thought desirable that states which are parties to a territorial dispute should work out an adjustment themselves. The great powers might facilitate the negotiations through direct assistance or moral pressure, but should initially avoid laying down a basis for settlement. Assistance might take the form of some *quid pro quo* offered to the state required to give up most.

The suggestion was made that boundaries tentatively agreed upon in advance of the armistice should become the administrative boundaries for occupying forces. In disputed areas, the parties concerned (except enemy states) should be expected to consult and arrive at an adjustment, aided by an international council or bureau on boundaries. If the disputants failed to reach a solution, that laid down by the occupying forces might continue. (...)

Box 59

****

§ Document 3 §

(Excerpt)

Secret T Minutes 17

August 21, 1942

Present:
Mr. Isaiah Bowman, presiding
Mr. Hamilton Fish Armstrong
Mr. Adolf A. Berle
Mr. Herbert Feis
Mr. John V. A. MacMurray
Mrs. Anne O'Hare McCormick
Mr. John Masland
Mr. Philip Mosely
Mr. Harley Notter
Mr. Easton Rothwell

(...) The chairman then introduced for reconsideration the problem of the Slovak-Hungarian frontier, and asked Mr. Armstrong to distribute and read a memorandum he had prepared on this problem. (T Document 49 — "Remarks on the Memorandum 'Hungarian-Slovak Frontiers: Alternative Territorial Solutions,' dated 21/VII/42." — Appended).*

Mr. Armstrong in presenting the statement explained that he had incorporated some of the suggestions made by Mr. Mosely but had also offered some solutions of his own.

When Mr. Armstrong had read his statement, Mr. Bowman asked Mr. Feis to state his judgment on the position tentatively taken by the subcommittee with respect to this frontier area. He pointed out that the subcommittee had agreed it would prefer to deal with the specific problems of particular areas rather than to consider the rectification of entire frontiers. All the various factors in a given problem-area would be studied, and the boundaries would be shifted only if that were indicated by the results of the examination. Mr. Feis said he thought such a procedure was desirable and that the need for it was suggested by Mr. Armstrong's statement. At the same time, he was not certain whether these procedures would accord with post-war emotional

---

*See Document 3, p. 190.

attitudes. If the war were a long one, the very existence of Hungary might be in question, rather than whether Hungary should be given a small slice of Slovakia. Mrs. McCormick replied that there would be little doubt as to the continued existence of Hungary, or at least of the Hungarian people. Mr. Feis then explained that he had not intended to make an issue of the possible disappearance of Hungary, but was in sympathy with the point of view accepted in the committee and expressed in Mr. Armstrong's memorandum. He thought that Mr. Armstrong's suggestion for compensating the side having to give up territory was a good one, but he questioned whether all the compensation should come from the outside and believed that Hungary should be required to make some compensation. Mr. Armstrong said that he had implied as much in suggesting that "a close study should be made as to whether any Hungarian *quid pro quo* might be available."

Mr. Bowman suggested that if the technique of dealing with specific problem-areas were applied to the Sudetenland's, it might develop that the problems of the Sudeten area were not boundary problems at all. In this connection, it would be of interest to know what concern the Germans had expressed for the Sudeten areas before Hitler's rise to power.

Returning to the Slovak-Hungarian frontier, Mr. Bowman asked Mr. Armstrong what areas besides the *Grosse Schuett* and the Hungarian plain might be considered eligible for transfer to Hungary. In response, Mr. Mosely explained that the predominantly Magyar areas would be found principally in the western part of the disputed zone. Beginning on the extreme west, the three administrative districts which comprise the *Grosse Schuett* were strongly (more than 75 per cent) Magyar. The three districts immediately to the east were also strongly Magyar. A line drawn to the east and north of these six districts would set off an area possibly eligible for transfer on the basis of 1930 census figures. These six provinces might be transferred to Hungary without injury to Czechoslovakia's railroad system. It might be assumed that by 1930 those persons desiring to change their nationality had already done so and that the ethnic figures have become relatively stabilized. Mr. Bowman asked whether the figures would be reversed in the adjacent row of districts on the east, but Mr. Mosely replied that in these districts, the ethnic division was not so clear. He explained that in the central section of the problem-area the districts of Levice, Lučenec and Modrý Kameň were Slovak in majority, with substantial Magyar minorities. On the other hand, the districts of Feledince, Moldava nad Bodvou and Tornal'a were strongly Magyar in character. In general, he reported, the problem-area consisted of a "southern" tier ten districts with strong Magyar majorities and a "northern" tier of fifteen districts, with a Slovak majority and substantial Magyar minorities. Presumably, he concluded, the two tiers of districts would be susceptible of different treatment in any settlement of the problem between Slovakia and Hungary.

The chairman stated that Mr. Mosely's explanation had given the committee a comprehensive view of the problem. Mr. Armstrong indicated that in the six districts first discussed, there were 40,000 Slovaks and 274,000 Hungarians. In the five administrative districts immediately to the north, however, there were 138,000 Slovaks as compared with 110,000 Hungarians. He believed that if the area to be transferred were to be restricted to a minimum, it would be desirable to register all persons living there with a view to determining those who would wish to migrate. Not all Slovaks would wish to leave, and the problem would be reduced in difficulty to that extent. It should also be noted, Mr. Armstrong added, that the transfer of the six southwest districts to Hungary would leave undisturbed the east-west railway line in Slovakia.

Mrs. McCormick asked whether the boundary drawn April 3, 1939 might not be presumed to be fair because it represented a frontier between two satellites of Germany. Mr. Mosely replied that the frontier had actually involved injustices to the Slovaks because it was based on the 1910 census which was heavily weighted in favor of the Magyars; moreover, taking 1910 as a base-line did not take account of the infiltration of Slovaks into the mixed regions between 1910 and 1939, or the higher of the vital excess of the Slovaks. In addition, parts of the boundary of 1939, especially in eastern Slovakia, were based on strategic considerations and had no ethnic justification.

Mrs. McCormick asked whether considerations other than ethnic distribution would not have to be taken into consideration in any boundary settlement. For instance, it would not be possible to move the boundaries to one or the other side of principal towns and cities without doing violence to established economic and other arrangements.

Mr. Bowman agreed, and said that ethnic facts could be regarded only as a starting-point for the examination of any problem-area. There would be needed, in addition, an intensive technical study of towns and cities affected, of transportation facilities, and of what might be termed strategic considerations.

At this point, Mr. Bowman said that he felt it would be useful to terminate the discussion of the Slovak-Hungarian problem for this meeting and asked Mr. Mosely to prepare for the meeting on Friday, September 4, a statement of nationality totals and subtotals within the particular problem areas of the frontier zone, as well, as an analysis of the specific transportation problems and those arising from the presence of cities and towns.

This phase of the discussion was completed by Mr. Armstrong who, after being assured by Mr. Bowman that transfers of population could be envisaged in this area because they were of relatively small scale, said that it would be desirable to block out the more desirable areas for territorial transfer, with a view to settling the rest of the problem by means of exchange of populations. (...)

x x x

SLOVAK-HUNGARIAN FRONTIER

Discussion of the Slovak-Hungarian frontier problem was opened by the reading of a specially prepared statement that enumerated reasons why only the most urgent ethnic considerations could justify the transfer of any territory to Hungary. Aside from the fact that Czechoslovakia had consistently followed more enlightened policies than Hungary and had been a victim of German and Hungarian aggression, any extensive adjustment of this frontier might lead to allegations that the Atlantic Charter had been violated and to the opening of boundary questions elsewhere. It might detract from the strength of the restored Czecho-Slovak State, as a factor in East European Federation. The statement suggested restricting any territorial adjustment to limited areas where transfer to Hungary was overwhelmingly indicated. These areas were subsequently shown to consist primarily of six administrative districts the *Grosse Schuett* and the area immediately to the east.

The statement further suggested that direct agreement between the disputants should be encouraged, that some form of *quid pro quo* should be arranged for Czechoslovakia, that any necessary exchange of populations should be effected, that Hungary should be required to adopt thorough-going land and political reforms, and that the diminished importance of all boundaries should be stressed. Further study was requested of ethnic and economic considerations, and of transportation and other factors in the districts most eligible for transfer.

Box 59

****

§ Document 4 §

(Excerpt)

Secret

T Minutes 18

August 26, 1942

Present:
Mr. Isaiah Bowman, presiding
Mr. Hamilton Fish Armstrong
Mr. Adolf A. Berle
Mr. Herbert Feis
Mr. Maxwell Hamilton
Mr. Stanley K. Hornbeck
Mr. John V. A. MacMurray
Mrs. Anne O'Hare McCormick
Mr. Leo Pasvolsky
Mr. Myron C. Taylor
Mr. Philip W. Ireland
Mr. William Koren, Jr.
Mr. Philip Mosely
Mr. Harley Notter
Mr. Easton Rothwell

Slovak-Hungarian Frontier

The chairman opened the meeting at 5:06 p.m.

The chairman introduced the subject of possible adjustments in the Slovak-Hungarian boundary, emphasizing for the benefit of those who had not attended previous meetings that the committee had adopted the policy of discussing boundary changes only with regard to specific problem-areas rather than reopening the question of frontiers as such. He noted that Mr. Mosely had prepared an additional note on the problems connected with the southern and northern tiers of administrative districts of the disputed area along the Slovak-Hungarian frontier of 1937.[1*] At this request, Mr. Mosely explained that in the southern tier of districts, there were six on the west, three in the center and one

---

[1]Document 48 — Hungarian-Slovak Frontier — Alternative Frontier Solutions — Additional Note

[*]See document 4, p. 193.

on the east, where the population was strongly Magyar; it was proposed that these ten districts, containing in 1930 309,306 Magyars and 59,757 Czechoslovaks, might be transferred to Hungary as part of a general settlement in that region. In answer to a question from Mr. Berle, Mr. Mosely explained that his recommendations took into consideration the transportation requirements of Slovakia; he believed that this transfer of territory would raise no local marketing problem since the districts concerned all included their own market towns.

At this point the chairman raised a question of principle with regard to decisions on boundary questions. It was his belief that at this stage the committee could profitably discuss only the issues involved in a given boundary problem; it should endeavor to make sure that these issues had been clarified and that all the relevant problems, such as the question of town-country relationships, transportation and the like, had been adequately studied. Final decision on the exact lines of a new frontier should, in his opinion, await study by a boundary commission in the field. Mr. Berle and other members of the committee assented to this proposition. Mrs. McCormick noted that in any case specific decisions would have to await the final determination of general principles and the over-all plan of the peace treaties.

Since Mr. Armstrong was not yet prepared to accept the proposed transfer of territory as outlined in Mr. Mosely's memorandum, the chairman suggested that the Slovak-Hungarian boundary problem be placed at the head of the agenda for the meeting of September 4. At that time he would except to poll the committee on the proposals submitted to it.

Mr. Armstrong indicated that he would like to ascertain the probable size of populations whose transfer might result from the adoption of Mr. Mosely's proposals for a new boundary and the practicality of such population transfers in this region. At the chairman's request Mr. Mosely undertook to prepare an additional memorandum on this question. He indicated orally that presumably there were now few Czechs or Slovaks living in the towns in the ten districts which it was proposed to transfer to Hungary. In his opinion, if a regional political organization were established for Eastern Europe and if internal social changes occurred in Hungary, this boundary question would be relatively unimportant. Mr. Armstrong did not agree that the populations concerned would consider boundaries of diminished importance, at least in the period immediately following the cessation of hostilities. Mr. Mosely noted that the proposed boundaries would effect no substantial change in the strategic relationships between Slovakia and Hungary. (...)

SLOVAK-HUNGARIAN FRONTIER

A proposal for the transfer of ten administrative districts from Slovakia to Hungary was introduced. These districts were all contiguous to the 1937 Hungarian frontier and were largely Magyar in population and self-contained so far as local marketing is concerned; their transfer would effect no substantial change in the strategic relationships between Slovakia and Hungary. Additional information was requested on the transfer of population which might follow such a rectification of the boundary. Final recommendation on this boundary was scheduled for the meeting of September 4.

Box 59

****

§ Document 5 §

(Excerpt)

Secret T Minutes 19

September 4, 1942

Present:
Mr. Isaiah Bowman, presiding
Mr. Hamilton Fish Armstrong
Mr. Adolf A. Berle
Mr. John V. A. MacMurray
Mrs. Anne O'Hare McCormick
Mr. Leo Pasvolsky
Mr. Paul Alling
Mr. Wallace Murray
Mr. Philip Ireland
Mr. Philip Mosely
Mr. Harley Notter
Mr. William Koren, Jr.

The chairman proposed to take up the agenda for the meeting in the following order: first, the question of the Slovak-Hungarian frontier;

second, Rumanian stability, on which Mr. Mosely would speak briefly; and third, the Near Eastern area with particular reference to Syria and the Lebanon; since Mr. Hornbeck could not be present, he proposed that the subcommittee discuss Thailand at a later meeting.

Slovak-Hungarian Frontier

On the invitation of the chairman, Mr. Armstrong read aloud remarks which he had prepared as a commentary on Mr. Mosely's memorandum on the Hungarian-Slovak frontier.[1*] Mr. Armstrong raised as a question of practical politics the difficulty of suggesting to an ally of the United States, the victim of aggression, that it transfer a section of its territory to a neighboring aggressor and enemy state. He thought that such transfers could be effected only in the cases and only if the ceding state were offered economic and financial advantages by the Great Powers and some *quid pro quo* by the state gaining territory.

Mr. Armstrong proposed, therefore, that the subcommittee recommend that the United States limit its attempts to bring about changes in this whole area to an effort to persuade the Czechoslovak Government to negotiate the cession of the six western districts of the southern border tier to Hungary as part of a general settlement of all outstanding Czechoslovak-Hungarian differences. This course would have the following advantages: first, that the ethnic argument for transfer is overwhelming; second, that the return of these districts to Hungary would represent a great psychological as well as racial gain for that country and should, therefore, go far towards mending Czechoslovak-Magyar relations from the Magyar end; third, that the main-line railway from Bratislava to Levice would remain in Czechoslovak hands; fourth, that administrative districts would be transferred in their entirety, in keeping with policy generally recognized by the subcommittee as advisable; fifth, that if no other alterations in this frontier were suggested, Czechoslovakia's public might regard this adjustment as the solution of a long-time "problem area" rather than as part of a general frontier change. Mr. Armstrong believed that transfer of the 40,000 Czechoslovaks who would then find themselves in Hungarian territory and of the 265,000 Magyars remaining in Czechoslovakia would not

---

[1]Document 48 — Hungarian-Slovak Frontier — Alternative Frontier Solutions — Additional Note.

*Mosely's memorandum and Armstrong's commentaries are presented as Document 4, p. 193 and Document 6, p. 202.

present in insuperable problem given the proper international assistance.

The chairman noted that Mr. Armstrong's remarks were in agreement with statistics as presented in Mr. Mosely's memorandum and asked the latter for his comments. Mr. Mosely believed that the subcommittee should consider this problem not merely in its aspect of a relationship between aggressor and victim but as part of a regional problem which required a certain number of internal adjustments in order to minimize friction within the regional political organization which the subcommittee had thus far envisaged. He considered that to leave in Czechoslovakia 265,000 Magyars subject to population transfer might be considered an invitation to future trouble.

The chairman requested that a new map be prepared of the ten districts which Mr. Mosely's previous memorandum had considered might be transferred to Hungary and the surrounding areas. This map should show the administrative boundaries and the number of Magyars and of Czechoslovaks who would be left as minorities if the line as analyzed by Mr. Mosely was approved by the subcommittee.

In answer to a question by the chairman, Mr. Armstrong repeated his belief that to transfer the ten districts which were located in three separate areas would give the impression of a general frontier change rather than of the adjustment of a problem-area. He, therefore, favored transfer only of the six districts in the westernmost group. The chairman, however, considered that problem areas might be plural in number along a given, frontier.

The chairman proposed that the committee's final recommendations on this problem await presentation of detailed geographic data by the Office of the Geographer. At this meeting, however, he thought that the subcommittee might make a preliminary recommendation to the general committee. Mr. Berle pointed out that if the present approach was followed, the subcommittee was no longer itself making a recommendation as to the transfer of territory, but merely recommending certain agenda for a Czechoslovak-Hungarian conference and providing documentation for those in charge of American policy should the advice of the United States be sought by the two negotiating parties. He pointed out that this new approach on the part of the subcommittee was in accord with the President's policy in April 1939, when he had urged that the interested parties confer directly, under the auspices of the Great Powers in order to guarantee a free and equal discussion. Mr. Armstrong agreed that this new approach as defined by Mr. Berle was the proper one and considered that it strengthened his previous remarks.

The chairman returned to the question of whether the subcommittee should recommend that direct negotiations between Czechoslovakia and Hungary concern themselves with the six districts in the west or with the three groups of six districts, three districts and one district, which he denominated respectively by the Roman numerals I, II and III.

Mr. Mosely outlined these areas on the map and indicated that the territory which should be under discussion for transfer to Hungary might include in addition a narrow border strip connecting these areas and certain parts of northern tier of districts contiguous to area I. If this latter adjustment were agreed upon, the main railway line of Bratislava to Levice would pass in part through Hungarian territory; this would alter the strategic picture to some extent but would not be a serious commercial handicap to Czechoslovakia since that country had constructed a parallel line to the north which would remain in its territory. The town of Nové Zámky, which would thereby be transferred to Hungary, had a slight majority of Magyars over Slovaks; the number of Czechoslovaks included a rather large proportion of officials and their families. In Galanta province, on the other hand, the Magyars outnumbered the Czechs almost two to one. In reply of these districts, Mr. Mosely informed the subcommittee that in the southern tier, which might be called the plains districts, the population was largely agricultural but that in the northern tier where the foothills began there was a more diversified economy, including extraction and metal-working industries. Nové Zámky itself included large railway shops and a number of small industries.

The chairman then put before the subcommittee the question of whether it was prepared to recommend that Area I, together with certain adjustments to the north, for final determination of which more data from the geographer's office was required, might be placed on the agenda for negotiation between Czechoslovakia and Hungary. The chairman pointed out that an affirmative vote meant that the subcommittee was merely formulating a recommendation to the President in respect to post-war policy. He supposed that the President would then pass the recommendation on to the organization established to deal with post-war problems. In this case the proposition before the committee as clarified by Mr. Berle was not that such and such a transfer of territory be made, but that negotiations on certain areas would be in order. Mr. Berle and Mr. Armstrong voted "aye". Mr. MacMurray thought it difficult to go farther than a mere suggestion, rather than a recommendation, that this solution of Czechoslovak-Hungarian friction be discussed. Mr. Pasvolsky agreed that the problem of Area I should be submitted to the interested parties for discussion but thought that the subcommittee could not yet recommend a policy to the American Government, should its advice be asked, since the subcommittee possessed only the arguments for transfer and not the Czech arguments for retention of these districts. The chairman agreed to the strength of this objection but pointed out that the American Government would not be bound by the subcommittee's recommendations. He and Mr. Armstrong and Mr. Berle believed that even before the Czech case was in hand, the subcommittee should take a stand on the basis of the information available to it. This was particularly necessary since the American Government might be presented with the necessity for making a sudden decision on this question and should not be left entirely without guidance by the subcommittee.

The chairman next posed the question of including Areas II and III in the agenda to be recommended to the Czechs and Hungarians. Mr. Armstrong was opposed to such inclusion. He and Mr. MacMurray were fearful lest it so incense the Czechoslovaks that they would refuse to discuss adjustments with respect to Area I. Mrs. McCormick felt that the subcommittee needed more specific information on Areas II and III before deciding on their inclusion on the agenda for direct negotiations. On the other hand, Mr. Berle felt that these two areas should be included on the agenda if only for their "trading-value". He pointed out that, conversely, even after Hungary and its associates had been defeated in the war, the Hungarian army might for some time remain the strongest force on the spot.

Mr. Pasvolsky was emphatic that the mere inclusion of Areas II and III on the agenda recommended by the United States would be regarded by Czechoslovakia and Hungary as an American commitment that this Government regarded their transfer as justified. The selection of negotiable questions was therefore one of the most important recommendations which the subcommittee could make. He did not agree with Mr. Berle that the inclusion of Areas II and III on the conference agenda was a commitment only that this Government believed that state of affairs existed in those areas which created friction. Furthermore, he felt that to inject discussion of these areas into a conference might create additional friction rather than eliminate it. He had approved the inclusion of Area I on the agenda for the hypothetical conference on the grounds that to discuss it would eliminate more friction than it would create. His view on the agenda question did not mean, however, that areas II and III should not receive the same detailed study as Area I. Mr. Armstrong welcomed the hesitation of Mr. MacMurray and Mr. Pasvolsky. He noted that Czechoslovakia had announced its intention of securing its pre-Munich frontiers before opening any negotiations with neighboring states. In his opinion there was one chance in three that the Czechs would negotiate over Area I and that there would be an even smaller chance of such negotiation if they were asked to discuss with the Magyars the future the status of Areas II and III.

The chairman concluded the discussion of this frontier with the statement that it was his understanding that in the light of its present knowledge the subcommittee would recommend the inclusion of Area I on the conference agenda but at the present time would reserve judgment on the inclusion of Areas II and III. (...)

x x x

Slovak-Hungarian Frontier

The subcommittee discussed the proper disposition of three frontier areas on the Hungarian border of Slovakia. A formal proposal was made that the subcommittee recommend that the United States encourage, as part of a general settlement of differences between these states, the negotiation of the transfer by Czechoslovakia to Hungary of the first or westernmost area, comprising six administrative districts. It was agreed in this proposal that, as a question of practical politics, the United States could ask no more concessions from an ally and victim state in favor of a late enemy and aggressor; this country, therefore, should no favor the transfer, or even the discussion of transfer, of the other two areas.

Subsequent discussion concerned four issues involved in this proposal: whether the United States should favor negotiations concerning the first area between Czechoslovakia and Hungary; whether the United States should favor such negotiation concerning the second and third areas; whether the United States should be ready to recommend the cession of the first area; and whether this Government should be ready to recommend the cession of the other two areas.

In part because the Czechs had in the past expressed a readiness to negotiate with Hungary over the first area, the subcommittee recommended that, in the light of its present knowledge, discussion of this area should be included on the agenda for a Czechoslovak-Magyar conference.

The subcommittee reserved judgment on whether the conference agenda should include discussion of Areas II and III. On the one hand, it was felt that the regional political institutions envisaged by the subcommittee would endure only if an attempt had been made to settle intra-regional causes of friction. Objection to such inclusion was raised on the ground that it would lessen the chances of the cession of Area I by Czechoslovakia, and that it would be regarded as a commitment by the United States that this country favored the cession of these areas.

The subcommittee postponed decision on the proper policy for the United States with regard to the ultimate disposition of all three areas until further material should have been prepared by the Office of the Geographer. An objection was raised against coming to any decision until the Czech case could be formally presented. It was felt, however, that the subcommittee would have to formulate a recommendation when the additional material requested was at hand, since the Government might be called upon suddenly to present its policy. The subcommittee would be free to alter its recommendation in the light of later information and developments.

Box 59

****

§ Document 6 §

(Excerpt)

Secret T Minutes 38

February 5, 1943

Not to be removed from the State Department building

Present:

Mr. Isaiah Bowman, presiding

Mr. Hamilton Fish Armstrong
Mr. Adolf A. Berle
Mr. John V. A. MacMurray
Mr. Anne O'Hare McCormick
Mr. S. Whittemore Boggs
Mr. Cavendish W. Cannon
Mr. Otto E. Guthe
Mr. C. E. Black
Mr. John Campbell
Mr. Richard Eldridge
Mr. David Harris
Mr. Harry N. Howard
Mr. Thomas F. Power, Jr.
Mr. Walter R. Sharp
Mr. Leroy D. Stinebower
Mr. Harley Notter
Mr. Philip Mosely
Mr. Easton Rothwell
Mr. William Koren, Jr.

(...) TRANSYLVANIA

The chairman asked Mr. Campbell to introduce the question of Transylvania. Mr. Campbell pointed out that the area of Transylvania was shaded in brown on the map.[1] The term Transylvania was used for purposes of discussion to mean the entire area which Rumania had acquired from Hungary after the World War. This included the Banat and other provinces. This was a rich area with a population of five and one-half millions. It included the center of Rumania's heavy industries. Its loss would therefore force considerable change in Rumania's economy.

---

[1]East European Series Map 13, Boundary Problems of East European States

The problem of the disposition of Transylvania tied in with the general problem of Eastern Europe, first because there was the possibility of both Rumania and Hungary becoming Communist, and secondly because both these countries were considered possible units in an East European Federation. The first possibility raised the question of what American and British policies would be concerning the extension of Soviet influence west of Russia's 1941 frontiers. Concerning possible federations it should be pointed out that Transylvania linked Hungary and Rumania. If Rumania retained this territory it would be one of the Danubian states. If it went to Hungary, then Rumanian interests would be more exclusively Balkan, and Rumania would be particularly close to Bulgaria, Greece and Yugoslavia. The suggestion had also been made that an autonomous Transylvania might form one of the units in an East European Federation.

Mr. Campbell suggested three possible solutions. The first would be the restoration of the 1939 frontier, thereby reconstituting Greater Rumania. This would be a settlement consonant with the principle of legality and that of minimum change in boundaries. It would, however, perpetuate a difficult minority situation since one million five hundred thousand Magyars would be left in Rumania. The second possibility was to transfer the entire area to Hungary. This was a very unlikely solution in view of the political situation and would have the disadvantage of transferring some three million Rumanians to Hungary. The third possibility was to perpetuate the present partition of Transylvania. This partition had been designed to connect the Magyar population in the Székely district, which formed the eastern tip of the Hungarian acquisition, with Hungary. This meant that Hungary acquired other territory in which the population was largely Rumanian and transferred in all approximately one million Rumanians to Hungary. This division was a strange line also from point of view of local economy and transportation since the Székely area had its trade connections to the southeast, with the Old Kingdom of Rumania.

The chairman asked how many of the one million five hundred thousand Magyars in Rumania had been transferred to Hungarian sovereignty by this territorial change. Mr. Campbell replied that Hungary had acquired approximately one million one two million and two million five hundred thousand. This total was a little less than one-half the population of Transylvania. Mr. Campbell continued that the idea of an autonomous Transylvania held certain attractions but it was hard to say how it would work since it would not be a satisfactory solution either to Hungary or to Rumania or to the local Magyar and Rumanian population. He admitted that there was some local feeling in the area but that the majority of either linguistic group would turn an autonomous Transylvania into an adjunct of either Rumania or Hungary.

Mr. Armstrong pointed out that the proposal for an autonomous Transylvania had been put forward by Otto of Habsburg as a way of detaching some territory from Rumania without creating too much of a row. The chairman pointed out that that would leave Transylvania to be fought over later. Mr. Campbell explained that this territory had been autonomous for some time at an early period in history. It had become a part of Rumania for the first time in 1919, except for the Rumanian claim that it had been joined to Hungary in 1868 as part of the compromise between Austria and Hungary. Before that it had been a separate Habsburg Grand Duchy. Mr. Campbell pointed out that it had for several centuries had close associations with Hungary and had really been run by the Magyars.

Mr. Armstrong thought that any idea of setting up Transylvania as an independent unit was remote, foolish and comic. Some of the best elements in Rumania and some of the strongest Magyar Patriots came from Transylvania. They did not have merely Transylvanian allegiance. He thought that the local feeling Mrs. McCormick referred to was really part of the feeling of the new Rumanians against the Rumanians of the Old Kingdom, who were in a less advanced state of civilization. Mrs. McCormick thought that in spite of these objections Transylvania might form one part of a large federation. Mr. Armstrong replied that this would not obviate the tensions between the Rumanian-speaking and Magyar-speaking Transylvanians. Mrs. McCormick considered that there would still be less friction than if the area were either under Rumanian or Hungarian sovereignty.

The chairman agreed with Mr. Armstrong that the pulls would be greater if the region were given autonomy.

Furthermore there would be the same objection to having such a unit in the East European Union as had been raised against the admission of East Prussia, namely that this would be a disturbing element in the Union. An East European Union would be difficult enough to set up in any case without adding these inexperienced units. Mrs. McCormick pointed out that there was a difference between East Prussia and Transylvania since the former was an area with a relatively unmixed population which was identical with that there had been no political separatist movement during the past twenty years. Mr. Campbell pointed out that there had been moves by the Magyars for autonomy but that this had been designed to increase their power and resulted from the fact that they thought as Hungarians, not as Transylvanians.

The chairman asked whether any difference of treatment in this area should derive from the fact that both of the contesting parties were enemy powers. Mrs. McCormick suggested that fact gave the United Nations more freedom of disposition than would otherwise be the case. The chairman was not sure that this was correct. He declared off the record that the territorial subcommittee was handicapped by the fact that in this as in many other cases it had received no recommendations from the security subcommittees. This left the territorial subcommittee "out on the end of a limb" and, so far as it prevented prompt decision, left a way open for action by those on the spot which might defeat the final recommendations of the territorial subcommittee and of the political committee.

The chairman continued that in spite of the recent announcement that the United Nations expected unconditional surrender from the enemies it remained proper to talk of an "armistice" in a conventionalized sense. Obviously an entire nation would not surrender to a group of powers and have it done as simply as Grant and Lee did at Appomattox.* The question would arise as to who had jurisdiction over particular areas. Unconditional surrender would not be equivalent to anarchy. Since the United Nations had to keep order, there would have to be some arrangements which should be technically spoken of as the armistice conditions. In Mrs. McCormick's opinion unconditional surrender meant an increase in the responsibilities of the United Nations. The chairman thought that this was relevant to the procedure to be followed in the case if this quarrel between Hungary and Rumania. If the armistice conditions restored the 1939 boundary, thereby returning Transylvania to Rumania, and negotiations were to proceed in that situation the conditions of negotiations would have in effect been written into the armistice terms. Hungary would therefore be tempted to use its remaining army.

---

*The reference pertains to the ending of the 1861-1865 American Civil War, when the commander-in-chief of the North, General Ulysses S. Grant, forced General Robert E. Lee to unconditional surrender. Once the capitulation documents had been signed, however, Grant treated the defeated very graciously. Officers, for instance, were allowed to ride home on their own horses and to keep their weapons. The term "unconditional surrender" was used at their January 14-24, 1943, Casablanca meeting by the President of the United States and the Prime Minister of Great Britain.

Mr. Berle suggested the following possible approach:

1. that the United Nations do not recognize the forcible seizure of territory, thereby restoring pro tempore the 1919 frontiers;
2. that the United Nations recognize that a problem exist in the ultimate disposition of this territory;
3. that the United Nations will establish a military government in Transylvania and will administer that territory for an indefinite period;
4. that at the appropriate time the United Nations will attempt to promote negotiations between the two parties, such negotiations to be delayed until both Rumania and Hungary had shown an ability to handle domestic problems without civil strife;
5. that the United Nations will supply the troops necessary to carry out this plan.

The chairman agreed that military occupation would prevent immediate fighting. Mr. Berle considered that such occupation would be necessary since a war would develop between Hungary and Rumania if no third party were in military control. At the present moment it was the Germans who were preventing the Rumanians and Hungarians from fighting. He did not think that the United Nations were prepared to have a local war decide the disposition of Transylvania. We should rather say to them that if you make war over Transylvania you will be making war on the United Nations. There would still remain, of course the problem of training these people to live together. Apparently the ethnic situation made it virtually impossible to draw a frontier which would be satisfactory to both sides. Neither was he in favor of shifting the two populations across the line of the Vienna award; that would raise a howl from both parties. Probably some three to five years of occupation would be necessary. The question was which powers would undertake this.

Mr. Armstrong pointed out that the desires of the population would be affected by the social policy of Rumania and Hungary. The latter would, and, as Mr. Berle said, should, go through a period of reform in land tenure laws which would certainly affect opinion in Transylvania, where the greater Magyar landowning counts were so important. Bethlen, Teleki and Horthy were all from Transylvania.

Mr. Mosely pointed out that prior to the war there had been an increasing split in Magyar opinion in Transylvania: on the one hand the landowning counts, the professional class and most of the townspeople, were, intransigently for rejoining Hungary; on the other hand, the peasantry, which had acquired some land by the Rumanian land reforms and which had found opportunity for cultural development, and rural improvement was essentially less irredentist in feeling. After the Vienna Award,* leaders of marked irredentist policies were placed in charge of Northern Transylvania, and more conciliatory Magyar leaders were deprived of authority. Mr. Armstrong noted that this was evidence that local irredentism was not strong enough for the government in Budapest. Mr. Mosely added that it was strongest among the wealthiest families who spent much of the year in the Hungarian capital.

Mrs. McCormick thought that it was too bad that the Magyar minority was so far inside Rumania. Mr. Campbell pointed out that, in addition to the Széklers, there were local concentrations of Magyars which created a border problem in Transylvania. In replying to a question by the chairman, Mr. Campbell pointed out that the predominantly Magyar cities of the area acquired in 1940 were Cluj, Satu Mare and Carei Mare. Of these only Cluj had a population of over one hundred thousand. In the Székely district the Magyar population totaled 90 percent of the whole. Mr. Mosely noted that in 1910, according to the Hungarian census, the district of Cluj had been 80 percent Rumanian but the city had been 80 percent Magyar.

Mr. Armstrong wondered whether this population balance would be offset by the different proportions of Hungarians and Rumanians who were being killed on the eastern front. Mrs. McCormick thought that far more Rumanians were being killed, but Mr. Campbell pointed out that most of the Rumanian troops in Russia were from the Old Kingdom. Mr. Cannon remarked that the Germans were reported to be placing the Magyar regiments in the most exposed positions but that there was no conclusive evidence to this effect. He noted that in the old days many leading German families had been close to the Magyars. He thought there might be a reversion to that situation once Hitler was thrown out.

Mr. Mosely explained that apparently nothing had been done to move the Germans of Transylvania back to Germany. Mr. Cannon added that they continued to have large privileges in Transylvania.

The chairman asked members of the subcommittee what they thought concerning Mr. Berle's proposals. Mr. Armstrong declared them sensible, and Mr. MacMurray said that something might be accomplished in that way. He could think of nothing else as a solution. Mr.

---

*August 30, 1940. German-Italian arbitration was unconditionally accepted in advance by both Romania and Hungary.

Armstrong thought that the only other possibility was the restoration of the 1938 frontier and that that would lead to local fighting.

Mr. Berle remarked that one might hope that in two to four years one could down somewhat these local antagonisms. Mr. Armstrong pointed out that after such an interim period the United Nations would know what the Rumanian frontiers would be in other directions and whether Rumania would be a part of the Soviet Union. Mr. Berle added that we would also know whether Hungary would be Communist. He thought that in Russian thinking and in the Czech plans there was a desire to prevent any strong unit in Hungary. Mrs. McCormick pointed out that the question remained as to which power would occupy Transylvania. Mr. Berle stated that his proposal had left that question open.

The chairman asked Mr. Mosely whether he had any suggestions to make on Mr. Berle's proposal. Mr. Mosely said that he had a few scattered remarks to present on the Transylvanian problem. He pointed out that the Germans in the area had been relatively well satisfied under Rumanian rule, that they had had adequate rights and had felt that there was greater danger of their denationalization if they came under Hungary. He thought this was a very wide-spread feeling among the Germans of Transylvania. The chairman noted that this might affect the final settlement. Mr. Mosely added that the Germans within Hungary had not been so well treated by the Magyars since 1918 and traditionally had been pro-Habsburg rather than pro-Magyar. As most of these Germans were in southern Transylvania and in the Banat, few of them had been absorbed by Hungary in 1940. They had subsequently been left in the area by Hitler in order to strengthen German control, being particularly helpful since many of them spoke both Magyar and Rumanian. Although they had traditionally formed non-commissioned cadres in the Habsburg armies, they had apparently not of their particular usefulness in Transylvania.

Mr. Mosely also pointed out that one of the difficulties with regard to a possible exchange of populations was the fact that the Magyars lived in the plains and valleys while the Rumanians lived in the uplands and mountains. Hence, neither linguistic group could easily make itself at home in the land inhabited by the other. This situation did not obtain in the Banat, where such exchanges could be effected more easily. These factors would of course be more important in the ultimate solution to be fixed after the cooling-off period.

The chairman asked whether there was any objection to Mr. Berle's suggestion for a cooling-off period.

Mr. Armstrong thought that the main point such a plan was that it perpetuated Transylvania as a center of conflict. Furthermore the United Nations might not wish to keep troops there for so long a period. The chairman agreed that it was not so easy to draw a positive conclusion, as was also true in the case of Teschen,* but thought that good use might be made of the period, during which attempts could be made to quiet the situation. It was to be expected that allied forces would be spread widely over Europe. He thought that Mr. Berle's proposal might constitute the recommendation of the subcommittee.

Mr. Armstrong urged that, while the subcommittee left its recommendation concerning the ultimate disposition of Transylvania open, there ought to be developed research studies concerning the policy which might eventually be adopted. It was his opinion that, with modifications, the boundary of the last twenty years did less ethnic injustice than any other. He thought that the 1940 boundary with its peninsula-like shape was essentially artificial and perhaps particularly designed to make trouble. He hoped that studies would be made to guide those who would eventually face the Transylvanian problem.

The chairman pointed out that one factor which could not be appraised at the present time was the action which the Hungarian army might take. The permanent solution might well reflect the situation brought about by the Hungarian troops if they got out of hand. Mrs. McCormick thought that it was unlikely that American or British forces would be the first United Nations troops to reach that area. Mr. Berle observed that it was yet too early to draw conclusions in this question. He agreed with the chairman that discussion of any future situation might be called academic at the present time. Mrs. McCormick and the chairman pointed that it was nevertheless necessary to begin thinking about Transylvania in order to have flexible material ready later for the actual negotiations. Mr. Armstrong hoped that particular study could be given to possible frontier lines in this area. Mr. Campbell explained that his study on this matter was in progress, and the chairman asked him to report on it at the next meeting. (...)

x x x

---

*A disputed border region between Czechoslovakia and Poland, which, until 1938, belonged to Czechoslovakia, and from 1938, in accordance with the Munich decision, to Poland.

Transylvania

The subcommittee reviewed briefly the historic claims of Hungary and Rumania to Transylvania and the raison d'être of the present division. It recognized that serious minority problems would result if the entire territory were assigned to either state and that Magyar concentrations in the Székely district well inside Rumania and certain cities surrounded by non-Magyar country districts made a reasonable ethnic boundary very difficult to draw. It understood that the concentration of Rumanians in the hilly country and of Magyars in the lowlands would complicate any plan for an exchange of populations. Magyar irredentism was thought, however, to have been weakened among the peasants by the acquisition of farms through Rumanian land reforms. The German minority was understood to fear forcible assimilation if Transylvania came under Hungarian rule.

The subcommittee believed that it was inadvisable to establish an autonomous Transylvania within an East European Union. Since there was little local patriotism, such a solution would dissatisfy both Rumania and Hungary and both the Rumanian and Magyar elements is Transylvania. Whichever one of the latter got the upper hand locally would try to turn Transylvania into an adjunct of either Rumania or Hungary.

The subcommittee held that no negotiated settlement in this area would be possible at the close of the war. It therefore recommended that a United Nations force occupy Transylvania for as long as five years, or until both Rumania and Hungary had shown an ability to handle their domestic problems and a reasonable attitude in their mutual relations. During this period the United Nations should do their best to promote an amicable settlement of the Transylvanian problem.

The subcommittee postponed formulation of a preliminary view on the most appropriate final disposition of Transylvania at least until the next meeting, when the full results of research undertaken in PS would be reported.

Box 59

****

§ Document 7 §

Secret T Minutes 39

February 12, 1943

Not to be removed from the
State Department building

Present:
Mr. Isaiah Bowman, presiding

Mr. Adolf A. Berle
Mr. John V. A. MacMurray
Mr. Leo Pasvolsky
Mr. Cavendish W. Cannon
Mr. Otto E. Guthe
Mr. C. E. Black
Mr. John Campbell
Mr. Richard Eldridge
Mr. David Harris
Mr. Harry N. Howard
Mr. Melvin M. Knight
Mr. Thomas F. Power, Jr.
Mr. H. Julian Wadleigh
Mr. Harley Notter
Mr. Leroy D. Stinebower
Mr. Philip Mosely
Mr. Easton Rothwell
Mr. William Koren, Jr.

EAST EUROPEAN BOUNDARY PROBLEMS, PART I

Transylvania

The chairman proposed that the subcommittee take up first the problem of Transylvania, which had been left in the air last week. He understood that Mr. Mosely and Mr. Campbell were prepared to discuss this area. He wondered whether the first question to be answered might not be whether there was any differentiation in the distribution of Magyars in the area given to Hungary by the Vienna Award, Was there any block of Magyar population in this territory? Mr. Mosely referred this question to Mr. Campbell, who had made a particular study of Transylvania. Mr. Campbell explained that the whole southeast of the ceded territory, the district of the Székely, had an overwhelming Magyar population. There was also a Magyar majority in a strip along the western frontier set up by the Treaty of Trianon. There was no way of drawing an ethnic line to connect the Székely district with other

Magyar areas since, in spite of the fact that some of the cities had Magyar majorities, northern Transylvania was largely Rumanian.

The chairman asked what the Vienna Award had actually provided. Mr. Campbell explained that by that Treaty Hungary and Rumania had accepted the arbitration of Italy and Germany concerning an adjustment in their common frontier. The Treaty provided also for the exchange of population and property. The chairman concluded that since Rumania and Hungary had already agreed to promote population transfers the way was for the United Nations to propose similar action. Mr. Campbell pointed out that such transfers might depend on the character of the frontier line drawn. Rumania had always favored the transfer of population when it had a majority of the disputed territory. At the time of the Vienna Award it had had to accede to such transfers although it objected to them since they would tend to perpetuate a frontier which Rumania regarded as unfavorable to its ethnic claims. Conversely, Rumania had accepted the exchange of populations after the loss of Southern Dobruja to Bulgaria.

Mr. Mosely pointed out that an exchange was difficult as the present boundary left 400,000 Magyars in Rumanian territory and 1,200,000 Rumanians in Hungary. An exchange was further complicated by the fact that the Magyars left in Rumania were markedly urban in character, while the Rumanians in Hungary were almost entirely peasants. In answer to a question by the chairman, Mr. Mosely explained that there were some 400,000 Magyars constituting 90 percent of the population in the eastern tongue of the territory which Hungary had acquired in 1940 (the Székely region). The chairman remarked that this concentration of Magyars was "damned inconvenient." Mr. Mosely added that the Székely district was in the geographical center of pre-war Rumania and that the Székely did not want to leave a land which had been their home for at least eight hundred years.

The chairman noted that numbers of the subcommittee would have to face the attitude of those who claimed that one would not get anywhere in these areas of mixed population by boundary shifts or population transfers, that the only possible way out was to have these people "learn to live together." He asked whether any members of the subcommittee could explain exactly what that phrase meant. Mr. MacMurray admitted that he had no clear understanding of its meaning. Mr. Knight remarked that Bulgars and Rumanians seemed to live happily together in southern Rumania, but the chairman pointed out that these were peasant populations. The peasants could always get along; trouble arose when there was a mixed industrial and agricultural population and when politicians entered the area. To move out the Székely would be a large-scale, violent operation and would still not solve the problem of the Magyars along the pre-war western frontier.

Mr. Mosely pointed out that an added difficulty in transferring the population in this instance arose from the fact that the region of Székely was relatively flat, whereas the areas inhabited by Rumanians were largely hilly. This resulted in a different standard of living and different type of farming for the two groups. Mr. Knight remarked that there was a considerable flat belt along the pre-war western frontier but Mr. Mosely pointed out that that also had a Magyar population. He explained to Mr. Knight that there had not been much Rumanian colonization in that region after 1920. Mr. Campbell explained that the Magyar majority was substantial because of Magyar concentration in the cities of Arad, Oradea Mare and Satu Mare. It had been suggested at Paris that this Magyar territory be included in Hungary but it had finally been decided that Rumania should acquire this region because an ethnic frontier would have deprived Rumania of the important north-south railway.

The chairman explained to Mr. Berle and Mr. Pasvolsky, who had just arrived, that the subcommittee was being bothered by the problem of what to do with the Magyars in the Székely district. There were 400,000 of these Magyars, who thus constituted the chief trouble in drawing a frontier in Transylvania. Mr. Berle noted that the Székely had been in their present home longer than the other Magyars had been in the Hungarian plain; moreover, their country was more hilly than Hungary proper. The chairman repeated the frequently given advice that we should teach these people "to learn to live together." Mr. Pasvolsky offered to enlighten him on that phrase. He had just come from a conference with a certain individual who had explained at some length that if we could get all of the religious and educational leaders of the world together and have them draw up universal plans of education, all would be well with the world. His thought had not reached the stage of providing machinery to carry out this universal plan. Mr. Berle remarked that after the second Epistle to the Galatians we would all be happy.

Mr. Berle suggested that it might be a more fruitful approach to the Transylvanian problem to abandon all efforts to disentangle the population and to start from the theory of constructing a state. By that method one would concentrate on what would appear to be the most powerful element in the population, the one most likely to maintain itself as a group, and turn over to that group a territory included within the frontier most likely to lead to its stability. This would mean either enlarging Hungary as far as the Carpathians or the recreation of Versailles' Rumania.

Introducing the problems which would arise during the period of occupation, the chairman suggested that to apply Mr. Berle's principle would require a return to the 1937 frontier. This was implicit in the declaration of the United Nations. Talk of new adjustments would come only after the restoration of the *status quo ante*. He did not think that after this war there would be much opportunity for self-determination arrived at by a plebiscite, since that had not seemed to solve problems in the past. Mr. Rothwell explained to Mr. Pasvolsky that the purple line on the map[1] indicated the boundary proposals made by the United States in 1919. This line had been drawn largely on an ethnic basis, Mr. Campbell explained, but had had the disadvantage of cutting the railway line at several points. Mr. Berle pointed out that the problem of this frontier would be more difficult after this war than in 1919 since both Rumania and Hungary were now on the same side.

The chairman considered that in the future the 1919 solutions would be criticized in the light of any principle of peace making. They had been adopted merely because all the other states surrounding Hungary had appeared first at Paris and presented their claims. Hungary received merely what was left. He added, off the record, that in his opinion Hungarian arguments against the 1919 frontiers were legitimate since in fixing them the Allies had contradicted their own principles. Mr. Pasvolsky suggested that this injustice could be redressed at the end of this war. The chairman pointed out that the difficulty arose from the fact that the Atlantic Charter made it necessary to return first of all to the 1939 boundary and that in this case that boundary was an unjustifiable line.* He supposed that the difficulty was somewhat mitigated by the conditions under which Hungary had entered the war and its behavior as a belligerent. He hardly thought that these gave any basis for leniency to Hungary. Mr. Pasvolsky remarked that both countries had behaved badly. While admitting that there was a residual balance of adjustment remaining from the last war he thought that the important thing was to find the line which would give the most chance of peace in the future.

The chairman noted that the sequence of events would entail first the occupation of Transylvania and secondly the restoration of the 1939

---

[1]Rumanian Series Map 4, Rumania: Eastern Frontier

*The signatories of the Atlantic Charter, which represented Allied war aims, sought "...sovereign rights and self-government restored to those who have been forcibly deprived of them." In Morris, *op. cit.*, 170.

line. Mr. Pasvolsky suggested that since the United Nations would occupy both Rumania and Hungary they could set the line between the two countries wherever they wished for the purpose of temporary administration. The question would arise whether the local machinery of government was to be used or whether it was to be changed and where the line would be drawn in terms of machinery which the occupying forces would use. In his opinion that was the time to shift the boundary. The change should first be made for administrative purposes only; the change of title and adjustments found necessary through experience would be made later. Mr. Cannon remarked that setting up two sections of occupied territory, a Rumanian and an Hungarian section, seemed a method of pre-indicating the frontier line.

The chairman thought that this was a good case to illustrate the fact that the final decision ought to be adumbrated in the action of the occupying authorities. We can't go into a territory saying that we know nothing about the area, the eventual settlement or even the principles of final settlement. Over and over again we would find that the limit of the militarily occupied zone would be the line which would be likely to have permanence. He thought that this discussions had advanced the position of the subcommittee somewhat since the previous week. Mr. MacMurray did not think there was any other thing which the subcommittee could do. Mr. Cannon asked whether the subcommittee could report that it found no solution possible along ethnic lines. The chairman was reluctant to make any such report since it was possible that later adjustments might be based on ethnic considerations. This was particularly true of the western limit of the area, where we were still faced with the problem left by the peculiar circumstances of the 1919 settlement.

PROCEDURE, PART I

Statement on Recommendations

The chairman suggested that the time had come when a statement ought to be made up on each point that had been agreed upon by the subcommittee. This should be done in the simplest terms and should be followed by a résumé of the argument on which the subcommittee's decision had been based. He thought that it was time that documents of this nature were accumulated. The subcommittee's decisions would not be considered as frozen in this form but as crystallized. Further investigation might cause changes or additions to these recommendations. Obviously such documents were not expected to summarize all the research work which lay behind the decisions of the subcommittee.

EAST EUROPEAN INTERNAL PROBLEMS, PART I

Székely Autonomy

Mr. Mosely suggested that, with regard to the settlement in Transylvania, the Székely might be treated separately since there was no minority problem within the Székely district, no rural-urban clash of nationalities and no conflict between two classes of peasants. Even after 1919 the Székely had enjoyed some cultural autonomy. It might be advisable to give them some autonomy in their local political life. This could be combined with a new frontier in the northwest and certain shifts of population in that region. He thought that such a combination would be better than an outright transfer of Székely or simple reincorporation in Rumania.

The chairman considered that the subcommittee should examine very closely the word autonomy. It raised the question of invasion of national sovereignty and the whole minority problem. He pointed out that such autonomy would be comparable to an international guarantees for the minority rights of French Canadians in New England. Any such international political action would be highly resented in the American melting-pot. He wondered how this difficulty could be circumvented. Mr. Mosely pointed out that the French Canadians had their own church schools and could elect local officials from their number, as in some towns of New England. The Székely would be content with comparable advantages and with the absence of discrimination against them in the national fiscal policy. The Székely had actually had autonomy for a very long period, unlike the inhabitants of the Banat and Macedonia. He did not think, he explained to the chairman, that it would be necessary to extend autonomous rights to other Magyar groups in Rumania.

Mr. Pasvolsky noted that this suggestion raised the question of the part to be played by the state in the maintenance of schools. In the United States schools were financed locally, but in Europe nationally. The question therefore arose whether public funds could be used for minority schools. Mr. Mosely explained that in Transylvania much of the support for the schools came through the church. Mr. Cannon pointed out that education in Europe was not a mere matter of teaching people to be literature but also a question of political activity. Schools were designed to instill nationalism. He knew of many cases where a dozen or so families had been planted in certain localities in order that they might claim after a few years that a school for them should be established in that town. In Transylvania the church had been used to promote nationalism. Mr. Pasvolsky pointed out that another question concerned the language which should be used in the courts of law.

The chairman suggested that in the interest of speed Mr. Mosely and Mr. Cannon should consult and bring in a recommendation next week for a solution of the Székely problem. Mr. Mosely and Mr. Cannon agreed to this suggestion. Mr. Knight declared that he would like to support Mr. Mosely's suggestion. He did not think that there was a complete parallel between the situations in Massachusetts and in Transylvania. In Massachusetts the French Canadians had come of their own will to a country whose laws they could learn before they arrived. In Transylvania, on the other hand, the Székely had been there before the formation of a Rumanian state and the latter had been imposed over their heads. This seemed to him to justify some degree of autonomy for the Székely. The chairman declared that Mr. Knight should be added to the Transylvania sub-subcommittee. He asked whether anyone else wished to speak on this subject.

EAST EUROPEAN BOUNDARY PROBLEMS, PART II

Yugoslav-Hungary Boundary

The chairman asked Mr. Black to enlighten the subcommittee on the situation in territory disputed between Yugoslavia and Hungary and on possible solutions with respect to that area. Mr. Black explained that there were five districts involved in this dispute, two in the northwest and three in the northeast. The American proposal in 1919 had given some of this territory, all of which was eventually included in Yugoslavia, to Hungary. The proposed American line had been drawn largely on ethnic grounds.

The two northwestern districts were Prekomurje and Medjumurje. The former of these had a population of slightly over 90,000 and had been occupied by Hungary in 1941. The population of Prekomurje was very largely Slovene. There were, however, twelve thousand Magyars in twenty-five communes along the Hungarian border. In these communes there were also approximately one thousand Slovenes. In three communes along the Austrian frontier there was a majority of German-speaking inhabitants. The total of Magyar and German minorities equaled approximately 15 percent of the population of Prekomurje. These two sets of communes could be detached from

Yugoslavia without doing any injury to the area in general. The railway lines through Prekomurje ran from southwest to northeast and were not in any case out by the Hungarian boundary. Medjumurje was almost entirely Croat in population. There was no commune with a majority of Magyars, who totalled only 6,000 or less than 7 percent of the total. There was no strategic, economic or ethnic argument for ceding any part of Medjumurje to Hungary. The Hungarian forces had occupied the district in 1941 for the "historical" reason that it had formed a part of Hungary proper before 1914.

Mr. Pasvolsky asked whether there were any Croats or Slovenes across the border in Hungary. Mr. Black explained that there were some 56,000 Yugoslavians of all groups in Hungary. These were in general scattered throughout the country and were not concentrated opposite the districts of Prekomurje and Medjumurje. The greatest concentration was in a north-south corridor leading to Czechoslovakia which had been the original excuse for a proposal which would link the two Slav states by a corridor between Austria and Hungary. Mr. Black added that almost all of the inhabitants of these two districts were Roman Catholic. The few Protestants in Prekomurje were mostly Magyars living along the eastern frontier.

Mr. Black then pointed out on the map[2] the location of the three northeastern districts, the Baranja, the Bačka and the Banat. The total population of this area in 1921, which was the date of the last census which showed language statistics, was 1,346,000. Various types of Slavs —Serbs, Croats, Slovenes and two minor groups, Sokci and Bunjevci— totalled 506,000 or some 38 percent of the entire population. The two minor Slav groups, Mr. Black explained, were concentrated in the northern part of the area and were Roman Catholic. Some 380,000 Magyars were scattered throughout the three districts. Hungarian revisionist maps which showed solid blocks of Magyar territory were deceptive. The largest city was Subotica, with a population of 100,000, most of whom were Yugoslavs. The Hungarians were concentrated in the southern parts of the three districts where the land was better than in the north. The Germans, of whom there were some 300,000, were most numerous in the Banat, where they constituted the largest single linguistic group. Hungary had occupied the Baranja and the Bačka. The Germans were said to have occupied the Banat and to have turned over the administration to the local German population. This, however, was uncertain.

---

[2]Yugoslav Series Map 1, Yugoslavia—Political Divisions.

This area had an extensive transportation system. The Danube and Tisza Rivers and the Francis and Francis-Joseph Canals were all internationalized. Communication could therefore remain free no matter which country had sovereignty over the area. The extensive railway system, which had been built largely when the area was under Hungarian rule, included four or five lines leading south from Subotica and two transverse lines. One of these was the Szeged-Temesvár-Bucharest line.

According to Mr. Black, population distribution was very complicated in these three districts. In the Baranja there was no districts which had a majority of any one of the three linguistic groups, Yugoslav, Magyar or German. The Bačka had a population of some 735,000, and in only two of the dozen districts of the area was there a majority of any language group. This majority was in both cases Serbo-Croat. In the eleven districts of the Banat each of the three ethnic groups had a majority in two districts. All this meant that it was impossible to draw an ethnic line through the area.

Economically, the area was valuable chiefly as wheatland. For this reason it was more important to Yugoslavia than to Hungary. Even within its reduced 1919 frontiers Hungary had had an excess of wheat. None of Hungary's lost forests and mines were located in these three districts.

Mr. Pasvolsky asked what had been the administrative picture in these three districts. Mr. Black explained that in 1920 Prekomurje had formed part of Slovenia, Medjumurje part of Croatia and the other three had formed an autonomous province within Yugoslavia. After King Alexander's reforms of 1929 Prekomurje had been included in the province of the Drava, Medjumurje in the province of the Sava, and the Baranja, the Bačka and the Banat had formed part of the Province of the Danube which had included Belgrade and north Serbia. The map showed the 1943 conditions of these areas. The first four had been occupied by Hungary, the Banat was variously reported to be occupied by Germans or to be under the rule of Nedič.*

Mr. Black suggested that there were three possible solutions with regard to the Baranja, Bačka, and Banat. The first was to return them all to Yugoslavia. This could be justified by Yugoslavia's part in the war and by its need for wheat. The second possibility was to return

---

*The "Yugoslav Banat" was never part of the jurisdiction of the Serbian government of Belgrade formed under the presidency of General Milan Nedić. Rather, it was governed directly by the occupying German command, with the collaboration of the representatives of the Swabian population.

them to Hungary in accordance with the claims of the Hungarian revisionists, who in fact desired all Yugoslavia north of the Danube and Drava. In this opinion there was insufficient ethnic or economic argument for such a shift. The third possibility was to divide these three districts, perhaps in accordance with the American proposal of 1919.* That would roughly equalize the minorities on both sides of the line; one-third of the Baranja and three northern districts in both Bačka and the Banat would be transferred to Hungary. This equalled one-fifth the area of these three territories, the least desirable area economically. The chief argument for such a division would be a desire to do justice to Hungary, based on the idea that Hungary had an ethnic claim to this area. It might also be argued that the Germans, who with the Magyars totalled 700,000 in the whole area, might prefer to be under Hungarian rather than Yugoslavian rule after the war.

Division in accordance with the 1919 American proposals would leave a minority of approximately 168,000 Magyars in that part of the district left to Yugoslavia and would transfer approximately 175,000 Yugoslavs to Hungary. This in turn might lead to forcible exchange of populations, to optional exchange of populations or to an optional exchange with a reciprocal minority treaty. The Magyars had argued in the past that a minority agreement with Yugoslavia would have been useless since Hungary's relative lack of a Yugoslav minority had prevented it from having any sanction over Yugoslavia's treatment of its Magyars. Mr. Black remarked further that there were some 75,000 Magyars in the rest of Yugoslavia and 56,000 Yugoslavs in Hungary.

There was one additional territorial problem in this area, Mr. Black explained. In the southern Banat some 80,000 Rumanians constituted an important minority. Through this area ran the railroad from Temesvar to the Danube River. Cession of this area to Rumania would be of economic help to Rumania. In 1919 the American Government had favored Rumanian sovereignty in this area.

The chairman thanked Mr. Black for his very clear presentation. He desired to suggest an amendment in terminology whereby reciprocal agreements concerning minorities might be referred to as "conventions." This would prevent them from being confused with the 1919 treaties. He accepted Mr. Pasvolsky's suggestion that they might be called "civic rights conventions." These would differ from the minority treaties in that their acceptance was not a prior condition insisted upon by the

---

*Cf. Map 6.

great powers as preceding a territorial cession. He then invited discussion on the problem of the Yugoslav-Hungarian frontier.

Mr. Berle asked whether this was not a typical case for indulging a presumption in favor of the 1919 border. Mr. Cannon declared that he would like to make several comments on the report. He pointed out that since April 1941 there had been a considerable exchange of population in this region. Although there were no statistics available he knew that many Yugoslavs had returned from Hungary. Concerning the economic status of the area, he thought that it should be pointed out that the Yugoslavs argued against the return of the disputed areas to Hungary partly because this would mean the elimination of the land reforms and would return the agricultural holdings to the great estates of Hungary. As a matter of fact, the Yugoslavian land reform had not accomplished very much.

Finally, Mr. Cannon pointed out that there had been in the months immediately prior to the outbreak of the war in 1941 strong indications that a basis had been laid for a Yugoslav-Hungarian understanding whereby the boundary would be shifted to a line which approached Mr. Black's compromise suggestion. Revival of such an agreement seemed, however, very difficult. Teleki, who had represented Hungary in the negotiations, and Prince Paul, who had represented Yugoslavia, were dead and in disgrace respectively. Mr. Berle pointed out that Teleki's suicide had resulted partly from the fact that Hungary had felt obliged to move in by force to settle a question on which he had reached a peaceful agreement. Mr. Cannon believed that the Teleki Treaty had been signed in December 1940.*

Mr. Mosely noted that Mr. Cannon had spoken of an exchange of population and wondered whether any Magyars from Yugoslav territory had returned to Hungary. Mr. Cannon believed that any movement in that direction had been very small. The Hungarian Government had not done much to promote immigration from Croatia or to the regions occupied by Hungary. Mr. Mosely supposed that the exodus of Yugoslavs from Hungary had been more in the nature of expulsion than in

*The Hungarian-Yugoslav Treaty of Perpetual Friendship was signed in Belgrade on December 12, 1940. It contained no reference to revisionism, although the matter had come up in the course of the preliminary discussions. Hungary wanted to get back the Murje region (Prekomurje and Medjumurje) along with two-thirds of the Baranja triangle and of the Backa (to the Francis Joseph Canal), while the Yugoslav party offered to return only the districts of Senta (Zenta) and Topolje (Topolya).

an exchange, and Mr. Cannon admitted that it had been accomplished by some massacres.*

In answer to the chairman's question concerning Hungarian-Yugoslav negotiations of 1940 Mr. Cannon explained that they had apparently been initiated by Hungary but that the full trustworthiness of his information was in question. Mr. Berle added that he had been given to understand that Teleki himself had taken the first steps. Mr. Pasvolsky pointed out that Yugoslavia would have been unlikely to initiate any negotiations which would result in the loss of Yugoslav territory. Mr. Cannon declared that he did not know the technical terms of the agreement nor the size of the population which was involved. The chairman explained that he desired as much information as possible concerning these negotiations since in these matters the subcommittee should be looking for a solution in terms of principle and since such a solution should have regard for the degree of freedom and sincerity of the interested parties when they had come close to a solution by direct negotiation.

Mr. Berle thought that whatever chances this agreement might have had in 1941 had now vanished. Hungary had broken its word and had behaved badly.** Now that Yugoslavia was in the war, could one do any more than return to the *status quo ante*? Personally he saw no compelling reason to do anything else. The chairman observed that such a solution followed Mr. MacMurray's ideas concerning the Polish-German frontier. Mr. Berle remarked that Yugoslavia might not be in a condition to behave quite as Poland did but asked what else any member of the subcommittee would propose. The chairman declared that if the United Nations made Yugoslavia the base of military operations yet gave part of Yugoslav territory away on the basis of a Yugoslavia-Hungarian agreement which had been made before the Hungarian atrocities in Yugoslavia, he would not know how to answer a Yugoslav who objected to this arrangement. Mr. Berle declared that he would not either. In his mind the real question was whether there was to be a Yugoslavia at all.

---

*According to Hungarian historians, about 3,000 Yugoslavs, mostly Serbs, were killed in these massacres. Recent publications based on hitherto secret Yugoslav documents estimate that late in 1944 and early in 1945, Tito's victorious partisans murdered 15,000 to 35,000 Hungarians in the same region. See, Tibor Cseres, *Vérbosszú Bácskában* (Budapest, 1991).

**The statement pertains to the fact that only four months after the Hungarian-Yugoslav treaty was signed, on April 11, 1941, Hungary joined in the German offensive against Yugoslavia.

GENERAL APPROACH TO TERRITORIAL PROBLEMS

Mr. Cannon asked whether all recommendations concerning frontiers reached by the subcommittee, even if agreed to by the policy-making officers of the Department, by the American negotiations and by the Peace Conference, were meant to be unalterable. The chairman answered that they were not. In his understanding, these recommendations were not to be imposed upon the smaller states. They were being discussed because the United Nations were ready to facilitate negotiations between interested powers. As Mr. Pasvolsky had declared at an earlier meeting, it was important that the subcommittee look at these matters not as possible items on the agenda for the Peace Conference but as agenda primarily for negotiation between two interested states. The important thing was that these negotiations be facilitated by the United Nations, not that the powers impose a settlement in the dispute. In the chairman's opinion, it was important to enunciate the principle of return to the 1937 frontiers, or otherwise the United Nations would have no restraint on a state which had local power at the close of the war. It was important to keep in mind the importance of the 1937 frontiers as a restraint upon both friend and foe. Mr. Pasvolsky noted that this would not prevent considerable flexibility, for example in Transylvania. He and the chairman agreed that the fact that both parties to the dispute were enemy states allowed a certain extra freedom.

Mr. Berle was of the opinion there was some difficulty in seeing the need for a Yugoslav-Hungarian frontier to appear on the agenda for the Peace Conference. Hungary's claim was historical, not ethnic or economic except in so far as recent population movements gave Hungary an ethnic claim. The United Nations should not indulge that sort of claim. Mr. Cannon added that negotiations at the end of the war would be impossible between these states. The chairman explained that according to the principles enunciated by Mr. Pasvolsky it was not a question of putting items on the agenda for the United States to bring up. Mr. Pasvolsky added that all the United States was interested in was an amicable solution of territorial disputes and that if we could use our good offices in furthering such a solution so much the better. The chairman pointed out that we acquired knowledge of situations in order to be able to use our good offices when required. There was no schedule of when any such negotiations should take place or whether they should take place at all.

Application to the Yugoslav-Hungarian Frontier

Mr. Pasvolsky thought that the five districts in dispute by the Yugoslavs and Hungarians could be relegated to that category of disputes which the United States had no reason to bring up. The chairman asked whether all the members of the subcommittee were agreed on that point. Mr. Cannon asked whether this decision was meant to include the Rumanian claims on the southern part of the Yugoslav Banat. The chairman answered in the affirmative.

EAST EUROPEAN INTERNAL PROBLEMS, PART II

Hungarian Land Holding and Land Reform

The chairman asked Mr. Power to introduce the subject of Hungarian landholding. Mr. Power explained that the Regency had carried out no real land reform in Hungary. More than 98 percent of the holdings were still in units of twenty-nine hectares or less. The average for this group was a holding of only 3.4 hectares. Only 5.5 percent of the agricultural land was in large farm holdings of between 29 and 58 hectares. The medium size estates comprised 85 percent of the holdings and 18 percent of the land. The large estates comprised less than 1 percent of the holdings but 29.5 percent of the land. Even the chart[3] did not show a true picture of the concentration of ownership, since in many cases one owner had several holdings.

Over half the arable land, Mr. Power continued, produced cereal crops. The land reform carried out between 1920 and 1925 had distributed only 666,000 hectares or 2 percent of the land.[*] These had been parceled out in very small plots insufficient to provide a living for a peasant family. The landless proletariat on the large estates had been particularly hard hit by the depression. These conditions of landholding made a program of land reform possible. If all medium and large estates, that is, those of 58 hectares and above, were broken up, 3,700,000 hectares of land suitable for redistribution would be available. The first difficulty in such a program arose from the fact that one-half of the land in these estates was entailed. It was held largely by the church and by municipalities, which rented it out in small lots. The

---

[3]Hungarian Series, No. 1, Hungary - Landholding, 1930.

[*]The land reform in the early 1920s affected not 2, but 8.5 percent of the country's arable land. This, however, was still a much lower proportion than the area of land subdivided in the neighboring countries.

redistribution of these 3,700,000 hectares would make it possible to increase 200,000 peasant holdings to a size which would provide an adequate standard of living. Mr. Power believed that the minimum size of the peasant holdings should vary from 8 to 50 hectares depending on the quality of land. A one-horse farm of 8 hectares on good soil would provide adequately for a peasant family. In northern Hungary, however, closer to 50 hectares would be needed. Furthermore the peasants would need financial assistance in order to acquire the necessary livestock and machinery.

At the same time, Mr. Power considered, an attempt would have to be made to diversify Hungarian agriculture. The peasants should change over from production of grain to the production of fruits and vegetables and the raising of livestock. He stated that up to the present time the large estates produced more per hectare than the small holdings, but at the same time they did not provide a decent living for the peasants who worked the land. The chairman asked Mr. Knight whether he cared to add anything to this report. The latter replied that he was not particularly acquainted with this area. The chairman then asked what could be considered the necessary number of acres for subsistence living according to Hungarian standards. Mr. Power replied that the German population in Transdanubia maintained a respectable standard of living on 15 acres. They were able to buy meat, coffee and sugar. It was worthy of note that their land was not exclusively devoted to grain since they raised considerable livestock. The problem following land reform and agricultural diversification would be to find the necessary markets. It might be that this would involve the industrialization of Hungary, lower tariffs in neighboring states and other adjustments.

The chairman asked what the interests of the United States were in this internal Hungarian problem. He hoped that some of the economic experts present would reply. Mr. Stinebower commented that this Hungarian problem had implications for commercial policy in the entire European area. Under one system the small countries devoted themselves largely to agricultural production for export and easily gravitated into making special arrangements with Germany which put them economically at the mercy of that industrial country. On the other hand, high tariff restrictions set up by these countries and attempts at increasing self-sufficiency tended to lower the standard of living and so to result by another route in a dangerous political situation. He did not suppose that the immediate social implications of Hungarian landowning were of importance to the United States.

The chairman commented that the primary interest of the United States was in the stability of societies all over the world. Mr. Stinebower pointed out the two main choices: first, a free trade economy leading to a higher standard of living but less stability in times of world crises and, second, a balanced self-sufficiency with a lower standard of living but more continuous stability. He wanted to point out that conditions in the surrounding area were relevant to the degree of stability which any state could attain. Mr. Wadleigh suggested that a rising standard of living in foreign countries might be more to the interest of the United States than mere economic stability. From the point of view of peace the choice was between stable, isolated societies and progressive societies linked with the outside world.

PROCEDURE, PART II

Economic Research and Discussion

The chairman observed that in the subcommittee's consideration of economic facts it should avoid the danger of jumping from the difficulties of a given country into a solution provided by world organization and the world situation. Any country's salvation would have to start with domestic developments. The world would not, of course, attain peace and a higher standard of living unless the nations agreed on some standard of international economic relations, on the importance of the principle of mutual advantages and rights. Nevertheless, we must not study the difficulties of one country only in world terms also in terms of the conditions within that country. He therefore suggested that PS and ES should present economic reports under two heads: (1) the scope of the economy of the given country and the remedial measures which it could take and (2) the relations of that state to the international economic organizations it is hoped to establish.

Mr. Pasvolsky considered that this statement of the chairman was very worthwhile, and added that Hungary was a good example. In spite of the predominance of agriculture in Hungary, only one-half the population depended on agriculture, if he remembered correctly. Mr. Power pointed out that the actual figure was 55 percent. Mr. Pasvolsky continued that that population produced an agricultural surplus for international trade. The problem had always been what to do with the Hungarian population. Could Hungarian agriculture, if built on a better system of land tenure and land exploitation, absorb more of the Hungarian population? If land reforms led to emigration from the rural districts, the Hungarians would be confronted with the problem of what to do with the rest of its economy. The subcommittee needed to explore the possibilities of Hungarian industry. This industry had been sufficiently advanced to produce goods for export. What had held it back?

Mr. Pasvolsky continued that the economic structure of a country was of the utmost importance for internal social and political conditions as well as for its international position. He thought that the United States was interested in the political and social stability of foreign countries and in their economic progress. He hoped that we could get away from the idea of economic stability and think in terms of economic progress [that] would attain political and social stability.

The chairman suggested to the members of PS and ES* that the time had come to develop a set of principles for discussion of economic conditions and economically important areas comparable to those which had been worked out for boundary questions. Only by this method could the subcommittee avoid the rather spasmodic discussion of economic matters which had taken place with regard to Upper Silesia and similarly important areas. He thought that the boundary principles arrived at by the subcommittee had enabled it to organize its thought rationally concerning frontier problems. He hoped that Mr. Mosely would be able to report at the next meeting on some such organization of principles for economic problems. This was a matter of codification rather than of research and should not be an arduous task. Mr. Pasvolsky expressed the hope that at the next meeting the subcommittee might spend a little time discussing what it wished to know about a country economically. The subcommittee had already set out a schedule of necessary political and boundary information. In order to complete the picture it would be necessary to figure out how best to enable the subcommittee to visualize the economic life of a country, say of Hungary behind its projected borders. The chairman considered that success in this matter would help the political committee in its discussion of an East European Union.

When Mr. Pasvolsky expressed the hope that Mr. Stinebower would present a statement on this question at the next meeting, the latter asked for further clarification of what was wanted. He asked whether the subcommittee desired an analysis and presentation of what it wanted to know concerning a country as it exists or of that country without pre-conceptions as to its boundaries. He noted that most boundary discussions which had occupied the subcommittee had not

---

*PS = Political Subcommittee; ES = Economic Subcommittee.

involved areas of great economic importance. On the other hand, in the relations of Germany, Czechoslovakia and Poland or of Germany, France and Belgium the major economic facts paid no respect to political boundaries, present or future.

The chairman replied that he understood Mr. Pasvolsky desired a study of the economics of a country within definite frontiers and that was what he himself had had in view. It was necessary to study the resources actually within the political boundaries of a given country. He was interested, for example, in learning the possibility of improved transportation and water power within Yugoslavia. He admitted that it was necessary to know how the economics of a country fitted into the world situation or regional groups in order to know completely what was economically feasible; nevertheless, he did not wish to have all discussions of a particular country's prospects left hanging on future world conditions and organization.

Mr. Pasvolsky remarked that what Mr. Stinebower had just said illustrated the kind of discussion which the subcommittee needed. It had to determine whether it was to deal with the facts of a nation's economy and with the facts of world economy on the one hand or with the facts of the overlapping of economic considerations across national frontiers. It was impossible to understand the economy of a country inside its frontiers and in relation to the world economy unless the subcommittee explored also the relations of that country to its immediate surrounding area.

Mr. Cannon added that in his opinion it was high time this discussion had taken place. He recalled that a few weeks ago the subcommittee had drawn a frontier in the Istrian Peninsula with the purpose of including the coal mines within Italy on the grounds of economic necessity. He remembered, however, that Italy had managed very well before 1914 when it had not possessed these coal mines. The chairman thought that Mr. Cannon had not given a completely fair picture of this boundary decision. According to him the subcommittee had awarded the local mines to Italy because of the sentimental value of this coal to the Italians. The subcommittee had specifically recognized that this coal represented only some 800,000 tons out of an annual consumption of approximately 15,000,000 tone. Mr. Cannon asked whether this sentimental principle was to be applied generally. The chairman declared that it was not. He admitted that it was arguable whether the principle which the subcommittee had applied was good or not. Mr. Pasvolsky pointed out that in making this boundary decision the subcommittee had made no real study of the economics either of Italy or of Yugoslavia.

The chairman remarked that the American Government was not expected to take up an unalterable stand on the basis of the subcommittee's recommendations. A shift in the major power situation would force an adjustment of the subcommittee's tentative conclusions.

Mr. Knight observed that a study of the 10,000,000 economic enterprises of Italy, even if it could be carried out with the limited staff of ES, would not constitute a description of the Italian economy. In his opinion these 10,000,000 enterprises did not have any organic unity which meant that they constituted an economy. It was in fact questionable whether there was any such thing as a national economy. The chairman replied that the subcommittee employed a loose layman's use of the word economy. He admitted, however, that in this subcommittee, no more than in any other committee of which he had knowledge, the members had faced up to the question of what to do within a country. In Hungary the problem sprang from the landholding situation.

EAST EUROPEAN INTERNAL PROBLEMS, PART III

American Interest in Hungary

The chairman continued that control of land policy in Hungary lay in the hands of the Hungarian government. He would like to know what place this landholding had in American interest and policy. Mr. Power explained that his memorandum on Hungarian Landholding had been begun as part of a study of the possibility of securing a more stable and prosperous Eastern Europe. In the case of Hungary a clear necessity was breaking the economic and thereby the political power of a ruling class which had been a trouble maker in Europe. It was felt that if no reform program with regard to Hungarian landholding was ready at the close of hostilities, the local population and neighboring states would alter the situation by force. He understood that a peaceful method of change was preferable. He also believed that only by the creation of a more democratic state based on a more equitable agrarian economy could Hungary have peaceful relations with its neighbors. Agrarian reform would also aid in the problem of disposing of the world wheat surplus. If the United States desired a stable eastern Europe, it would have to back some group which stood for the four freedoms for which the United States declared it was fighting. The only way that such a group could win power in Hungary would be on a program of land reform. He did not mean that officers of the Department of Agriculture would go to Hungary and supervise the breaking up of large estates and their redistribution among the peasants. It was rather a matter of supporting a group which would carry out such policy. At the same time it was only realistic for the American Government to make a study of what would be practicable in the way of land reform.

William Koren, Jr.

x x x

PROCEDURE

Statement on Recommendations

The subcommittee agreed that a summary statement should be prepared of its recommendations and of the arguments supporting them

Economic Research and Discussion

It was suggested that studies of a country's economy should consider first, the remedial measures which that country was capable of undertaking and second, its relations with projected international economic organizations. The question was raised whether there was any such thing as a "national economy" or whether the business enterprises did not have to be considered as part of a functional structure which transcended political boundaries. It was agreed that a country's economy must also be considered in terms of the surrounding economic region.

It was hoped that at the next meeting there could be presented for criticism a set of principles for the discussion of economic problems comparable to those which had been successfully elaborated for the discussion of boundary problems.

GENERAL APPROACH TO TERRITORIAL PROBLEMS

It was understood that the subcommittee should discuss all territorial problems likely to arise after the war. In many cases, however, the subcommittee undertook its study merely in order that, should two disputants choose to negotiate a settlement and call upon the good offices of the United States, this government would possess the necessary data.

EAST-EUROPEAN BOUNDARY PROBLEMS

Transylvania

The subcommittee resumed discussion of the population distribution in Transylvania. It took note of the concentration of Magyars in the Székely districts and along the Trianon frontier, where the railway was of considerable importance to areas inhabited by Rumanians. It recognized that any exchange of populations would involve a revision of the economic life of the people concerned and that the Vienna award left three times as many Rumanians as Magyars outside the territory of their respective states.*

It was suggested that the subcommittee abandon the ethnic approach and decide either to give all the land up to the Carpathians to Hungary or to restore the pre-war frontier. Such a solution rested on the principle that the more stable element should be given optimum frontiers and entrusted with the construction of the state. Assuming that the United Nations would occupy both Rumania and Hungary, the subcommittee recognized that the view of the United Nations concerning the proper frontier between them might well be embodied in a temporary administrative boundary within the area of occupation.

Yugoslav-Hungarian Frontier

It was explained that five areas in northern Yugoslavia were claimed by Hungary. In, Prekomurje 25 border communes had a population over 90 percent Magyar, and three on the Austrian border had a German-speaking population. These could be detached without economic damage to Yugoslavia. There was no adequate strategic, ethnic or economic argument for Hungary's claim to Medjumurje. The Baranja, Bačka and Banat had a mixed Yugoslav, Magyar and German population; the Yugoslavs were the largest group but only 38 percent of the total. Local subdivisions showed an equally indecisive ethnic distribution. In the southern Banat was a concentration of Rumanians in an area important to Rumania by reason of its railway. Economical-

---

*The statement is inaccurate. According to the Romanian (!) census of 1930, 1,149,000 Romanians got annexed to Hungary, and 444,000 remained in Romania. Counting the few thousand Romanians living in Hungary after Trianon, too, the ratio is 2.5:1. However, taking into consideration the migrations of the 1940s, as well as the distortions of the Romanian statistics, it is evident that Romanian "predominance" was exaggerated.

ly, these three wheat-growing areas were more essential to Yugoslavia than to Hungary. The navigable rivers and canals were all internationalized. It was pointed out that since April 1941 there had been a considerable withdrawal of Yugoslavs from these territories under Hungarian rule.

The subcommittee took note of the fact that the American representatives of 1919 had proposed to leave some of the Baranja, Bačka and Banat in Hungary and to award a portion of the Banat to Rumania, and that Yugoslavia and Hungary had reached agreement in December 1940 for adjustment of the frontier.* It recommended a restoration of the 1920 boundary.

EAST EUROPEAN INTERNAL PROBLEMS

Székely Autonomy

The subcommittee discussed briefly the possibility of granting autonomy to the Székely in the event that Rumania obtained the major portion of Transylvania. The chairman referred this question to a sub-subcommittee composed of Mr. Mosely, Mr. Cannon and Mr. Knight, which should report at the next meeting.

Hungarian Landholding and Land Reform

It was explained that 98 percent of agricultural landholdings in Hungary were in holdings of less than 29 hectares. The peasants farming them or working on the large estates were impoverished. If estates of over 58 hectares were broken up, 3,700,000 hectares of agricultural land would be available for distribution, or enough land to provide farms of between 8 and 50 hectares for 200,000 peasant families. The technical difficulties of such a program included the fast that much of the land was held by the church and municipalities, the cost of supplying the necessary livestock and machinery, the necessity of persuading the peasants to take up a more diversified agriculture, and the need to prepare for repercussions on Hungarian industry and trade.

It was suggested that the landholding system of Hungary was of interest to the United States since, by retarding economic progress in

---

*The Hungarian-Yugoslav Treaty of Perpetual Friendship signed on December 12, 1940, did not contain any reference to boundaries.

that country, it promoted a condition leading to social and political instability and thereby constituted a danger to peace. Since support of an Hungarian political group dedicated to land reform seemed the most that this country could conceivably do to alter this situation, it was important to study the practical possibilities of land reform.

Box 59

****

§ Document 8 §

Secret T Minutes 40

February 19, 1943

Present:
Mr. Isaiah Bowman, presiding

Mr. Hamilton Fish Armstrong
Mr. Adolf A. Berle
Mr. John V. A. MacMurray
Mrs. Anne O'Hare McCormick
Mr. Leo Pasvolsky
Mr. Myron C. Taylor
Mr. Cavendish W. Cannon
Mr. Otto E. Guthe
Mr. C. E. Black
Mr. John Campbell
Mr. Norris B. Chipman
Mr. Richard Eldridge
Mr. Leon W. Fuller
Mr. David Harris
Mr. Harry N. Howard
Mr. Melvin M. Knight
Mr. Thomas F. Power, Jr.
Mr. Andreas G. Ronhovde
Miss Julia Schairer
Mr. H. Julian Wadleigh
Mr. Harley Notter
Mr. Leroy D. Stinebower
Mr. Philip Mosely
Mr. John Masland
Mr. Easton Rothwell
Mr. William Koren, Jr.

TRANSYLVANIA

The Possibility of Autonomy, Part I

The chairman noted that at the close of the last meeting the question of Transylvania, and particularly the possibility of establishing Székler autonomy, had been referred to a sub-subcommittee. He asked Mr. Campbell to report the findings of this group. Mr. Campbell noted that the sub-subcommittee had had to assume the retention of this area by Rumania. Given that sovereignty there were two possible forms of autonomy: (1) an autonomy on a territorial basis, which would give extension to the local self-goverment of the Széklers within Rumania so that they had certain rights as citizens of Rumania and others as citizens of the area; (2) autonomy in religious, educational and social matters in conjunction with all Magyars in Rumania, i. e., an attempt to force Rumania to take the idea of nationality out of its basic state doctrine. Under this second alternative Rumania would not try to establish a strictly Rumanian national state. He repeated that the question of autonomy arises if the territorial solution of the Transylvania question between Hungary and Rumania follows the 1919 line or some compromise different from the Vienna Award. It would not exist if the Széklers and Magyars were transferred to Hungary. He pointed out that there was particular difficulty in transferring the Széklers since they numbered one-half million persons, they had had exceptionally long residence in their home and that home was located in the geographical center of Rumania.[*]

The chairman considered that a brief description of possible solutions previously discussed would help later discussion in detail on the autonomy issue. The subcommittee had previously discussed the possibility of a division of Transylvania along nationality lines, the possibility of making permanent the 1940 line and the possibility of the restoration of Transylvania to Rumania with some provision for autonomy. Such autonomy might restore the historical privileges enjoyed by the Széklers in cultural matters and might perhaps extend local privileges in accordance with a new bill of rights. Mr. Campbell observed that if autonomy were granted on a territorial basis Székler autonomy would remain a Rumanian question. By the second system of autonomy, Transylvanian autonomy would be put under some general

---

[*] Campbell and his group's written proposal is presented as Document 8, p. 221.

scheme for the treatment of minorities. He explained once more that the subcommittee had assumed that the boundary between Rumania and Hungary would be west of the Székely district, since otherwise no question would arise of Székler autonomy.

The chairman asked Mr. Cannon what his reflections were on this question of autonomy. He wondered what advantages or disadvantages Mr. Cannon saw with respect to autonomy population in accordance with 1919 principles. Mr. Cannon replied that in his opinion the best regime for the region would be a system of autonomy under which similar regimes would be applied both to the remainder of Rumania and the remainder of Hungary. He expected that Rumania would be considerably truncated even if it existed at all after the war. He noted that before 1848 the Széklers had had more independence than other Hungarians. He considered this historical cohesion of considerable importance. The 1919 frontier had been, in his opinion, drawn too far to the west. In some respects the Vienna Award of 1940, under which some Magyars still lived in Rumania, had not been too bad a compromise. Almost any line would inevitably leave minorities on both sides. Geographical conditions made an exchange of these populations impracticable.

For these reasons he favored autonomy for the whole region of which the Székely districts was only a part. Instead of minority rights in the 1919 sense he wanted equal rights for all individuals. It had been proved that special minority legislation was not satisfactory in a democratic country which had majority rule. In his opinion the whole region of Transylvania might become a unit within which all elements would be assured adequate rights by a general bill of rights. By such a scheme the Széklers would obtain a large measure of political power.

The chairman explained to Mr. Taylor, who had just arrived and had not been present during previous discussion of the Transylvanian problem, the difficulties which the subcommittee faced in this matter. Mr. Armstrong asked who would be sovereign and who would enforce the necessary rights in an autonomous Transylvania. Mr. Cannon replied that he thought of an autonomous Transylvania as an administrative section of a lower Danubian federation made up of Hungary, Transylvania and the remainder of Rumania. Mr. Armstrong observed that Transylvania would therefore be considered a bridge between Hungary and Rumania, and Mr. Cannon added that it would be almost that. He did, however, see unitary policy-making in such matters as the defense of these three regions.

The chairman considered that Transylvania would be one of the most critical areas in the whole region of Europe. In the case of

Bukovina, another critical area, the power situation at the end of the war would be the controlling element. In Transylvania, where the population distribution was so mixed, it was extremely difficult to provide a territorial solution which separated the peoples. It was therefore necessary to discuss some alternatives to the 1919 system of minority protection.

The German Minority

The chairman suggested that it might be illuminating to concentrate for a time on another Transylvania minority, namely the Germans, concerning whom Mr. Mosely had recently given him some particularly interesting information. He thought that these Germans would have an important place in the scheme outlined by Mr. Cannon. Mr. Mosely explained, with reference to the map,[1] that in eastern Transylvania proper there were some 250,000 German descendants of settlers who had some in the 12th and 13th centuries. They had always enjoyed considerable autonomy in local administration, church affairs and education. In fact, in recent centuries, membership in the Lutheran Church had been the basis of their autonomy rights. In the Banat there were some 350,000 Germans whose ancestors had settled there during the 18th and 19th centuries. These Germans were Roman Catholic and did not have a degree of autonomy equal to that of the first group.

In Rumania as a whole the German-speaking population was approximately 800,000. They had formed the German Pets people's Party, which had acted as a unit in politics in spite of the diverse makeup of the German population. The Saxons, or Germans in historic Transylvania, lived in mixed villages, which they shared largely with Rumanians rather than Magyars. After September 1940 they had enjoyed particular privileges. Their leader, who was appointed directly by Hitler, was empowered to issue decrees binding on German communities in Rumania. Mr. Mosely thought that this establishment of a state within a state might so have exasperated the Rumanians that they would demand the expulsion of these Germans after the war. The German-speaking minorities in Bukovina, southern Bessarabia and southern Dobruja had already been evacuated to Germany.

The chairman declared that he had also been interested in the way taxes paid by these Germans found their way back as revenue for the

---

[1]Rumanian Series, Map 5, Transylvania: Population according to declared nationality.

German communities. Mr. Mosely explained that the Saxon church organization controlled the local schools. It was empowered to assess taxes for the maintenance of the church and the schools, which were collected by the Rumanian state. They were then turned over to the German "University" in the medieval sense of a Corporation.

Mr. Taylor asked what was the total population of Rumania. Mr. Mosely explained that in 1930 the total population had been 18 millions, of whom 5 1/2 millions lived in Transylvania. So far as was known here, none of the Germans in Transylvania had been repatriated, Mr. Armstrong wondered whether the fact that these Germans had been left, whereas those in Rumania east of the Carpathians had been repatriated, did not shed some lights on the division of spheres of influence between Germany and Russia which had apparently been worked out in the Russo-German understanding at the beginning of the war. Mr. Berle agreed that that understanding had probably included provisions concerning Rumania. Mr. Mosely pointed out that the Germans in Rumania had in general been very discontented because they had lost the dominant position which they had enjoyed before 1919. Universal suffrage had brought about a condition in which the Rumanians could outvote the Germans in local elections. This population was rising far more than the Rumanian population.

The Possibility of Autonomy, Part 2

The chairman considered that the subcommittee was now in a better position to look at the question of autonomy for Transylvania. He had understood Mr. Cannon to say that the principle of autonomy should affect a tri-partite bloc made up of Hungarians, Transylvanians and Rumanians. Mr. Cannon noted that his autonomy proposal was not intended to be accompanied by any effort to segregate the different elements in Transylvania. When they had gotten along best it was by direct bargaining. He hoped that they could revert to that system and that the Powers and the Hungarian and Rumanian governments would allow them to work out their local problems. It would be impossible for this country to impose any solution. He hoped that the different groups would bargain for position on the basis of equal rights for all individuals in the various groups. Mr. Armstrong observed that that would become a pretty bloody sort of bargaining, given the bitterness between Rumania and Hungary. Mr. Mosely explained in answer to a question by Mrs. McCormick that Transylvania had been practically independent for three hundred years although nominally under ottoman suzerainty.

The chairman asked Mr. Cannon what he proposed to do concerning the boundary problem within his tripartite bloc. In particular where was the eastern boundary of Hungary to be? Mr. Cannon admitted that he had not thought his scheme in all details. He was inclined to restore the 1919 frontier of Hungary. The chairman thought that, inasmuch as Transylvania was being set up as a unit, it would be reasonable to give it as a boundary on the west the 1919 Rumanian-Hungarian boundary and on the east the 1914 Rumania-Hungarian boundary.

Mr. Mosely observed that when he had been in Transylvania he had often asked Germans and Magyars how they felt concerning autonomy. Usually they were not favorable to the idea because they believed it would still leave them subject to the Rumanian majority in Transylvania. They also felt that they got along better with Rumanians of the Old Kingdom who were sent in as administrators and who could be more easily influenced or bribed. The Transylvanian Rumanians were less easy to circumvent. Mr. Cannon admitted that that was a consideration which argued against a scheme of autonomy.

The chairman observed that in some respects the line was very fine between autonomy and minority treaties. The latter had included a court of appeal to which a minority might take its case and which therefore helped to make the majority behave. Autonomy would have no such a sort of charter. Mr. Cannon pointed out that the population would be bound to respect this as individuals rather than as members of minority groups. The chairman thought that such a scheme might be made manageable, in part through a process of "reasoning". If autonomy concerning cultural matters such as courts, schools and religion went hand-in-hand with an autonomy which permitted the levying of special minority group taxes, then the situation obtaining in the United States would be approached. Mr. Mosely observed that the main difficulty concerning church schools was that the Saxons were doubly taxed, once for the Rumanian state schools and once for their own church schools. The chairman remarked that since our own practice was the same the United States could not well give advice on this issue.

Mr. Campbell declared that the autonomous scheme of Mr. Cannon might create a political vacuum and a field of unrest between Hungary and Rumania. An autonomous Transylvania would therefore require strong buttressing from the outside in order to enforce the original agreements. Rumanian and Magyar groups both inside and outside Transylvania might strive to disrupt the autonomous scheme. Mr. Cannon pointed out that his scheme presupposed some regional arrangement in Eastern Europe. Transylvania would be an autonomous unit of such a regional arrangement and would therefore have international status. Mr. Berle asked why Mr. Cannon's scheme was not worthy of study. In his opinion, since we were seeking international security, areas which threatened international security became of international interest and remained so until they reached some angle of political rest. He thought the United Nations had the right to interfere in order to make sure that Hungary and Rumania did not fight over Transylvania.

Mr. Pasvolsky agreed that Transylvania could not be allowed to become a source of war. Mr. Armstrong asked whether it would be more satisfactory to deal with Hungary and Rumania alone or to have to deal both with them and with an amorphous unit within which the United Nations had guaranteed that something would happen but where they would have to use force to see that it did happen.

The chairman asked whether the autonomy of Transylvania should be considered as autonomy relative to an international organization or to some international sovereign. Mr. Pasvolsky thought that the question could be framed by asking what would be an autonomous Transylvania's first court of appeal. He would also like to know how the troubles of the Germans and Magyars would be solved according to this scheme. The conflict was between Rumanians and Hungarians and "Saxons"; all these three units would still be thrown together in Transylvania. He asked whether the proposition was to take the whole of Transylvania and make it autonomous of 1914 Rumania.

Summary of Possible Solutions

The chairman explained that the proposal for autonomy had arisen after last week's discussion and examination of the map showing the 1940 boundaries of Hungary and Rumania.[2] The first question was whether the subcommittee was prepared to say that for the peace of the world and for the decent treatment of the local population the 1940 boundary should be approved. Secondly, if that was not satisfactory, did the subcommittee wish to out off the southeastern extremity of territory gained by Hungary in 1940. The difficulty in that was that this area constituted the principal Székler bloc. If Hungary was to be extended to include these Magyar-speaking people a boundary line very much like that of 1940 was inevitable. The third solution would be the transfer of populations. This had seemed difficult since the Széklers were as

---

[2]Rumanian Series, Map 4, Rumania: Eastern Frontier.

rooted as a population can be and therefore transfer of populations had not appealed to the subcommittee. Fourth, the subcommittee had raised the question of whether within the 1940 boundaries or the 1919 line there were possibilities and advantages in the principles of autonomy. He explained to Mr. Pasvolsky that the meeting had opened with a brief report on the Szeklers by Mr. Campbell and on the German minority by Mr. Mosely. He did not think there was any need to consider the Rumanians separately. In sum, the three possible solutions were based, respectively, on territorial changes, on transfers of population, and on autonomy. The third possibility raised the question in relation to what sovereignty Transylvania would be autonomous.

The Possibility of Autonomy, Part 3

Mr. Pasvolsky asked what area was to be made autonomous. The chairman replied that it would be the whole area of Transylvania as shown by the map.[3] Mr. Taylor remarked that that constituted nearly one-half of all Rumania without Bessarabia. Mr. Pasvolsky asked how the autonomy of this bloc of territory was going to solve the relations of the three peoples within that territory. In answer to Mr. Taylor's question, the chairman noted that there were five and one-half million people in all Transylvania, of whom approximately 3,400,000 were Rumanians, 1,500,000 Hungarians and 600,000 Germans. Mr. Taylor asked whether the scheme of autonomy was designed because of the pressure of the German minority. The chairman replied that it was not, but that account had to be taken of historical community life in Transylvania.

Mr. Armstrong asked whether the subcommittee had discussed the previous whether the 1919 frontier had been too far to the west. Personally he thought there was some justification for a change and noted that Temperley and others who had taken part in the peace conference were doubtful over the merits of this boundary decision.* The chairman explained that this question had been raised at the last meeting when a map was displayed showing the 1919 American

---

[3]Rumanian Series, Map 5, Rumania: Population by declared nationality.

*As concerns Hungary's 1920 frontiers, it was the changing of primarily the Czechoslovak-Hungarian borders that Harold Temperley considered possible and desirable. He also brought up the matter of taking the strip of land between Arad and Szatmár away from Romania. See Harold Temperley, "How the Hungarian Frontiers Were Drawn," *Foreign Affairs*, (April 1928), 441-446.

proposal.[4*] By that proposal some 250,000 Magyars would have been transferred from Rumania to Hungary. Mr. Taylor asked what would happen if nothing was done about changing the 1919 frontier. The chairman replied that that would turn the territory back to Rumania but that if no United Nations force was in the area it would be invaded by the Hungarian Army without the slightest delay. Such an invasion was likely to take place the moment that at the last discussion the subcommittee had been in favor of occupying all Transylvania and returning at last temporarily to the 1919 boundary. Mrs. McCormick observed that under Mr. Cannon's proposal this area would be considered apart from Hungary and Rumania. In reply to Mr. Armstrong's question, Mr. Mosely explained that in the area awarded to Hungary at Vienna in 1940 there were approximately a million Hungarians and 1,200,000 Rumanians.[**]

Mr. Cannon pointed out that any boundary solution would present this phenomenon of mixed populations. If the end war found any military strength remaining to these two states it would be followed, as Mr. Berle predicted, by an armed invasion by Hungary. If the Soviet Union occupied Bessarabia or Bukovina, some solution by which the Carpathian area could be detached from Rumania would be a helpful move and eventually of advantage to Rumania; otherwise the U.S.S.R. might acquire Transylvania as well. Mr. Armstrong remarked that a mountain barrier was not sufficient to stop a Russian invasion. Mrs. McCormick declared that she was unable to envisage a Transylvania autonomous with respect to both Hungary and Rumania. She could understand an autonomous Transylvania only within a larger bloc of states.

Mr. Cannon agreed. He declared that his tentative proposal was operative only if similar arrangements were made elsewhere in eastern Europe. Such a unit of three as he proposed should be tied up with other similar units of three. It would be an impossible solution if it were unique in Europe. He replied to Mrs. McCormick that he was in favor of similar solutions for other areas of mixed population. Mr. Berle suggested that it would be worthwhile studying autonomy relative to two sovereignties where a territorial solution was impossible. Study

---

[4]Rumanian Series, Map 4, Rumania: Eastern Frontier.

[*]*Cf.* Map 6.

[**]According to the Hungarian census of 1941, there were 1,343,000 ethnic Hungarians and 1,069,000 Romanians living in Northern Transylvania. According to the Romanian census of 1930, the one Mosely is referring to, the figures were 909,000 and 1,149,000, respectively.

should be made of autonomy in relation to a court of appeal of which both sovereign states could take cognizance.

Economy of Transylvania

Mr. Taylor asked what was the relative economic value of this area to Hungary and to Rumania and what was the likely economic future of an autonomous Transylvania. Mr. Cannon replied that, although Mr. Mosely was better acquainted than he with the economy of Transylvania, he would like to point out that one of the greatest troubles in the Danubian basin had been the lack of forest and river control since the last war. Rumania's actions had resulted in flooding parts of Hungary. Deforestation had had important effects on the water supply and river flow. The flow of silt through the iron gates of the Danube had reached twenty times its pre-1914 level. He thought that the mineral and forest wealth of Transylvania would be beneficial to both sides under a scheme for autonomy. He referred the chairman to Mr. Mosely for an answer concerning the exact location of resources.

Mr. Mosely pointed out that Hungary had claimed Transylvania on economic grounds because of its forest wealth and because of the water control of Hungarian rivers. So far as industry was concerned, Transylvania was very important to Rumania since it contained most of Rumania's heavy industry and some of its light industry. These had been developed largely since Rumania had acquired sovereignty over the areas. In terms of agriculture, western Transylvania produced a surplus of grain; central and eastern Transylvania were self-sufficient in grain and exported animal products.

Views of Subcommittee Members

The chairman remarked that in the Political Committee he would be asked for a solution, not to lay out the elements of the problem. He suggested therefore polling the committee on their views. He noted that Mr. Armstrong had added to the suggestion for autonomy a rectification to the western boundary of Transylvania. He asked whether any member of the committee was prepared to express a preference. Mr. Armstrong replied that he would make a proposal. He preferred the return of Transylvania to Rumania, with a rectification of Transylvania's western frontier in favor of Hungary. He was definitely not in favor of the creation of a lot of small states such as East Prussia, Slovakia and Albania, Croatia, Transylvania, etc. He thought that the creation of such states would aggravate the Balkanization of Europe, which had already proved so unfortunate.

Mrs. McCormick confessed that she could not think of any single solution which was more satisfactory than another. If we made this area autonomous we would get twenty similar autonomous regions in Europe. On the other hand, the unsatisfactory conditions would not be altered by restoration of the Rumania and Hungary. She thought that there would be some amelioration by the temporary solution of allied occupation previously proposed by Mr. Berle. This could be justified because Transylvania constituted a danger spot for peace. Mr. Berle explained, upon being questioned by the chairman, that he had thought of the occupation of only that part of Transylvania which had been awarded to Hungary in 1940. Mr. Taylor declared that he had not been present at previous discussions of this problem and therefore did not feel competent to express his views.

Mr. Berle admitted that no solution was satisfactory; therefore it was particularly important that some solution be adopted rather than that an attempt for the impossible postpone all decision. He thought that in this case a territorial solution was at its weakest. Two contingencies would justify two different solutions. If a Balkan Federation turned out to be a going concern, he was in favor of autonomy. If there was no such Federation he was in favor of Mr. Armstrong's solution. Of the two he hoped that the former would be possible. Mr. MacMurray declared that he felt utterly hopeless concerning any solution. In the absence of one he thought it best to build on whatever had been established in the way of adjustment during the years since Rumania had ruled Transylvania. He was therefore in favor of the return to the 1919 boundary.

The chairman declared that before Mr. Pasvolsky left the meeting he had expressed his hope that the subcommittee would provide an answer to his question on how autonomy for Transylvania would improve Hungarian-Rumanian relations.

Mr. Cannon pointed out that at present Transylvania constituted an issue between Hungary and Rumania. By creating an autonomous Transylvania the question would be transferred to one of the relations of Magyars, Germans and Rumanians in that territory. If they could work out a solution under international guarantee, it would be only instead of a Hungarian-Rumanian problem. He was opposed to the establishment of autonomy where populations would be segregated. In those cases administrative measures could be expected to solve the problem.

Mr. Armstrong explained that he agreed in part with Mr. Cannon but felt that Hungary and Rumania would continue to interfere in the affairs of Transylvania. Mr. Cannon pointed out that that was the reason why he desired his scheme to be put in force inside a larger political organization. Mr. Armstrong asked whether it was better to begin with something which was admitted not to be satisfactory than to leave the question open for later decision. When Mr. Berle asked whether this problem had ever been settled by any boundary solution Mr. Armstrong pointed out that the war did not begin over Transylvania. The chairman recalled that before 1919 there had been a Rumanian minority within Hungary but after 1919 conditions had been revised to that there was a Hungarian minority within Rumania and that since 1940 there had been minorities of countries on opposite sides of the frontier. Mr. Berle admitted that settlements had been made but was not sure that the area had ever settled down. Mr. Armstrong thought that there had been some degree of settling down in the last two years and that it would have been greater if there had been fewer Hungarians in Transylvania. He asked how many Hungarians would be restored to Hungary by a rectification of the frontier.

The chairman pointed out that this was a key area for minority questions, territorial questions, cultural questions, and the relations of two states. Mrs. McCormick thought that since centralization had not worked there might be some hope in decentralization. Mr. Armstrong declared that we might hope for better regimes in Rumania and Hungary than had been in power in the past. The overthrow of Hungarian feudalism would be a step in this direction. It might be that the territorial reduction of Rumania would also be helpful.

The chairman asked Mr. Knight whether there was anything in the economic situation of the area which indicated a particular solution. Mr. Knight replied that he did not think the purely economic situation was so important. He thought that some improvement might be expected if one adopted the American proposal of 1919 and tried to give Rumania the areas of 75 percent Rumanian population and Hungary the areas of 75 percent Magyar population. He pointed out that the mines were found largely in the Transylvanian Alps. He did not think that much would be left of Rumania of the larger part of Transylvania was taken away. He pointed out that although there was a sharp natural boundary of Transylvania on the east he could not envisage that territory out off from Rumania and set up as an autonomous unit. He did not think that that would bring peace. Mr. Campbell pointed out that the southern half of Transylvania contained most of the mines and industries and that therefore Rumania had not been industrially damaged by the Vienna Award.

Transylvanian Politics

The chairman concluded that the committee was divided in its views on Transylvania. Mr. Knight added that one couldn't move the Szeklers any place. Mr. Cannon pointed out that Transylvania was also an example of an area where political demagoguery among Hungarians, Rumanians and Germans had reached an apogee. He thought that if the local population had been left in peace a satisfactory political situation would have resulted. The trouble was that it had been disturbed by elements both from within and from without Transylvania. Mrs. McCormick added that there might be more chance for peace if neither Hungary nor Rumania had a chance to interfere.

Mr. Mosely pointed out that the Rumanians in Transylvania disliked the interference of Rumanians from the Old Kingdom in Transylvania affairs. On the other hand, for them to return to Hungarian sovereignty would mean giving up the advantages which they had secured since 1918. They would fear a reversal of the land reforms and the reimposition of cultural disabilities. They would therefore be opposed to Transylvanian autonomy if that meant the predominance of the Magyars. On the other hand, if the Rumanians would still be dominant in an autonomous Transylvania it would be a satisfactory solution to the local Rumanians. Mr. Taylor concluded that an autonomous Transylvania was impracticable without outside pressure and asked who would really run such an autonomous state. It was pretty far away from Washington.

Suggestion by the Chairman

The chairman declared that he was going to propose a solution in the form of a question directed to Mr. Mosely. He asked the latter whether he would be satisfied with a solution which would rectify the western boundary by shifting it eastward a little in order to take in perhaps one-fourth to one-third the area of the Vienna Award, and then establish the rights of the Germans and Székler in the rest of Transylvania along the lines of their former rights and privileges. Mr. Mosely thought that might work very well. It would result in the shift of some 300,000 Magyars and 100,000 Rumanians to Hungary. The latter might be exchanged for 100,000 Magyars still in Rumania. Such an exchange would of course leave the Szeklers untouched. The chairman reminded

Mr. Mosely that the Szeklers would retain their historical rights and privileges.

Mrs. McCormick observed that the Szeklers constituted the most nationalistic group of Magyars in Rumania. Such a solution would therefore not remove the trouble. When asked by the chairman what solution she preferred she replied that she favored a solution within a large regional grouping. When the chairman remarked that it all seemed to come back to an international organization to maintain the peace. Mrs. McCormick concurred and pointed out that without force the settlement would not stick. The chairman expressed the hope that the committee would cease referring local problems to a solution in world wide terms.

Mr. Mosely pointed out that there could be no solution unless the Magyars and Rumanians could get over their mutual irredentism. The trouble was that Hungarian irredentism would last as long as the Székler continued in their present home. It might, however, be lessened by social reforms in Hungary and by local autonomy for the Széklers in Rumania. For example, the Szeklers might be permitted to study at the University of Budapest and then return to practice law in the district, rather than be forced to attend Rumanian universities and study law in the Rumanian language. In answer to Mrs. McCormick's question as to who would guarantee such an arrangement, Mr. Mosely declared that it might be the obligation of a regional organization.

Mr. Notter suggested that since the tangle was so bad alternative solutions might be presented to the political committee, 1) in the event that a regional structure was possible and, 2) in case it proved impossible. He reminded the subcommittee that there was one constant, namely the thrust of the Soviet Union. The binding force which would guarantee a solution might be outside military pressure; but it might be a common fear. If the Széklers were left in Rumania they would either be discontented and subject to exploitation for political purposes by the U.S.S.R. or they would maintain good relations with the Rumanians out of a common fear of Communism.

Postponement of Decision

The chairman concluded that he would ask the members of the subcommittee to think this problem over for a week. He would ask each member for his views at the start of the next meeting. He thought that sometimes people had more confidence in their conclusions if allowed time for reflection. He reminded them that the documentation would help with the necessary facts.

RELATIONS OF CZECHS AND SLOVAKS

The chairman suggested that the subcommittee consider next the relations of Czechs and Slovaks. These were relevant to the consideration of the East European Union which was scheduled for discussion in the political committee the next day. This East European Union would have special problems in the areas which bordered on Germany. The subcommittee had already looked at the problem of Czech boundaries but had not looked inside of Czechoslovakia to study the political forces and the possibility of establishing or re-establishing Czech-Slovak relations. He understood that Mr. Howard had information and views on this subject.

Basic Data

Mr. Howard explained that there were three special problems in Czechoslovakia. First, the relations of Czechs and Slovaks; second, the relations of Czechs and Germans; and third, the relation of Ruthenia to the Czech state. The first had been one of the greater problems in the effort of making a Czechoslovak state. The Slovaks had joined with the Czechs of their own free will in accordance with the declaration of Turčiansky Svätý Martin in October 1918.* From 1918 to 1940 there had been a dispute over whether the constitutional structure of Czechoslovakia should be unitary or federal. The Slovak Autonomists had been organized in the Slovak Popular Party led by Father Hlinka. They had formed the largest Slovak Party but had never had a majority in Slovakia and had ceased to grow after 1935. From 1927 to 1929 they had shared in the government and Slovaks in general had taken a large share in the government of the state. The last prime minister of Czechoslovakia had been a Slovak, Milan Hodža. In 1927, an administrative reform had gone part way to meet the demands of the Slovaks. It had set up four provinces; Bohemia, Moravia-Silesia, Slovakia and Ruthenia. With the rise of Hitler and the greater demands of the Sudetens, Father Hlinka and his party had also increased their demands on the state. During the premiership of Dr. Hodža there had been moves by the Government tending toward autonomy for Slovakia. This scheme had, however, never passed Parliament. In 1938, at the time of the Munich crisis, the extremist wing among the Autonomists, had

---

*The Declaration of Turčiansky Svätý Martin, deciding on Slovakia's secession from Hungary, and its annexation to the Czechoslovak state, was signed by the representatives of the Slovak political parties on October 30, 1918.

allied with the Magyars and Sudetens to carry out their demand for independence.

Mr. Howard believed that there were four possible solutions of the Slovak problem. The first was to set up an independent Slovakia. This had very doubtful chances of success without German aid. The present puppet-state of Slovakia was a totalitarian state which had never rested on free elections. The second solution was to return Slovakia to Hungary, to which it had belonged in 1914. There was little evidence of any desire for this in Slovakia except for the Magyar elements. According to the 1930 census the Magyars constituted only 600,000 out of a population of 3,300,000.* Third, there was the possibility of a connection with Poland. There was no reason for this or desire for it within Slovakia. Finally, there was the possibility of restoration of Czechoslovakia under some kind of decentralized structure.

Discussion

The chairman asked for Mr. Cannon's opinion on this issue. The latter saw no reason why Czechoslovakia could not be reconstructed as a going concern. He thought that the Slovaks had learned a lesson from their experience of "independence". They were gentle people who had been politically undeveloped because of their long period of rule by Hungary. He thought the Czechs would have been willing to allow more Slovak self-government if adequate Slovak political leadership had existed.

Mr. Cannon preferred the frontiers approximately as they were in 1919, with the idea that adjustments might be made at a later date. Personally he was in favor of some adjustments of the Slovak-Hungarian frontier in favor of Hungary. He did not think, however, that we should take any steps in that direction at the present time. He noted that Beneš was already declaring that the Czechoslovak government-in-exile could not make commitments affecting the position at home. In November, however, he had gone so far as to speak of decentralization. Mr. Cannon pointed out that the agitation for Slovak autonomy originated in part with the Slovaks in the United States, who were ready to raise a fuss although they were not prepared to go back to Slovakia and help solve its political problems. The chairman remarked that they seemed to act just like the alumni of a university.

---

*The data exclude Subcarpathian Ruthenia.

Mr. Cannon continued that he was hopeful of very tolerable relations between the Czechs and Slovaks. He admitted that the Czechs had been guilty of some tactlessness or stubbornness and that the Slovaks generally did not trust the Slovak members of the government-in-exile, who, they claimed, were too Czechified. He thought, however, that there were other Slovaks in exile who were inclined to cooperate in favor of Czechoslovakia. These included Hodža and Osuský, the former Czechoslovak Minister in Paris. The difficulty was that the latter was in an advanced state of personal enmity with Beneš and that Hodža was not on good terms with Beneš. Masaryk was, however, confident that a good arrangement could be made.

The chairman pointed out that on the assumption of an allied victory the terms of surrender must be specified at the close of hostilities and then applied over a period of time. This application must progress logically step by step. Reference of the importance of this to the tongue of Hungarian territory in Transylvania had been made at the last meeting. It applied equally to other areas in Europe. This meant that although the subcommittee could analyze and theorize, the effect of the final terms of surrender would be such that the United Nations ought to have an opinion on the ultimate solution of territorial problems at the time of the surrender. Furthermore, these solutions should be adumbrated in the steps taken as a result of the terms of the surrender. All this pointed up the difficulties which resulted from the fact that the different leaders of European countries were in disagreement and that because they were in exile they were not sure of home opinion or home support. Mr. Armstrong believed that Osuský did not count for very much. The chairman continued that, on the supposition that the United States Government favored the restoration of Czechoslovakia with possible modest boundary rectifications, it had to be decided how far we would carry our conclusions into action at the moment of surrender when the United Nations would be predominant. The United Nations would have to have an idea on what they favored. He recognized that even a tentative conclusion bristled with difficulties.

Mr. Pasvolsky asked who would oppose the restoration of Czechoslovakia. The chairman suggested that perhaps the Slovaks would. Mr. Pasvolsky then asked what we meant by the restoration of sovereignty to those peoples who had not been forcibly deprived of sovereignty. If the Serbs and Croats or the Czechs and Slovaks wanted to part company, was that not acceptable unless they insisted upon fighting a war on the question? He did not think that we could adjudicate Slovak claims to independence at this time. The chairman suggested that one must start by considering the wishes of the peoples, but Mr. Pasvolsky pointed out that one people might wish to separate and another to continue union. Mr. Pasvolsky thought that in that case we would have to step in. Mr. Berle pointed out that if we occupied we did it nominally for military reasons. The military administration of a unified Czechoslovakia would be followed by an invitation to hold an election in which the issue could be framed so that it concerned Czechoslovakia as a whole. Mr. Pasvolsky declared that this constituted the restoration of Czechoslovak sovereignty.

PROGRAM OF ACTION IN TERRITORIAL QUESTIONS

The chairman concluded that past discussions had showed that the subcommittee had agreed on the necessity of a certain succession of procedures with respect to the countries which they had considered, France, Italy, Poland, Czechoslovakia, et cetera. The first necessity was for the restoration of the pre-war frontier; second, there must be provided the means for complete order; third, there must be provided conditions under which the people might express their political views; fourth, the code under which the people were going to live would have to be provided, whether it was the old code or something worked out ad hoc.

He asked whether the members of the Committee agreed with this summary. Mrs. McCormick declared her agreement but pointed out that the Czechoslovak problem was far different from that of Transylvania. The Slovaks would be satisfied with additional local autonomy, gains which they were already acquiring. The chairman added that the Czech problem concerned two blocs of peoples rather than a mixture. He then asked the other members of the subcommittee what they thought of his general review. Mr. MacMurray expressed out that on almost every case the subcommittee had recommended minor boundary changes for the purposes of amelioriating local conditions. Mr. Taylor being informed that this formula excluded the Sudeten question, agreed with the chairman's summary. Mr. Berle and Mr. Pasvolsky also concurred.

William Koren, Jr.

x x x

PROGRAM OF ACTION IN TERRITORIAL QUESTIONS

The subcommittee agreed that necessary steps to be taken in areas where territorial disputes existed could be summarized as follows: first, restoration of the pre-war frontiers; second, guarantee of complete internal order; third, establishment of conditions under which the people might express their political views; and fourth, reestablishment of the old code of laws or provision of an ad hoc temporary code.

TRANSYLVANIA

Basic Data

The subcommittee was informed concerning the numbers, location and history of the German minority in Rumania. It was pointed out that the "Saxons" of Transylvania had always enjoyed special privileges and that at present they constituted virtually a state within a state since a leader appointed by Hitler was empowered to issue decrees governing their affairs.

The mineral, forest, agricultural and industrial wealth of Transylvania was briefly indicated. It was pointed out that careless forest policy in Transylvania caused floods in eastern Hungary. The Vienna Award had left the major portion of the mines and heavy industry of Transylvania to Rumania.

Summary of Possible Solutions

It was considered that because the Rumanian-Hungarian rivalry over Transylvania made that area a possible danger to peace, the United Nations had a legitimate excuse for actively concerning themselves with it until it reached some angle of political rest.

Possible long-term solutions were thought to include: first, boundary rectifications; second, transfers of population; third, autonomy. Having considered the inadequacies of the first two at the previous meeting, the subcommittee devoted most of its attention to the possibilities of an autonomous regime.

Schemes For Autonomy

Four schemes of autonomy were suggested: one would provide for the continuation of traditional Szekler and Saxon privileges in conjunction with a small territorial adjustment on favor of Hungary; the second would provide an autonomous regime for the Székely district within Rumania; the third proposed "denationalization" of Rumania so that the national minorities would be protected by a bill of rights which applied to them as individual citizens; the forth proposed that Transylvania be established as an autonomous unit of a tripartite state composed of Hungary, Transylvania and Rumania.

The subcommittee felt that the last scheme would be impracticable unless similar arrangements for areas of mixed population were made in other parts of Europe. Its chances of success would be improved if the proposed tripartite state formed part of a Balkan Federation. Autonomy in this sense did not rule out rectification of the eastern frontier of Hungary.

Criticism of Autonomy

The subcommittee was not convinced that the creation of an autonomous Transylvania would eliminate the struggle between Rumania and Hungary or the rivalries of the local national groups. The Transylvanian Rumanians might welcome the elimination of domination by the Old Kingdom, but the Magyars and Germans would probably prefer the relatively mild rule of the latter. Social reform in Hungary and the chastening of Rumania by loss of territory to Russia were uncertain guarantees of a détente between the two states. Autonomy could probably be maintained only by outside pressure.

Doubt was also expressed over the advisability of aggravating the "Balkanization" of Europe, even within the framework of a regional federation.

Postponement of Decision

In view of the divergence of opinions expressed by members of the subcommittee, it was decided to postpone decision on this issue until the next meeting.

RELATIONS OF CZECHS AND SLOVAKS

Basic Data

It was explained that the Slovaks had freely entered the Czechoslovak state and had taken a considerable share in its government. Their subordinate position was largely the result of their lack of political experience under Hungarian rule. The Slovak Popular Party led by Father Hlinka, which had stood for Slovak autonomy had never had a majority in Slovakia and had ceased to grow after 1935. The independence achieved in conjunction with German and Hungarian action was the work of extremists. Slovak nationalist movements were to a large extent fomented by Slovak organizations in this country.

Future Probabilities

There seemed to be little popular support for the maintenance of an independent Slovakia after the war and still less for the incorporation of Slovakia in Hungary or Poland. In spite of friction between exiled Slovaks and the Government-in-exile headed by President Beneš, difficulty in re-establishing Czechoslovakia was not anticipated. The constitution and boundaries of the state would have to await the expression of the will of the inhabitants. Action by the United Nations would be required only if Czechs and Slovaks threatened to go to war.

Box 59

Chapter II

Proposals and Remarks to the Subcommittee on Territorial Problems

§ Document 1 §

T Document 21
July 16, 1942

THE SLOVAK-HUNGARIAN FRONTIER, 1918-1939

Summary and Recommendations

1. The boundary as drawn in 1919 was over-favorable to the Czechoslovak ethnic claims. At Paris it was assumed that the needs of Czechoslovakia as a Danubian power could only be served by giving her, not only an outlet at Bratislava, but also the north bank of the Danube from the Morava River to the Ipola River, together with the almost purely Magyar island of the *Grosse Schuett.* East of the Ipola it was assumed that the need for east-west communications in Czechoslovakia should have precedence over ethnic considerations. An argument which seems fallacious but which carried considerable weight in drawing the new boundary was that Czechoslovakia should receive Magyar population in "compensation" for the preceding Magyarization of considerable numbers of Slovaks.

2. The boundary drawn on November 2, 1938 erred in favor of Hungary, mainly because the Axis powers insisted on taking the Hungarian census of 1910 as a basis.

3. It would be consistent with the principle of minimum boundary change to provide for the return to Hungary of the *Grosse Schuett* and

of a narrow strip of almost purely Magyar rural population along the southern frontier of 1937.

4. A by-product of this slight shift would be to prevent Czecho-Slovakia from again becoming self-sufficient in foodstuffs, while Hungary's export problem would in turn be increased. If properly manipulated, this factor might operate to promote closer economic cooperation among the Danubian countries after the war.

THE SLOVAK-HUNGARIAN FRONTIER, 1918-1939

I.
Temporary Frontiers, 1918-1919

Upon the proclamation of the independent Czechoslovak state and the dissolution of the Austro-Hungarian Empire it became necessary to draw at least a provisional line of demarcation between the Slovakian part of the new state and the remainder of Hungary. Unlike the situation in Bohemia-Moravia-Silesia, there was no "historic" boundary to refer to, as Slovakia had been governed for centuries as an integral part of the lands of the Crown of St. Stephen. Prior to the definitive fixing of the new frontier by decision of the Big Four at Paris, on June 13, 1919, three different and temporary lines were drawn to separate the areas of Czechoslovak and Hungarian administration.

1. *The Beneš-Pichon Armistice Line of November 27, 1918.* This line followed the historic boundary between Hungary and Galicia the length of the Carpathians, and the historic boundary between Hungary and Moravia to the Morava River and down the Morava River to the Danube; thence, it followed the Danube River to its junction with the Ipola (Eipel, Ipoly) River; then the Ipola to Rimavská Sobota (Rimaszombat); thence, as the crow flies, to the junction of the Už and the Bereg, and the line of the Už up to the watershed of the Carpathians.[1] This line left the island of *Grosse Schuett* (Csallóköz, Zitny Ostrava) to Hungary.

2. *The Hodža-Bartha Line of December 6, 1918.* This line, negotiated directly between the Slovak leader. Hodža, and the Foreign Minister of Hungary, Bartha, left Bratislava (Pressburg, Pozsony), the *Grosse Schuett*, and Košice (Kassa) to Hungary. It was disavowed by the Czechoslovak Goverment.[2]

3. *The Vix Note Line of December 23, 1918.* This line of demarcation was imposed on Hungary by the Allies in a note delivered by the head of the Inter-Allied Mission in Budapest on December 23, 1918. It included in Czechoslovakia the city and district of Bratislava; the railway through Galanta and Nové Zamky (Érsekújvár); Komárno (Komárom); the line of the Danube to the Ipola; Ipolské Šahy (Ipolyság); Balasšké D'armoty (Balassagyarmat); Lučenec (Losonc); Salgotarján (Salgótarján); Rimavská Sobota; Rožňava (Rozsnyó); Košice; Čop (Csap); Užhorod (Ungvár).[3] It did not include the *Grosse Schuett* in Slovakia, but it included in Slovakia a few sectors, such as Salgótarján, which were later awarded to Hungary.

II.
The Drawing of the Definitive Boundary

The definitive boundary between Slovakia and Hungary was announced to the Government of Béla Kun on June 13, 1919, as a result of negotiations between the Allied and Associated Governments, on the one hand, and the Czechoslovak Government, on the other. It was not changed during the subsequent negotiations which led up to the signing of the Treaty of Trianon on June 4, 1920.

1. *Czechoslovak claims.* In addition to the territory which the Czechoslovak state finally received its representatives asked for certain territories south of the main branch of the Danube, considerable territory east of the Ipola River, and a much more southerly line from the easternmost bend of the Danube to the boundary of Ruthenia.[4] These claims were sharply curtailed by the Allied negotiators, especially to the east of the Ipola. In the opinion of Seton-Watson, a severe critic of the Magyar regime, it would have been unjust to deprive Hungary of the coal-mines of Salgótarján, the vineyards of Tokaj, the genuinely Magyar towns of Vác, Miskolc and Sárospatak. The town of Sátoraljaújhely was also left to Hungary; its railway station, one mile distant, together with the junction of Čop and the line connecting Čop with Košice, went to Czechoslovakia.[5]

2. *Disagreements within the Committee on Czechoslovak Frontiers:*

a.) *Bratislava.* There was no disagreement over the necessity for assigning Bratislava to Slovakia, although the largest single linguistic group, according to the Hungarian census of 1910, was made up of German-speaking persons (32,790 as against 31,705 Magyar speaking, and 11,673 Slovak-speaking). However, a majority of the Magyar-speaking people also spoke Slovak, and could be considered as bilingual Slovaks who, for various reasons, had declared Magyar as their preferred tongue.

b.) *The area north of the Little Danube from Bratislava to the junction of the Ipola River.* While it was recognized that there were very many Magyars in the southern parts of the counties of Nitra (Nyitra) and Tekov (Bars), it was felt that Czechoslovakia needed an extended outlet to the Danube River; that the economic unity of the left bank of the Danube should not be disrupted; that the railway system should not be disrupted unnecessarily; and that a very large part of the Magyar-speaking population was made up of Magyarized Slovaks.[6]

c.) *Grosse Schuett.* This large island, extending from a few miles east of Bratislava to Komárno (about 100 km. long; average width 25 km.; 1910 population: 101,839 Magyars, 2884 Germans, 453 Slovaks) provided grounds for sharp contention in the Committee. The reasons for assigning it to Czechoslovakia were: (1) the southern or main branch of the Danube was "the only possible frontier"; (2) its economic ties were with Bratislava and the north bank; (3) without it, Czech access to the Danube might have been seriously curtailed.[7] The French representatives wished to give the *Grosse Schuett* to the Czechs; the Americans, to the Magyars. The British Empire members were divided. Harold Nicolson thought, on balance, that it should be left to Hungary; Sir Eyre Crowe and Sir Joseph Young insisted on giving it to the Czechs. The *Grosse Schuett* was assigned to the Czechs.[8]

d.) *The line from the Ipola to the Už (Ung).* The Czech claims reached far south both of the ethnic or linguistic line and of the line finally drawn. The American proposal was to take a more northerly line, following the ethnic cleavage at the cost of cutting the railways. The British representatives proposed leaving the Komarno-Košice railway to Czechoslovakia. Eventually, the Americans agreed to include Ipola in Czechoslovakia; the British, to leave Miskolc to Hungary. While the question of railways was of decisive importance in drawing this eastern half of the frontier, Nicolson later learned from General Mance, a British expert on the railway systems of Europe, that "with very little expense, an alternative railway could be constructed in Slovakia whereby many thousand Magyars would be saved from incorporation /Into Czechoslovakia/."[9]

3. *The Smuts Mission.* In April 1919 General Smuts visited Prague on his way back from Budapest. According to Nicolson's account, Smuts urged President Masaryk to give up the claim to the *Grosse Schuett,* and Masaryk agreed that he would do so, provided Czechoslovakia, in compensation, were given a bridgehead at Bratislava. At the Council of Five meetings on May 3 and May 5, 1919, however, Beneš, backed by Pichon, denied that Masaryk had made any formal offer, and the southern frontier of Slovakia was confirmed by the Five as drawn in the Committee.[10]

Lloyd George defines very differently the territory under discussion between Smuts and Masaryk. "According to his (Smuts') report to us, President Masaryk agreed and said that he would prefer to waive all claims to the Magyar territory and withdraw the Czech frontier to the North, so as to leave all this ethnologically Magyar territory to Hungary; but he made one condition that, in exchange, Czechoslovakia should get a small strip of Hungarian territory south of the Danube at Pressburg.[11] Nicolson's version, according to which only the *Grosse Schuett* was discussed with Masaryk, has greater probability.

4. *Magyar Counter-Proposals:*

a.) *Demand for plebiscites in all areas to be ceded.* The Hungarian peace delegation demanded that, in accordance with the principle of national self-determination, the population of all areas to be ceded should be allowed to vote freely, under international guarantees of impartiality, to determine its future status.[12] This demand was rejected.

b.) *Maximum compromise offer of April 23, 1920.* Encouraged by the more friendly attitude of Paléologue, the Hungarian Peace Delegation hoped that some of the territory assigned to Czechoslovakia by the draft treaty of peace might be returned to Hungary. By instructions of April 23, 1920, Apponyi was authorized to ask for the return of a broad belt of territory including Pozsony, Moder, Nyitra, Bélabánya, Korpona, Nagyröcze, Dorsina, Kassa, Ungvár and Munkács, most of eastern Slovakia and all of Ruthenia.

c.) *Minimum compromise offer of April 23, 1920.* By the same instruction the Hungarian delegation was empowered to abandon, without referring back to Budapest, Pozsony and surroundings, together with eastern Slovakia. The minimum retrocessions which Hungary regarded as indispensable for any successful negotiations were: the

Grosse Schuett, parts of the Little Hungarian plain (norths of the Danube) parts of the counties of Hont and Nógrád, and Ruthenia.[13]

5. *The Millerand Note.* In a note accompanying the transmission of the final terms of the Treaty of Trianon, Millerand suggested that slight local changes of frontiers could still be made under the Treaty by the Boundary Commission. The Hungarians later claimed that this Commission should have proceeded to effect extensive transfers of territory. However, neither the Commission was empowered to make other than local changes with a view to minimizing local inconveniences.

III.
Proposals for Partial Revision

Between 1920 and 1938 numerous proposals for a partial revision of the frontier were put forward. Hungarian public opinion, at bottom, would not have been reconciled to anything short of "total" revision. Most of the arguments put forward in favor of revision applied only to total revision: e.g., historical traditions, mystical unity of the lands of the Crown of St. Stephen, "enlightened" minority policy of old Hungary, economic unity of the Danubian area, defense of the Carpathians against the "Tartars" and against Russia, and so forth. Nevertheless, for tactical reasons, Hungarian leaders kept the idea of a "partial" revision, to be based on ethnic justice, to the fore. They probably assumed that even a partial revision would greatly weaken the Succession States internally and would split up the Little Entente, thus preparing the way for a later total revision. Similarly, it became a part of the Hungarian tactic to minimize their claims against Yugoslavia and to center their hostility on Czechoslovakia and Rumania; Hungary even signed a Treaty of Perpetual Friendship with Yugoslavia.* Four of the many proposals for a partial revision are summarized below.

1) *Rothermere Line.* In June 1927 Lord Rothermere became an advocate of partial revision. The so-called "Rothermere Line" would have returned to Hungary a broad strip of southern Slovakia, including the cities of Bratislava, Nitra, Lučenec, Košice, Užhorod, Mukačevo, and Hust. This line differs from the present boundary, established in April 1939, in that it would have given to Hungary Bratislava and a slightly

*December 12, 1940.

wider strip north of Nitra and Lučenec, while it would have left to Czechoslovakia eastern Slovakia and the mountain area of Ruthenia.[14]

2) *The Bethlen Solution.* The point of view presented to the western powers by the former Prime Minister, Count Stephen Bethlen, called for a new distribution of territory under which "about as many Rumanians, Serbs and Czechs (*sic*) should be put under Hungarian rule as there would be left Magyars under the dominion of Rumania, Serbia, or the Czechs."[15] This solution would have left the frontier considerably to the south of the present Axis-imposed boundary.

3) *The Temperley Proposal.* In retrospect, Harold Temperley, a member of the British delegation at Paris, came to the conclusion that several small areas could be returned to Hungary without endangering the viability of the Czechoslovak state. "The chief evil of the whole Hungarian settlement was the cession of the *Grosse Schuett* to Czechoslovakia, and it would certainly be an advantage if this island were handed back to Hungary...A careful reexamination...would reveal cases where small Magyar areas could be safely handed back to Hungary...Counties are mixed...But parishes are not mixed...The frontier could be differently drawn so as to restore a number of Magyar parishes to Hungary without much deranging the Czechoslovak state."[16] Temperley's article gave no consideration to the question of whether such a relatively trifling correction of the frontier would have been a sufficient inducement to persuade Hungary to cooperate with the states of the Little Entente.

4) *The Macartney Proposal.* One of the most thorough students of the problem of Hungary and her neighbors came to a conclusion similar to Temperley's, except that, for economic reasons, he believed that Ruthenia should also go to Hungary. Macartney would return Ruthenia to Hungary under a rigidly controlled statute of autonomy, preferably supervised by a resident commissioner of the League or of the great powers, and would add the left bank of the Tisza (Rumanian Maramureş) to Ruthenia, for economic reasons. The southern frontier of Slovakia should also be corrected so as to return to Hungary the purely Magyar districts, without, however, cutting the east-west communications between the valleys.[17]

IV.
Partial Revision of 1938 and 1939

1. *Vienna Award. November 2, 1938.* As a corollary of the Munich "settlement" of 1938, it was insisted upon by Germany and Italy, and agreed to by England and France, that the principle of demarcation applied in separating the Sudeten German areas from Czechoslovakia should also be applied to the areas inhabited by Poles and Magyars. Promptly thereafter, on October 2, 1938, Hungary presented far-reaching claims:

(1) all areas which showed a Magyar-speaking majority according to the Hungarian census of 1910 were to be returned at once to Hungary;

(2) plebiscites were to be held in the rest of Slovakia and Ruthenia to determine their political allegiance;

(3) a settlement was to be negotiated without delay and along these lines.

In the negotiations of October 9 to 13, the Slovaks, to whom the Prague Government now transferred direct responsibility for the settlement, made a number of counter-propositions. First, they offered autonomy for the Magyars within Czechoslovakia; second, they went on to offer Ipola, together with a railroad station adjoining; third, they added the *Grosse Schuett*; and fourth, they offered an additional area along the southern frontier amounting to about 5,400 sq. km. with a 1910 population of about 350,000. The final Slovak offer was for the cession of about 11,300 sq. km. of territory. On October 24, 1938 the Hungarian Government accepted this offer as a basis of negotiation, and proposed the holding of plebiscites areas outside the area already offered.

By the Axis award of Vienna, of November 2, 1938, Hungary received about 12,000 sq. km., with a population of 1,027,000, stretched along the entire southern frontier of Slovakia and Ruthenia. According to the Czechoslovak census of 1930 the area thus ceded contained

587,558 Magyars, 288,611 Czechs and Slovaks, 51,578 Jews, 35,250 Ruthenes, and 13,481 Germans.*

2. *Hungarian-Slovak Protocol of April 3, 1939.* As a consequence of the German seizure of Bohemia-Moravia, Premier Paul Teleki announced, on March 16, the incorporation of Ruthenia into Hungary; the Hungarian army then proceeded to overcome the brief but bitter resistance of the small Ruthenian army, supported by the semi-military Sich and by Czech officers. On March 24 the Hungarian troops also invaded eastern Slovakia and occupied strong defensive positions west of the Už (Ung) Valley. In addition, along the central part of the Slovak border the Hungarian advanced their previous line of occupation to the north, thus straightening out the somewhat saw-tooth border of the preceding November. On April 3, 1939, Hungary and Slovakia, which had in the meantime proclaimed its "independence" under a German protectorate, signed a protocol confirming Hungarian possession of an area of about 386 sq. miles.[18]

3. *Criteria for drawing the new frontiers.* The cession of November 2, 1938 was justified by Hungary on the grounds of ethnic justice. However, taking the Hungarian census of 1910 as a basis for partition was unjust to the Slovaks. Even of "mother tongue" could, under Hungarian census practices, be accepted as a reliable index of nationality, reliance on this census gave Hungary the full benefit of several preceding generations of Magyarizing Slovaks, Germans and Jews. Scores of thousands of Slovaks, who had been registered as Magyar-speaking in 1910 would have claimed Slovak nationality in 1938. The numerous Jewish element would also have been reluctant, on the whole, to rejoin the new Hungarian state with its copies of the Nürnberg laws. In addition, the much higher birth-rate of the Slovaks was ignored in returning to the 1910 figures (in 1936 the vital excess for Czechoslovaks in Slovakia was 59,937 births - 34,667 deaths or 25,270; that for Magyars in Slovakia was 13,006 births - 8,928 deaths or 4,078). No plebiscites were held, contrary to a long-standing Magyar demand. Finally, the strategic and communications necessities of Slovakia were everywhere sacrificed to Hungarian advantage, except that Bratislava was left to Slovakia.

---

*According to the Hungarian census of 1941, the region had a total of 1,062,000 inhabitants, with declared native languages in the following distribution — Hungarian: 892,000; Slovak: 116,000; Ruthenian: 23,000; Yiddish: 10,000; and German: 9,000.

The cession of April 3, 1939 was justified by Hungary solely on strategic and communications grounds. By taking a strip of eastern Slovakia, in addition to the remainder of Ruthenia, Hungary secured a fairly extensive common frontier with Poland, together with three railroad lines traversing the Carpathians.

V.
Possible Bases of Post-War Settlement

1. *Restoration of the 1937 boundary.* This solution is claimed by the Czecho-Slovak Government-in-Exile on the grounds that the Munich and related settlements have lost whatever legal validity they may have had for a time in the eyes of some of the democratic powers. Unofficial Czechoslovak spokesmen have expressed a willingness then to see the *Grosse Schuett* and a strip of the southern frontier returned to Hungary, provided the latter accepts the new settlement loyally and cooperates for regional and European security and prosperity. It is understood that the great powers among the United Nations are pledged to restore the independence of Czecho-Slovakia, but not to restore any definite frontiers.

2. *Restoration of Czechoslovakia as a unitary state.* The ambition of the Czechs and of the Slovak centralists to restore the pre-1938 internal structure would be greatly favored if they were able to restore the Slovak frontier pretty much as it was in 1937. In general, Slovaks tend to be either more anti-Magyar or pro-Magyar than do the Czechs, and the decision on the frontier problem might affect greatly the question of whether centralist or autonomist groups would get the upper hand in Slovak politics.

3. *Federation of Slovakia with Hungary.* If Hungary is able to husband her military resources till the end of the war, and if the present Slovak leaders feel that their lives and political fortunes are endangered by Czech more than by Magyar ascendancy, they might prefer to federate with Hungary rather than with Bohemia-Moravia. In this case Hungary might be willing to return to Slovakia a part for a close political and military association with Slovakia. If the great powers wish to prevent this solution from being at least attempted, it seems evident that they should be ready, in advance of the cessation of fighting to state their policy concerning the future relationship of Slovakia to Czechia and Hungary.

4. *Federation of Slovakia with Czechia and with Poland.* While the Czechs in exile assume that Czecho-Slovakia will enter as a unit into the proposed Czechoslovak-Polish confederation, some Poles seem to hope that Czechia and Slovakia will enter it as separate units. Poland might then try to use her double position as protector of the Slovaks and as a traditional friend of Hungary to effect a lasting compromise between Slovaks and Magyars by moving the present Slovak frontier somewhat to the south.

5. *Incorporation of Slovakia into a Danubian state or confederation.* This solution would presumably be accompanied by a boundary adjustment favorable to Slovakia, and/or by the setting up of internal conditions within each member-state which would allow free expression of national-cultural allegiance and equal opportunities for cultural and economic development.

6. *Consideration in drawing a purely ethnic frontier between Slovakia and Hungary:*

a.) The Czechoslovak census of 1930 offers, generally speaking, a sounder basis for partition than the Hungarian census of 1910.

b.) Greater weight should be given to the ethnic distribution of the rural population than to that of the urban population. This area has no genuine urban areas of the western type, except Bratislava and Košice; the other small towns serving as commercial and administrative centers, tend, over a period of years, to take on the ethnic color of the surrounding rural groups.

c.) Problems of communications can be overcome by various types of agreement, such as the Rumanian-Czechoslovak agreement for the upper Tisza railway, provided the will to agree is present.

d.) Strategic considerations can now have little weight in determining frontiers within the area bounded by the Carpathians.

16.VII.42.
Sr:PEMosely:VVP

NOTES

1. Macartney, C. A., *Hungary and Her Successors* (London, 1937), p. 105.

2. *Ibid*, p. 107.

3. *Ibid*, p. 107.

4. Raschhofer, Hermann, ed., *Die Tschechoslowakischen Denkschriften für die Friedenskonferencz von Paris 1919-1920*, (Berlin, 1937), p. 178-181.

5. Seton-Watson, R. W., "The Formation of the Czecho-Slovak State", in *A History of the Peace Conference of Paris*, edited by H. W. V. Temperley (London, 1921), IV, 271-272.

6. *The Hungarian Peace Negotiations* (Budapest, 1920), I, 508-510.

7. Seton-Watson, *op.cit.*, IV, 271-272.

8. Nicolson, Harold, *Peacemaking*, 1919 (New York, 1939) p. 275, 279-280.

9. *Ibid*, p. 275, 279-280, 130.

10. *Ibid*, p. 323-325.

11. Lloyd George, David, *The Truth about the Peace Treaties* (London, 1938), II, 941.

12. *The Hungarian Peace Negotiations*, I, 494-505.

13. *Papers and Documents Relating to the Foreign Relations of Hungary, 1919-1920*, published by the Royal Hungarian Ministry for Foreign Affairs, edited by Francis Deák and Dezső Újváry (Budapest, 1939), I, 250-252; see map opposite p. 250.

14. Rothermere, Harold Sidney Harmsworth, first viscount, *My Campaign for Hungary* (London, 1939) see map on back papers.

15. Bethlen, István, *The Treaty of Trianon and European Peace* (London, 1934), p. 186.

16. Temperley, Harold W. V., "How the Hungarian Frontiers Were Drawn," *Foreign Affairs* (April, 1928), VI, 438, 445, 446.

17. Macartney, *op.cit.*, p. 247-248.

18. Taylor, Paul B., "Germany's Expansion in Eastern Europe," *Foreign Policy Reports* (May 15, 1939), XV, 51-52, 58.

Box 60

****

§ Document 2 §

Secret

T Document 24
July 21, 1942

HUNGARIAN-SLOVAK FRONTIER. ALTERNATIVE TERRITORIAL SOLUTIONS

Stated schematically, three alternative territorial solutions present themselves:

A. return to the 1919-1938 boundary;
B. preservation of the present (1939) boundary;
C. establishment of a compromise boundary between the boundary of 1937 and that of 1939.

I.
Ethnic Quantities

A. If the boundary of 1919-1938 is restored, Czechoslovakia will again rule a half-million Magyars (571, 988 according to the Czechoslovak census of 1930) in Slovakia, most of them located along her southern border. It can be assumed that those who registered themselves as Magyars in 1930 represented an irreducible nucleus of Magyardom within Czechoslovakia, and that changes of political and ethnic allegiance to the advantage of Czechoslovakia, such as were common after 1918, were no longer operative by 1930. Accordingly, Czechoslovakia would again govern Magyar majorities in the following districts:

District	Magyars	Total (citizens)
Dunajská Streda	39,070	44,296
Feledince	25,195	32,565
Galanta	41,474	66,922
Komárno	53,154	64,098
Král'ovsky Chlmec	29,832	37,817
Moldava nad Bodvou	16,737	29,739
Parkan	39,483	48,413

District	Magyars	Total (citizens)
Šal'a	28,431	51,192
Šamorín	27,030	35,135
Stará Ďala	36,940	52,676
Tornal'a	17,701	21,297
Vel'ké Kapušany	11,314	20,304
Želiezovce	24,164	30,227
Total	**390,525**	**534,681**

B. If the boundary of 1939 is allowed to stand after the war, Hungary would then govern a number of predominantly Slovak districts, together with parts of other districts, Slovak in majority.

District	Slovaks	Total (citizens)
Košice urban	42,245	63,967
Košice rural	50,188	55,715
Krupina (part)	28,945	47,489
Levice (part)	30,651	44,410
Lučenec	49,302	71,699
Modrý Kameň (part)	23,898	35,508
Nové Zámky	9,561	21,939
(in this district balance between 9,561 Slovaks and 10,193 Magyars is held by 1,609 Jews and 256 Germans.)		
Revúca (part)	18,777	21,815
Rimavská Sobota	40,324	48,093
Rožňava	34,417	42,131
Vráble (part)	25,744	35,817
Totals (app.)	**343,052**	**488,583**

If a new boundary were run so as to leave a maximum number of Magyars to Hungary and a maximum number of Slovaks to Czechoslovakia, it would lie somewhere between the boundary of 1937 and that of 1939. Presumably, it might run from the present Slovak-Hungarian boundary on the main branch of the Danube norths-eastwards, leaving Galanta and the city of Zámky Nové to Hungary (the northern part of the Zámky Nové district to go to Slovakia), leaving Levice City and the northern two-thirds of Levice province to Slovakia, leaving all of

Krupina district and all except of a southern strip of Lučenec province to Slovakia, leaving all except a southern strip of Rimavská Sobota province to Slovakia, together with all of Košice district. By this new line of demarcation Hungary would recover the predominantly Magyar districts of the *Grosse Schuett*, most of the Little Hungarian Plain and a small strip of ethnically Magyar territory running eastward to the boundary between Slovakia and Ruthenia. The remaining minorities on both sides of the frontier would then be approximately equal in size, and a certain amount of exchange of population and of farm properties might then be effected without undue compulsion, in order to reduce still further the size and importance of the respective minority problems.

II.
Occupations

A. If the frontier of 1937 is restored, Czechoslovakia will recover a preponderantly rural population, also engaged in a certain amount of lumbering along its northern strip and in household industry in the foothill villages. It would recover the small mining district of Rimavská Sobota and the small diversified industries of Košice.

B. If the frontier of 1939 is retained, Hungary will have added slightly to its population engaged in mining, small industry and lumbering and substantially to its agricultural population.

C. Under a compromise arrangement, Hungary would receive almost nothing in the way of population engaged in lumbering; Czechoslovakia would receive a slight increment of persons engaged in mining, in consumption-goods industries and in lumbering. Under any alternative the bulk of the rural population affected is engaged in agriculture, and the bulk of the small urban population is engaged in commercial, artisan, administrative, and cultural occupations.

III.
Experience of Government since 1918

A. If the boundary of 1919 is restored, Czechoslovakia will again have within its boundaries a fairly large, compact and indigestible nucleus of Magyar irredentists. While the generally efficient level of Czech administration also applied in this border region, administrative efficiency often worked against Magyar interests and was therefore not appreciated by the Magyar minority. Since all Magyar national activities were at least potentially, and sometimes actively, irredentist, they were closely supervised and restricted. While the allotment of land to Magyar peasants lessened somewhat irredentist feeling in the villages, no feeling of real gratitude or of attachment to the Czechoslovak state was created, except in a small section of the minority, as most Magyars felt that Slovak peasants had been treated more generously and all Magyar groups resented the colonizing of Czech legionaries on the so-called "remnant estates" located in strongly Magyar areas. The Magyar Socialists came closest to preferring Czechoslovak to Hungarian rule, because of the character of the internal regime in Hungary; even they did not stress loyalty to the new state, and, in any case, they were few in numbers. The failure of the Magyars in Czechoslovakia to develop any really non-irredentist leadership was, and would presumably remain, a barrier to granting them any genuine autonomy. Restoration of the frontier of 1937 would therefore restore the compact Magyar minority to its former position of "fellow-travelers" on the Czech ship of state, and would recreate the vicious circle making the grant of autonomy conditional on proof of loyalty to the Czechoslovak state.

B. If the boundary of 1939 is retained, a large and fairly compact Slovak minority will be left under Hungarian rule. While most Slovaks did not object very vociferously to Magyar rule before 1918, the situation is quite different now. Twenty years of national education and of widened opportunities for advancement in all fields have pretty much eliminated the old humble attitude of the Slovaks towards the Magyar "ruling race." Since the Magyar system of local self-government eliminates non-Magyars from a voice in public affairs even more effectively than the Czechoslovak system of allowing free elections to a national parliament dominated by Czechoslovak parties, the Slovaks are not likely to be reconciled to Hungarian rule.

C. Under a compromise settlement, negotiated or imposed as part of a general settlement, irredentism on each side of the frontier would lose most of its sustenance. The presence of approximately equal minorities on each side of the frontier might lead to more favorable treatment in linguistic, cultural and local-government matters. The important factor in any settlement which would be tolerable to the local minorities would be to assure both them and the majorities that irredentism was now neither a hope nor a peril. From this realization might flow a relaxation of both majority vigilance and of minority irreconcilability.

IV.
Transportation

A. Under the boundary of 1937 Czechoslovakia would retain the principal east-west railway south of the Tatras, from Bratislava to Komárno, to Rimavská Sobota and Košice. Hungary would continue, as before 1938, to utilize its fairly dense railway network centering on Budapest.

B. Under the boundary of 1939 Czechoslovakia's principal east-west railway south of the Tatras would be cut by the loss of Lučenec, Rimavská Sobota and Rožňava. She would still hold a new line connecting Bratislava with the Váh River line, and with the main east-west Tatra line, but connections of the southern parts of the highlands with the Danube and with Bratislava would be roundabout and costly.

C. Under a compromise line which would leave Nové Zámky to Hungary, Czechoslovakia would be fairly well equipped with railroads along her southern border. The areas left to Hungary would be excellently equipped with main and branch-lines providing easy connections with Budapest, and with the Danube ports. Presumably special facilities should be provided at Komárno (Komárom) for the transshipment of Slovak timber which is rafted down the Váh River during spring and autumn floods.

V.
Natural Resources

A. Under the boundary of 1937, Czechoslovakia would retain some very productive farming country, in the *Grosse Schuett* and in the Little Hungarian Plain. She would retain a small mining center at Rimavská Sobota and small amounts of timber accessible to rivers.

B. Under the boundary of 1939, Hungary would retain valuable farming areas, considerable timber resources and a small amount of mineral resources.

C. Under a compromise line, Czechoslovakia would retain most of the timber and minerals and part of the rich farming country, while Hungary would hold the richest grain and livestock area. Under B or C, Czechoslovakia would presumably cease to be self-sufficient in grains, and would have to increase her imports of sufficient and fodder; this would be a factor encouraging her to cooperate more closely with Hungary and other Danubian states, or with Poland. Hungary's problem of disposing of her agricultural surpluses would be somewhat increased under B or C. Her requirements in lumber and minerals would not be satisfied to any applicable under B or C.

VI.
Considerations of Security

A. The boundary of 1937 gave Czechoslovakia a greater sense of security as against Hungary, for it brought her frontier down into the plains and opened up an easy route to Budapest. In the event, Hungary proved to be merely a subsidiary menace to Czechoslovakia's existence.

B. The boundary of 1939 provided Budapest with a considerably extended zone of defense, and brought Bratislava within range of Hungarian attack. However, it still left to Slovakia the main east-west railway through the Tatras, covered by fairly extensive and difficult approaches; it also leaves to Czechoslovakia several alternative lines of egress to the Hungarian plain and Budapest.

C. A compromise boundary would deprive both Czechoslovakia and Hungary of any substantial advantages of terrain. In the central sector, between Levice and Lučenec, the Czechoslovak frontier would again jut out somewhat, as before 1938, against Budapest. The Hungarian salient stretching west from Vác along the northern bank of the Danube would be exposed to a southward sally from Czechoslovak territory. On the other hand, Bratislava would again be within easy range of Hungarian forces.

VII.
Economic Considerations

A. A return to the boundary of 1937 would restore to Czechoslovakia a prosperous farming region with a high level of consumption of manufactured goods. It would also recover an important secondary center of consumption-goods industries, at Košice, and a small mining center at Rimavská Sobota. If postwar Czechoslovakia returns to its former policy of agricultural protection, the farming population of its Magyar-inhabited areas would be, as before, in a much more favorable position than the farmers of Hungary proper.

B. Preservation of the frontier of 1939 would add considerably to Hungary's exportable surplus of cereals and animal products. This would be an advantage only of Hungary were assured of foreign outlets for its surpluses. The present frontier would leave to Hungary the consumption-goods center of Košice, which is hardly able to complete with similar industries of Budapest, together with a small increment of mining around Rimavská Sobota.

C. A compromise frontier would leave to Hungary most of the plains area, with its marketable surpluses of grain, while Czechoslovakia would recover the mainly mixed-farming areas of the valleys and foothills. Košice would presumably continue to develop as a subsidiary center of consumption-goods industries for Eastern Slovakia and Ruthenia. The mining of Rimavská Sobota adds very little to Czechoslovak total.

VIII.
Commitments

In extending full recognition to the Provisional Czechoslovak Government in London, the United States Government, in aide-memoire of July 31, 1941, specifically refrained from entering, even by implication, into any commitment respecting the future frontiers of Czechoslovakia. The aide-memoire stated, in part: "...The relationship between our two Governments does not constitute any commitment on the part of the American Government with respect to the territorial boundaries of Czechoslovakia or the juridical continuity of the Czechoslovak Government headed by His Excellency Dr. Beneš. The American Government considers that the occasion for more formal reservations on these points has not arisen."

IX.
Regional and Political Implications

A. The restoration of the boundary of 1919-1938 would satisfy the Czechoslovaks' demand for the recognition of the legitimacy of their Republic in its full territorial extent, a demand which is deep-seated in the Czech way of thought. It would likewise satisfy the natural desire to avoid penalizing the victim of an aggression after a victory over the most naked and unscrupulous forms of aggression.

In domestic Czechoslovak politics the restoration of the *status quo ante-Munich* would undoubtedly bring great prestige to Dr. Beneš personally. It would greatly facilitate the reestablishment of a unitary regime, or at least tend to hold to a minimum Slovak demands for autonomy. Within Slovakia the recovery of the boundary of 1937 would strengthen the Slovak Centralists and weaken the Independentists, for it would be regarded as an achievement of the Czechoslovak orientation, in contrast to the territorial losses suffered by autonomous and later "independent" Slovakia.

On the other hand, under this solution it would be difficult, probably impossible, as it was before 1938, to reconcile the compact population of the Magyar minority to Czechoslovak rule. Nor could one then expect Hungary to cooperate with its neighbors better than it did prior to 1938, regardless of the internal regime in the country.

In discussions of the projected Czechoslovak-Polish Confederation the Czechs assume that Czechoslovakia will enter as a single unit into any such union. Some Poles would prefer to see separate Czech and Slovak units as members of it, as this would enhance Polish leadership. A restoration of the Slovak frontier of 1937 would tend to strengthen Czechoslovakia in acting as a unit towards Poland and towards the proposed confederation. Conversely, any severe limitation of Slovak territory might make the idea of direct Slovak-Polish cooperation more attractive to Slovaks.

B. The perpetuation of the 1939 frontier would undoubtedly weaken considerably the Czechoslovak orientation in Slovak politics. Slovaks tend to be either more anti-Magyar or more pro-Magyar than do Czechs, and a pro-Magyar Slovak leadership might emerge. Even the present Slovak leaders, if they saw their political fortunes and their lives endangered by a Czechoslovak triumph, might choose the pro-Magyar path, especially if it were made smooth by territorial concessions by Hungary. It would be a clever maneuver if Hungary were able to confront the victors with a Slovak-Hungarian federation as a fait accompli.

C. The enforcement of a compromise settlement based primarily on ethnic considerations would probably leave both Slovaks and Magyars disgruntled. However, under whatever territorial arrangement is adopted, strong therapeutic measures in the fields of security and economics will be required and will be decisive for the permanence of the settlement. Such treatment would have better prospect of lasting success if the minority problem were first reduced to its smallest possible proportions.

One very serious objection to making any change in the 1937 boundary is that, upon the abandonment of the principle of the legitimacy of the frontiers of 1919, the way would be open to call into question the legitimacy of boundaries elsewhere. However, frontiers can more reasonably be classified "stable" and "unstable" rather than as "legitimate" and "illegitimate." "Illegitimate" frontiers lose the bar sinister with time and custom; "legitimate" frontiers may become untenable under new conditions having nothing to do with the equity of the frontier itself.

Unofficial Czechoslovak spokesmen have on occasion indicated a willingness to sacrifice some Magyar-inhabited areas for the sake of a reconciliation with Hungary.* The real question, which remains unanswered, is not whether the Czechoslovaks will be more or less reasonable, but whether the Magyars can be brought to accept wholeheartedly a final and amicable settlement with each of their neighbors. Since Czechoslovakia must "live dangerously" of it is to live at all, it may find advantage in cutting its political risks along its exposed south-eastern frontier.

21/VII/42.
SR/PEMosely/JRB Box 60

****

*A statement of this sort was made by almost every member of the Czechoslovak government-in-exile. For details, see the Introduction.

§ Document 3 §

Confidential

T Document 49
August 21, 1942

REMARKS ON THE MEMORANDUM "HUNGARIAN-SLOVAK FRONTIERS: ALTERNATIVE TERRITORIAL SOLUTIONS," dated 21/VIII/42

I.

In connection with probable Hungarian claims to former Czechoslovak territories, the following considerations might be kept in mind:

1. Czechoslovakia had been the object of German and, in effect, Hungarian aggression, and only the clearest sort of ethnic requirements should lead us to reward the aggressors. The door to reaching a modus vivendi with Hungary, including even frontier rectifications, had never been closed definitely by Masaryk and Beneš. Their position before the present war was that formal negotiations could never begin because the Magyars maintained the whole of their national claims integrally.

2. In Hungary the non-Magyar sections of the population were effectively precluded from having a voice in public affairs; the rural population is still kept in hand by Magyar landlords through the system of public voting in elections; and as no land reform ever was instituted in Hungary the Slovak peasants remain on much the same economic level as formerly.

Czechoslovakia, on the other hand, has demonstrated a respect for the cultural, political and economic rights of minority elements; has maintained a system of free elections by secret ballot; and after the last war instituted a broad system of land reform.

3. Partly because of the above, there never was any very articulate irredentist movement among the Magyars in Czechoslovakia. The cry, "nem, nem, soha," (no, no, never) raised in Budapest found no clear response across the northern Hungarian frontier.

4. Some accommodation of interests had been achieved locally in the course of the living together of the Magyar and Czechoslovak populations during the twenty years between the wars. To whatever

extent this accommodation is a fact, it should not unnecessarily be destroyed and the same problem of adjustment posed afresh.

5. There is an advantage in not raising the problem of the whole Czechoslovak-Hungarian frontier, as such, after this war. To do so would provoke serious Czechoslovak complaints based (whether entirely justifiably or not) on the allegation that the general implications of the Atlantic Charter had been violated. The Czechoslovak Government would find support in that position from a number of other directly interested states, including Poland and Yugoslavia, and probably also from Soviet Russia and perhaps Great Britain (*cf.* Eden's recent reaffirmation of the British repudiation of the Munich "Settlement"). Simultaneously, all the other states which would like to open or re-open boundary disputes with their neighbors would be galvanized into greater activity; Germany and Italy, to mention no others, would have new grounds on which to argue that annexations, or plebiscites preliminary to such, be recommended in areas such as Danzig, Alsace, Eupen and Malmedy, Nice, Corsica, Tunisia, et cetera.

6. We are committed to the restoration of the Czechoslovak state. Presumably, then, we intend that it shall be strong and prosperous. If the Czechoslovak Government-in-Exile, or any successor group engaged in peace negotiations, were unable to prevent what seemed like an extensive amputation along the Hungarian frontier, it would tend to lose Slovak support and the future unity of the Republic would be impaired and perhaps destroyed. This is a factor to be weighed in connection with plans for an Eastern European Federation.

With the above in mind, I suggest that in considering the future relations of Czechoslovakia and Hungary, we would do well to avoid, so far as possible, any appearance of opening up the whole question of the Czechoslovak-Hungarian frontier. Instead, we might identify one or two areas of fairly limited size where the ethnic situation is such as to indicate overwhelmingly the wisdom of including them in Hungary in the interest of future amicable relations between the two neighboring peoples (e.g. the *Grosse Schuett* and perhaps an adjoining section of the so-called Little Hungarian Plain).

II.

If this general course were adopted, I suggested more specifically that:

a) American policy aim to facilitate a direct agreement between the two parties on the limited territorial question involved;

b) offers of American economic and financial assistance help to "sugar the pill" for Czechoslovakia, not only in broad terms but specifically for the construction of new railway, airport and other facilities to replace those lost to Hungary;

c) a close study be made as to whether any Hungarian *quid pro quo* might be available, even if of minor importance, to save face for Czechoslovakia;

d) in connection with this limited transfer of territory an exchange of populations be effected therein, as well as in other Czechoslovak and Hungarian border regions under international auspices and with international help—all of which would benefit Czechoslovakia in the long run by removing a former source of weakness in the Czechoslovak state;

e) Hungary's adoption of a thorough-going land reform and the reform of her voting system be considered a necessary preliminary to any transfer of Czechoslovak territory to her;

f) in general, a vigorous effort be made to prove, not only to the two nations here involved but to all the states of Europe, that under the new international regime coming into effect after this war, security will be guaranteed and frontiers as such will be less important.

H.F.A.*

Box 60

****

---

*Hamilton Fisch Armstrong

§ Document 4 §

Secret

T Document 48
August 24, 1942

HUNGARIAN-SLOVAK FRONTIER. ALTERNATIVE FRONTIER SOLUTIONS. ADDITIONAL NOTE

I.

The Hungarian-Slovak problem-area falls into two categories: a southern tier of predominantly Magyar districts, and a northern tier of mixed Slovak-Hungarian districts. These two tiers of districts may be susceptible of different handling in case an effort should be made to resolve the Hungarian-Slovak dispute by direct negotiation or by a compromise settlement induced through the efforts of the leading members of the United Nations.

II.
Southern Tier

1. In the western section of the southern tier there are six districts, which together contain most of the *Grosse Schuett* and over half of the Little Hungarian Plain. According to the Czechoslovak census of 1930, they contain the following ethnic quantities:

Name of District	Total	Czechoslovak	Magyar
Šamorín	35,135	3,994	27,030
Dunajská Streda	44,296	2,196	39,070
Komárno	64,098	7,910	53,154
Stará Ďala	52,676	14,536	36,940
Parkan	48,413	7,532	39,483
Želiezovce	30,227	4,503	24,164
Total	**274,845**	**40,671**	**219,841**

In 1938 all of these districts were taken by Hungary, except for about one-twentieth of Želiezovce district.

The transfer of these six districts to Hungary would leave intact in Czechoslovak hands the main-line railroad from Bratislava through Galanta and Nové Zámky to Levice. It would place in Hungarian hands (1) most of a subsidiary railroad from Bratislava to Komárno, which traverses the *Grosse Schuett*; (2) the main-line railroad southeast of Nové Zámky to the former frontier station of Szob; and (3) a branch-line northward in the direction of Levice. No serious adjustments in transportation and local marketing arrangements would be needed, except that Slovakia should be provided with transshipment facilities at Komárno for the handling of lumber floated down the Váh River to that Danubian port.

2. In the central section of the Slovak frontier of 1937 there are three districts of markedly Magyar population:

Name of District	Total	Czechoslovak	Magyar
Feledince	32,565	4,551	25,195
Tornal'a	21,297	2,629	17,701
Moldava nad Bodvou	29,739	7,937	16,737
Total	**83,601**	**15,117**	**59,633**

Of these three districts, all except about one-fifth of the Moldava district were annexed by Hungary in 1938.

The transfer of these three districts to Hungary would leave intact in Czechoslovak hands the existing railroad system connecting Levice, Lučenec, Rimavská Sobota, Revúca, and Rožňava, It would place in Hungarian hands three branch-lines closely connected with existing Hungarian lines and with Budapest.

3. In the eastern section of the frontier of 1937 the district of Král'ovský Chlumec is overwhelming Magyar in character. Of its total population of 37,817 in 1930, 3,969 were Czechoslovaks and 29,832 were Magyars. This entire district was annexed by Hungary in 1938.

The transfer of the district of Král'ovský Chlmec to Hungary would cut the main-line connecting Košice with Užhorod and Ruthenia, but would leave an alternative through-line in Czechoslovak hands. The section of the main-line lying within this districts would, however, be cut off from the Hungarian network. If a narrow southern strip of Trebišov province were added to Hungary, this section could be connected with the important junction of Sátoraljaújhely and with the main Hungarian network.

III.
Northern Tier

1. The western section of the Hungarian-Slovak problem-area consists of five districts of strongly mixed population:

Name of District	Total	Czechoslovak	Magyar
Galanta	66,922	21,161	41,474
Šal'a	51,192	20,726	28,431
Nové Zámky	62,107	39,724	19,629
Vráble	35,817	25,744	9,208
Levice	44,410	30,651	12,190
Total	**260,448**	**138,006**	**110,932**

Of these districts, considerable portions were annexed by Hungary in 1938; four-fifths of Galanta, three-fifths of Šal'a, nineteen-twentieths of Nové Zámky and of Vráble, and one-fifths of Levice district.

Slight adjustments of frontier could be made in this section, particularly in the districts of Galanta, Šal'a and Nové Zámky, if it should be desired, to transfer a number of strongly Magyar communities to Hungarian rule. However, the drawing of an ethnic line of demarcation would place the cities of Galanta and Nové Zámky in Hungary, thus depriving Czechoslovakia of its main-line eastward from Bratislava to Levice, while leaving to it a well-developed but more roundabout line to the north.

2. In the central section of the northern tier there are five districts of strongly mixed composition:

Name of District	Total	Czechoslovak	Magyar
Krupina	47,489	28,945	17,279
Modrý Kameň	35,508	23,898	11,025
Lučenec	71,699	49,302	18,502
Revúca	21,815	18,777	2,094

Name of District	Total	Czechoslovak	Magyar
Rožňava	42,131	23,417	14,767
Total	**218,642**	**144,339**	**63,667**

Considerable portions of these districts were annexed by Hungary in 1938; about one-third of Krupina and of Modrý Kameň, about two-fifths of Lučenec, one-fourth of Revúca, and one-half of Rožňava

Slight adjustments of frontier could be made in the southern portions of the districts of Krupina, Modrý Kameň, Lučenec and Rožňava, to transfer a few mainly Magyar communes to Hungarian rule, and without dislocating the system of railroad transportation.

3. In the eastern section of the ethnically mixed area the following districts with small Magyar minorities are involved:

Name of District	Total	Czechoslovak	Magyar
Košice Urban	63,967	42,245	11,504
Košice Rural	55,715	50,188	3,546
Trebišov	47,417	40,057	3,971
Vel'ké Kapušany	20,304	7,457	11,314
Michalovce	50,238	42,533	3,066
Total	**237,641**	**182,480**	**33,401**

Of these districts Hungary, in 1938 and 1939, annexed all of Košice Urban, nine-tenths of Vel'ké Kapušany, two-thirds of Košice Rural, one-third of Trebisov, and one-fifth of Michalovce. A small rectification could be made in the district of Vel'ké Kapušany to leave a few Magyar villages to Hungary, without injuring the Czechoslovak railroad system.

IV.

The difference in the relative importance of the ethnic quantities involved is a significant one. The southern tier, comprising ten districts, contained a total population of 396,263 (census of 1930), of which 309,306 were Magyars and 59,757 were Czechoslovaks. The northern tier, on the other hand, includes fifteen districts with a total population of 716,731, of which 464,825 were Czechoslovaks, and 208,000 Magyars (1930).

The retrocession to Hungary of the districts of the southern tier would not impose any great difficulties of transportation on Czechoslovakia; the retroceded areas would return to their pre-1918 gravitation towards nearby Hungarian market-towns and towards Budapest. The return to Hungary of any substantial part of the Magyars contained in the northern tier of districts would, on the other hand, necessitate considerable adjustments in the Czechoslovak railroad system; even in this area certain small sections of compact Magyar settlement could be transferred to Hungary without serious inconvenience. In this connection, it must be remembered that some of the district boundaries were redrawn in a somewhat gerrymandered manner after 1920, apparently with a view to diluting the volume of the Magyar element in some of the disputed districts.

SR/PEMosely/JRB
24/VIII/42. Box 60

****

§ Document 5 §

Secret T Document 61
September 3, 1942

Not to be removed from the State Department building

HUNGARIAN-SLOVAK FRONTIER: PROSPECTS FOR AN EXCHANGE OF MINORITIES SUBSEQUENT TO FRONTIER-RECTIFICATION

I. *Southern and Northern Tier in the Problem-Area*

In a memorandum entitled "Hungarian-Slovak Frontier; Alternative Frontier Solutions; Additional Note" (T Document 48; August 24, 1942), a distinction in regard to possible post-war treatment was drawn between the southern tier of ten districts bordering on the Slovak-Hungarian frontier of 1937, and the northern tier of fifteen districts adjoining the first group. It was suggested that the southern tier might be assigned to Hungary, the northern tier to Czechoslovakia.

It was found that the ten districts of the southern tier contained, in 1930, a total population of 396,263, including 309,306 Magyars and 59,757 Czechoslovaks. The northern tier, it was ascertained, contained 716,731 inhabitants, of which 464,825 were Czechoslovak and 209,000 were Magyars by nationality.

If the sixty thousand (59,757) Czechoslovaks living in the southern tier of districts were exchanged for an equal number of Magyars of the northern tier, there would be no Czechoslovaks left in the strip of territory ceded to Hungary. The number of Magyars left in the Czechoslovak-held northern tier would thereby be reduced to about one hundred and fifty thousand (148,243). The total number of Magyars left would then be about two hundred thousand (202,925), of whom 54,692 lived (in 1930) scattered elsewhere in Slovakia, outside the northern and southern tiers of frontier districts.

If the transfer of the southern tier of districts to Hungary should not be followed by the compulsory exchange of the sixty thousand Czechoslovaks of this tier for an equal number of Magyars of the northern tier, Slovakia would still contain 262,682 Magyars, compared with a 1930 total of 571,966.

II. *Possible Bases for a Further Exchange of Slovak and Magyar Minorities*

If an attempt were made to redraw the Hungarian-Slovak frontier, taking into account only the twenty-five districts of the southern and northern tiers, so as to leave approximately equal minorities on each side of a new frontier, certain sections of the northern tier would have to be transferred to Hungary. The following approximate areas with a 1930 Magyar majority would be involved in the first instance:

Western section:		
Galanta	(two-thirds)	41,474 Magyars
Šal'a	(three-fifth)	28,431 Magyars
Nové Zámky	(one-third)	19,529 Magyars
Eastern section:		
Vel'ke Kapušany	(one-half)	11,314 Magyars

By this sectioning of four additional districts, an area containing about one hundred thousand (100,848) Magyars could conceivably be transferred to Hungary.

By assigning to Czechoslovakia the remaining area of the same four districts, 89,068 Czechoslovaks would come under Czechoslovak sovereignty. At this stage in the study, these estimates are of course based on district totals; although somewhat simplified, they may serve to give some indication of the ethnic quantities involved. In any actual division of these four districts between Czechoslovakia and Hungary, only an examination of the area commune by commune would indicate just where the line of division would run within the four districts, and what minor minority quantities would be then subject to exchange.

If the 59,757 Czechoslovaks of the southern tier (1930) were exchanged for a number of Magyars located in the northern tier outside of the additional area assigned to Hungary, and if 100,849 Magyars of the northern tier were also transferred to Hungarian rule by shifting the frontier, the number of Magyars then left in that part of the northern tier assigned to Czechoslovakia would be reduced to 47,395. Even added to the 64,682 scattered Magyars who, in 1930, lived in Slovakia outside the northern and southern tiers, a total minority of 102,077 dispersed Magyars would present no problem from the point of view of possible future claims for territorial or autonomous self-determination. By the same token, no Czechoslovak minority would remain in that part of the problem-area assigned to Hungary.

Thus, even the transfer to Hungary of the predominantly Magyar sections of these four districts of the northern tier would fall short of establishing complete equality of minority quantities on each side of the new frontier. To achieve such equality, it would also be necessary to transfer to Hungary narrow southern strip of some of the remaining eleven districts of the northern tier. The approximate territorial division which would be required under this solution has been outlined roughly in a memorandum entitled "Hungarian-Slovak Frontier; Alternative Territorial Solutions" (T Document 27), and need not be repeated here."

III. *Occupational Factors in a Possible Exchange of Minorities*

On to this point the discussion of possible exchanges of minorities contingent upon a redrawing of the Slovak-Hungarian frontier has been in terms of numbers involved. In practice, the problem of the occupational stratification of the exchangeable populations is of equal or greater importance.

The first step in a study of this aspect of the problem is to determine the structure of the population in terms of nationality and occupation. However, in order to make a really usable analysis of the problem, it would be necessary to refine the study even further. One would need to know, for example, how far peasants accustomed to raising wheat in the plains can be set down in the place of uplands peasants accustomed to mixed farming, and vica versa. A detailed analysis might show, for instance, that a plains peasant, transferred to the uplands, would need to have a larger cultivable area and a smaller capital equipment at his disposal taking, if he was to maintain his accustomed standard of living. An experienced mechanic, moved from a more industrial town of the foothills to a more primitive market-place on the plains, might not find employment for his acquired skill and at his customary wage-level. However, even without entering, at present into these further refinements of analysis, it is possible to indicate some of the occupational quantities involved in an exchange of "remnant" minorities of this problem-area.

Combined data of nationality and occupation are available for some, but not all, of the districts in question. For purposes of illustration the relevant data for two districts are presented here. Stará Ďala is a typical plains districts of the southern tier. Nové Zámky is a somewhat more industrialized district, partly plain and partly foothills, fairly typical of the northern tier. Only Czechoslovaks and Magyars are taken into account; in the following table the data refer, not to persons actually engaged in the occupation indicated, but to those "dependents" on it for their livelihood.

	Stará Ďala Czecho-slovaks	Magyars	Nové Zámky Czecho-slovaks	Magyars
1.) Farming, cattle-raising, gardening	11,870	30,109	19,080	9,364
2.) Lumbering, hunting, mining	39	179	97	58
3.) Industry	891	3,957	7,499	4,851
4.) Commerce and private transport, banking, hotelkeeping	278	638	2,167	1,830
5.) Government service, incl. post office, railroad, army	995	754	7,522	815
6.) Free professions	20	294	269	277
7.) Living on investments or charity	335	884	1,999	1,777
8.) Independent domestic service, hospitalized, students, barbers	34	129	532	360
9) No occupation designated	93	300	754	615

While these figures offer no basis for a planned exchange of minorities according to occupations, as they refer to only two districts, they may serve to indicate some of the discrepancies involved. More particularly for industry, commerce, and the free professions the differences in quantities are significant. Such qualitative discrepancies within the "remnant" minorities, like the quantitative disproportions mentioned above, would be greatly diminished in their extent, and thus rendered more tractable, if certain southern strips of the districts of the northern tier were also assigned to Hungary. For example, in Nové Zámky district 10,193 of the 19,629 Magyars of the district live (1930) in the city of Nové Zámky, located in the southeastern corner of the district adjacent to the southern tier.

SR/PEMosely/JRB
3/IX/42 Box 60

****

§ Document 6 §

T Document 64
September 4, 1942

REMARKS OF H.F.A. ON THE CZECHOSLOVAK-HUNGARIAN FRONTIER

We have been asked to express our individual views as to the best solution of the problems presented in Mr. Mosely's detailed memorandum on the Hungarian-Slovak Frontier (T-48, August 24, 1942). My response is conditioned by one general consideration which seems to me of considerable significance.

Like other members of the Subcommittee, I am anxious to see some adjustments made after the war in border areas where the population is overwhelmingly of a different race from that of the nation in which it is included. Such adjustments would facilitate the consolidation of national states; lessen the need for prolonged international measures to protect minority rights; and remove causes of international friction.

The prospects are, however, that we shall encounter great difficulties in securing any adjustments whatsoever which involve transfers of territory from our allies, the victims of aggression, to neighboring states which have recently despoiled them. I do not raise this here as an issue of morals, but of practical politics. It seems most unlikely that our Government would attempt to coerce our recent allies, or that the American public would support it if it did.

In these circumstances, the best chance of our securing any territorial adjustments of this sort at all will probably be for us to pick out a small number of areas of limited size where the ethnic situation is beyond dispute; and to attempt to bring about adjustment there through direct negotiations between the two interested parties. This course might succeed if: (a) the sacrifice suggested to any one state did not involve more a single area; (b) we were able to offer that state economic and financial advantages on the side; (c) the state gaining territory offered some face-saving *quid pro quo*, to the state making the cession. If any other course is adopted, I should think it highly unlikely that, in most cases, any readjustments of territory whatsoever will be effected.

Applying the above considerations to the problem under discussion, I suggest that we concentrate our attention on the six administrative districts of the Southern Tier described in Section II of Mr. Mosely's memorandum; and that we limit our attempt to bring about changes in this whole area to an effort to persuade the Czechoslovak Government to negotiate the cession of these six districts to Hungary as part of a general settlement of all outstanding Czechoslovak-Hungarian differences.

Specifically, this course would have the following advantages:

1) These six districts, by the Czechoslovak census of 1930, contain about 219,000 Magyars to about 40,000 Czechoslovaks. The ethnic argument for the transfer therefore is overwhelming.

2) They compose most of the *Grosse Schuett*, which figured particularly prominently in discussions at the last peace conference and since, as well as more than half of the so-called Little Hungarian Plain. Thus their return to Hungary would represent a great psychological as well as racial gain for that country, and should go far towards mending Czechoslovak-Magyar relations from the Magyar and (especially as such a transfer would be an act of unexampled generosity from one state in this area towards a defeated enemy).

3) The transfer of these six districts would leave the main-line railway from Bratislava to Levice intact in Czechoslovak hands.

4) Arguments have been advanced in our discussions in favor of transfers of whole administrative districts. The transfer suggested would meet that requirement (except as a small enclave might have to be left to Czechoslovakia, opposite Bratislava, in order not to out off a suburban area from the city).

5) Finally, if no other alterations in the 1937 status of Czechoslovakia were suggested (she might, of course, wish voluntarily to make slight changes in the Erzgebirge), the transfer of these six districts might successfully be presented to the Czechoslovak public as the solution of a long-time "problem area" rather than as a part of a general frontier change in favor of the Hungarian state which only recently had been able, through Nazi help, to seize many preponderantly Czechoslovak areas.

The transfers of these six districts to Hungary would mean that 40,000 Czechoslovaks might wish to be repatriated to Czechoslovakia. And the maintenance intact of other parts of the pre-1938 frontier would mean that 265,000 Magyars might wish to be repatriated to Hungary. In practice, the numbers doubtless would be much smaller. In any case, they are not too great for transfer under humans conditions with the proper international assistance.

H.F.A.
Box 60

****

§ Document 7 §

Confidential

T Document 235
February 3, 1943

YUGOSLAV-HUNGARIAN FRONTIER: ETHNIC COMPOSITION OF THE DISPUTED AREAS

I. *THE HUNGARIAN AND YUGOSLAV CENSUSES*

1. *Hungarian Census of 1910*

This census[1] gives detailed information on the distribution of the population by mother-tongue and by religion. While it may be biased in favor of the Magyar claims, it appears to give a fairly accurate picture of the numerical strength of the Slavic and other minorities in the territories involved.

2. *Yugoslav Census of 1921*

The first Yugoslav census[2] is, in most respects, as complete and satisfactory as that of 1910. Comparison of the two censuses reveals remarkably few discrepancies.

3. *Yugoslav Census of 1931*

While this census[3] is more detailed than that of 1921, the figures on distribution by native tongue have not been published. The most recent statics on language are thus those of 1921. The figures for religious distribution useful as a check on the language figures because of the confusion of language and religious groups in the areas under consideration.

II. *ZONES OF ETHNIC COMPOSITION*

1. *Prekomurje*

The language statistics both for 1910 and for 1921 indicate that the whole area is predominantly Slovene-speaking. The Hungarian figures listed 20,110 Magyar inhabitants and some 2000 Germans out of a total of 88,671. The bulk of the population 4,34 – 66,410 – is classified as "Others". The Hungarian government, at the time of the Peace Conference in 1919, insisted that these peoples were Wends, Slavic-speaking but unrelated to the other South Slavs.[4] The Yugoslav government and disinterested outside authorities, on the other hand, are agreed that these Wends are closely akin to the neighboring Slovenes.[5] The census of 1921 classified them as Slovene-speaking. Of a total population of 92,295 it listed 74,199 as speaking Slovene as their native tongue, 14,065 speaking Magyar and 2,540 speaking German.

In two small sections of Prekomurje, the Magyar and German languages are clearly in preponderance. The greater part of the Magyar-speaking population is concentrated on the eastern frontier contiguous to Hungary. A line drawn to the west of the communes (opštini) of Hodoš, Krplivnik, Domanjšovci, Središče, Prosenjakovci, Pordašinci, Dobrovnik, Radmožanci, Kapca, Kot and Petišovci separates from the rest of Prekomurje the predominantly Magyar zone, with a Magyar-speaking population of 12,410 in twenty-five communes. Scattered through this Magyar area, there are also some 2,450 Slovenes and 180 Germans.

Somewhat over one-half (1,304) of the German-speaking population of 2,504 is concentrated in the three contiguous communes of Kramarovci, Ocinje and Fuksinci. These communes are located on the Austrian frontier and include only 35 Slovenes.

2. *Medjumurje*

In the case of Medjumurje, all the statistics agree that it is overwhelmingly Croat in composition. In 1910 there were 82,829 Croats and 6,766 Magyars out of a total of 90,387. By 1921, the total population had risen to 96,892, and included 93, 623 Serbo-Croats and 1,904 Magyars. In no one of the twenty-six communes of Medjumurje are the Magyars more than a small minority.

3. *The Baranja*

According to the census of 1921, the distribution of the population by language shows an almost equal proportion of Serbo-Croats, Magyars and Germans in the Baranja. Out of a population of 49,452, 16,638 spoke Magyar, 16,253 German and 15,604 Serbo-Croat. As compared with the Hungarian census of 1910, these figures represent a certain relative gain for the Slavic-speaking population. In the earlier census, 20,134 were Magyars, 13,908 Germans, 7,913 Serbs and Croats and some 7,400 Šokci,[6] out of a population of 50,797. This last-named group consists of Slavs of the Catholic faith who moved into the region to the south of Pécs in the seventeenth century, migrating presumably from Dalmatia. Despite the Hungarian claims to the contrary, the Šokci are generally considered to be one of the South Slav peoples, akin to the Croats, and they are treated as such in the census of 1921.[7]

As for population trends after 1921, the figures on religious distribution offer some further evidence. Whereas the Roman Catholic and Protestant faiths showed remarkably little change, the Orthodox religion, which had 6,448 adherents in 1910 and 6,782 in 1921, rose to 11,314 in 1931, while the total population of the area rose only slightly. From this evidence it may be concluded that the Serbian elements in the population underwent a small relative increase in the ten-year period.

The Magyar, German and Serbo-Croat nationality groups are so intermingled in the Baranja that no clear zones of ethnic distribution can be defined. The Magyars are distributed in the southeastern section of the southern district (srez) of Darda, and in particular in the towns of Bilje, Kneževi Vinogradi and Lug. There are also smaller Magyar settlements in the northern district of Batina, in the towns of Batina, Duboševica and Suza. Serbs and Croats, on the other hand, are concentrated in the north in the regions bordering on Hungary. The German-speaking peoples form a plurality in the southern district, where they are strongly represented in the railroad centers of Beli Monastir and Darda. In general, almost every one of the thirty communes in the Baranja, has a sizable proportion of Slavs, Magyars and Germans living together.

4. *The Bačka*

The census of 1921 reported for the Bačka a total population of 735,117 comprising the following language groups: 260,998 Magyars, 246,598 Serbs and Croats, 173,796 Germans, 30,993 Czechs, 10,999

Ruthenians and 4,850 Slovenes. In the cities of over 20,000, of which the Bačka has five, the Slavs form two-thirds of the population of the important railroad centers of Subotica, these Slavic groups include a substantial number of Šokci and Bunjevci.[8] There is in addition a plurality of Slav-speaking peoples in Novi Sad, in the south, although her both Magyars and Germans are also well represented. The Magyars form almost the entire population of the cities of Senta and Stara Kanjiza in the northeastern part of the Bačka.

In the rural areas, the Serbs and Croats are in a majority in the districts of Titel and Zabalj in the south, and they are well represented in the districts of Apatin, Novi Sad, Palanka, Sombor and Stari Bečej. The Magyars predominate in the districts of Senta, Stari Bečej and Topola, in the northeast, and are represented in smaller numbers throughout the region. The districts of Apatin, Kula, Odzaci, Palanka and Sombor form the German-speaking strongholds. The Czech minority is concentrated chiefly in the districts of Novi Sad and Odžaci, and the Ruthenians in the district of Kula.

The figures on religious distribution contribute little to the clarification of the ethnic problem. Despite a small decline in the number of Roman Catholics, and a corresponding rise in the number of the Greek Orthodox, the relative sizes of the various religious groups remained remarkably stable between 1910 and 1931. The Catholic population includes both Croats and Magyars, the Orthodox are predominantly of Serb nationality, whereas both Germans and Magyars are included in the Protestant faith. The comparative figures follow:

	1910	1921	1931
Roman Catholics	438,521	449,083	402,143
Orthodox	144,866	159,919	182,965
Protestants	98,798	98,668	95,571
Others	18,233	27,447	31,187
Totals	**700,418**	**735,117**	**711,866**

The ethnic fragmentation is illustrated by the fact that of the 105 communes in the Bačka, the Germans are in a majority in 36, the Slavs in 31, the Magyars in 23 and the Czechs in 7, while in 8 communes no one language-group predominates. Of the eleven administrative districts into which the Bačka is divided, the German-speaking communes are in a majority on Odžaci and Palánka, the Serb and Croat in Zabalj and Titel and the Magyar in Senta and Topola. In the remaining five districts, the communes of no single language group are in predominance.

6. *The Banat*

In the Banat, no single language-group has a clear majority. Of a population of 561,958, as of 1921, the Serbs and Croats led with 240,213. They were followed by the Germans, with 126,530, the Magyars, with 98,471 and the Rumanians, with 67,897. There were also Czechs, Slovenes, Albanians, Turks, Poles, Italians, French and Ruthenians in smaller numbers. As compared with the last Hungarian census, the total population had increased by some 37,000 from a figure of 522,907 in 1910. Of the individual language-groups, the Serbo-Croats and the Germans had each increased some 20 percent since 1910, while the number of Magyars and Rumanians had declined somewhat.

The figures on religious distribution show a gradual relative decline in the number of the Protestants, who are chiefly Germans and Magyars, and a corresponding rise in that of the Orthodox, most of whom are Serbs and Rumanians. These shifts were not sufficiently great between 1921 and 1931, however, to warrant any more significant conclusion than that there was probably a small influx of Serbs into the Banat:

	1910	1921	1931
Orthodox	288,757	306,414	321,262
Roman Catholics	188,756	209,370	196,087
Protestants	37,379	39,226	37,179
Others	8,015	6,948	11,932
Totals	**522,907**	**561,958**	**566,460**

The national groups in the Banat are, if possible even more inextricably intermingled than are those in the Baranja and the Bačka. The Serbo-Croats are concentrated chiefly in the districts of Velika Kikinda and Novi Bečej, in the norths, and in the districts of Kovačica and Kovin, in the south. The Germans are heavily represented in the towns of Vršac and Bela Crkva and in the districts of Jaša Tomić and Velika Kikinda, while the Magyars are in a majority in the district of Nova Kanjiza and are strong in Veliki Beckerek, in the central part of the Banat. The Rumanian minority is concentrated in the southern part of the province in the districts of Pančevo, Alibunar and Vršac without, however, being in a majority in any one district.

Of the 169 communes in the Banat, 61 are predominantly Slav-speaking, 29 German, 27 Magyar, 24 Rumanian, 3 Czech and 25 mixed. The ethnic confusion is illustrated by the following table which shows the distribution of communes by dominant language groups within each of the eleven administrative districts of the Banat:

	Distribution of Communes					
District	Serbo-Croat	Magyar	German	Rum.	Czech	Mixed
Alibunar	7		2	4		4
Bela Crkva	13		1	2		3
Velika Kikinda	3	2	1			3
Veliki Bečkerek	6	6	9	4	1	1
Vršac	4	1	4	11		7
Jaša Tomić	2	4	6			4
Kovačica	9	1		1	2	
Kovin	5	1	1			2
Nova Kanjiža	3	8				
Novi Bečej	6	2				
Pančevo	3	2	5	2		1
Totals	61	27	29	24	3	25

In the cities, of which the Banat had five, the same balance among ethnic groups exists. While the Slavs and the Germans have small majorities in the cities of Velika Kikinda and Bela Crkva respectively, no one language group is predominant in the three remaining cities. In addition, it should be noted that while the Magyars form 18 percent of the total population of the Banat, they are poorly represented in the urban areas. This is illustrated by the following chart showing the distribution of language groups within the cities:

	Percentage of Ethnic Groups				
Cities	Serbo-Croats	Magyars	Germans	Rum.	Others
Vršac	36	9	49		6
Pančevo	48	8	37		7
Bela Crkva	28		54	7	11
Velika Kikinda	58	16	21		5
Veliki Beckerek	39	27	28		6

PS:CEBlack:VVP

NOTES

1. *Magyar statisztikai közlemények* (Hungarian statistical publications), Vol. 42 (Budapest, 1912).
2. *Kraljevina Jugoslavia. Opsta drzavna statistika. Definitivni rezultati popisa stanovistva od 31 Januara, 1921 god* (Kingdom of Yugoslavia. General government statistics. Definitive results of the census of January 31, 1921) (Sarajevo, 1932).
3. *Kraljevina Jugoslavia. Opsta drzavna statistika. Definitivni rezultati popisa stanovistva od 31 Marta, 1931 godina* (Kingdom of Yugoslavia. General government statistics. Definitive results of the census of March 31, 1931), Vols. I, II and IV, (Beograd, 1937-40).
4. Royal Hungarian Ministry of Foreign Affairs, *The Hungarian Peace Negotiations*, 3 vols. in 4 (Budapest, 1921-22), I, 447-451.
5. C. A. Macartney, *Hungary and Her Successors: The Treaty of Trianon and its Consequences*, 1919-1937 (London, 1937), 379.
6. In a number of communes the Hungarian census gives only the figures for a mixed population of Šokci and Gypsies, so that the exact figure of the former cannot be accurately calculated.
7. Macartney, *op. cit.*, 382-383; *Hungarian Peace Negotiations*, I, 538-541.
8. The Bunjevci are Serbs from Bosnia who moved north in the seventeenth century, and who adhere to the Roman Catholic faith. They and the Šokci are distinguished from the Serbs and Croats in the census of 1910, but not in that of 1921.

Box 62

****

§ Document 8 §

Secret

T Document 248
February 18, 1943

TRANSYLVANIA: THE PROBLEM OF THE SZEKLERS

I. *AREA AND POPULATION OF THE SZEKLER DISTRICTS*

The Szeklers inhabit an area in the southeastern corner of Transylvania, covering approximately 13,000 square kilometers and consisting of the three counties of Háromszék (Trei Scaune), Udvarhely (Odorhei) and Csík (Ciuc), together with a part of the county of Marostorda (Mureş). Their origin and the time of their ancestors' arrival in this region is uncertain. They are apparently of Turanian stock, closely akin to the Magyars, although they have probably assimilated a considerable Rumanian element in the course of some ten centuries of residence in this area. They speak the Magyar language and are strongly Magyar in national sentiment.*

The Szeklers number about half a million and make up the overwhelming majority of the population in the above-named districts. The Hungarian census of 1910 and the Rumanian census of 1930 both report over 85 percent of the inhabitants of the three Szekler districts as Magyar-speaking.[1]

---

* The origin of the Székelys (Szeklers) is still a question of historical debate. The chronicles of the Middle Ages hold them to be the descendants of the Huns, i.e. of Attila's people. Over the years, this conjecture became folklore. Various 19th and 20th century historians have related them to the Pechenegs, the Jazygians and the Kabars. Many believed, and still do, that the Székelys came to the Carpathian Basin with the conquering Hungarian tribes at the end of the 9th century, and had always spoken Hungarian. According to a more recent hypothesis, which is gaining ground, the Székelys are descendants of the Hungarian-speaking Avar tribes which arrived in the Carpathian Basin already in the late 6th, or early 7th century and which, as a matter of course, joined the other Hungarian tribes when they arrived at the end of the 9th century.

1 The census of 1930 gives the Magyars only 85 percent on the basis of declared nationality. These figures give some support to the Rumanian contention that a part of the Magyar-speaking total consist of Rumanians who have adopted the language of the surrounding majority, although part of the difference is represented by Magyar-speaking Jews and Gypsies.

The Szeklers occupy the upper valleys of the Maros (Mureş), Nagy Küküllö (Târnava Mare) and Aluta (Olt) Rivers. The more thickly settled parts of the area are comparatively flat; other parts are hilly and some are mountainous, since these districts lie in the great bend of the Carpathians.

II. *HISTORICAL BACKGROUND*

For many centuries, both when Transylvania was under the Hungarian Crown and when it was independent, the Szeklers enjoyed the privileges of self-government in these districts, as did the Saxons in the areas where they were settled. The Magyars, the Szeklers and the Saxons were the three "recognized nations" represented in the Transylvanian Diet. However, the Szeklers gradually lost most of their ancient privileges and became entirely assimilated to the Magyars, the dominant element in Transylvania. The Act of Union of Transylvania with Hungary in 1867 abolished all special national privileges and proclaimed the equality of all Hungarian citizens.

III. *THE PERIOD OF RUMANIAN RULE. 1918-1940*

The Minorities Treaty signed by Rumania and the Principal Allied and Associated Powers on December 9, 1919, provided that Rumania should "accord to the communities of the Saxons and the Szeklers in Transylvania local autonomy in regard to scholastic and religious matters, subject to the control of the Roumanian State." This vague obligation had little meaning in practice, and the Szeklers did not press their rights under it since they wanted to avoid any split with the rest of the Magyars of Transylvania.

The Szeklers, while under Rumanian rule, were subjected to a certain amount of persecution by officials on the ground that they were really Magyarized Rumanians who should be "re-Rumanized," by force if necessary. Some were compelled to change their names or their religion. In the matter of education, the Rumanian Education Act of 1924 provided generally for teaching in the language of each particular community or sufficiently numerous linguistic group, but made an exception in the case of "citizens of Rumanian origin who have lost their mother tongue"; these had to send their children to schools where instruction was exclusively in Rumanian. The Szekler districts were included in a special "cultural zone", in which many new Rumanian schools were created, although in general the Szeklers enjoyed the use of their language in school and church and in village administration.

IV. *ALTERNATIVE SOLUTIONS IN THE EVENT OF THE RETURN OF THE SZEKLER DISTRICTS TO RUMANIA*

1. *Removal of the Szeklers to Hungary*

The removal of one-half million Szeklers to western Transylvania or to Hungary proper would be a tremendous and difficult undertaking because of their numbers, their attachment to the region they have inhabited for centuries, and the problem of finding an area in which they could settle without great dislocation of their established mode of life. It is doubtful if they would leave their homeland voluntarily, and a compulsory exchange of populations would involve great hardship.

2. *Autonomy within the Rumanian State*

To be effective, a guarantee of autonomy for the Szeklers would have to be more specific than that which was embodied in the Minorities Treaty of 1919. In view of the solidly Magyar character of the population of the Szekler districts, this autonomy would have a territorial basis, with local self-government in a specific series of matters such as education, policing, public welfare, and so forth.

The success of such an experiment would depend largely on the satisfactory solution of two other aspects of the Hungarian-Rumanian problem: 1) the Rumanians would have to abandon the idea of forcible assimilation of the Szeklers and respect their rights both as citizens of Rumania and as citizens of the autonomous area; 2) there would have to be a fundamental solution of the conflict of claims to Transylvania which would remove the possibility that the Szeklers might become involved in a new campaign of Hungarian irredentism.

As an alternative to autonomy on a territorial basis, there is a possibility that the language, religion and customs of the Szeklers could be protected by the existence of a Magyar national cultural association (open on a voluntary basis to all Hungarians in Rumania), which would have jurisdiction over education and similar matters. The success of such an arrangement would be doubtful in the absence of certain fundamental changes in the modes of political thought and action which have been characteristic of Eastern Europe since the rise of nationalism. The Rumanians would have to accept the limitations which this arrangement would impose upon their conception of Rumania as a national state. The Szeklers and other Magyars left within Rumania would have to abandon the idea of using their cultural organizations as a means of working for territorial revision in favor of Hungary.

Either one of these types of autonomy for the Szeklers would certainly require international guarantees and a workable method of making those guarantees effective.

PB:JCCampbell:VVP:MT

Box 62

****

§ Document 9 §

Secret T Document 259
Preliminary March 2, 1943

TRANSYLVANIA: ALTERNATIVE TERRITORIAL SOLUTIONS

I. *OCCUPATION BY UNITED NATIONS FORCES*

Upon the collapse of Germany military power in the Danubian area, both Hungary and Rumania will presumably be occupied by forces of the United Nations. The close of formal hostilities is likely to be followed by rapidly changing and revolutionary events in this area. The forces of occupation will have the task of preserving order and of preventing groups representing either nation from jeopardizing the chances of reaching a solution that will minimize the dangers to the future peace of Europe.

To reinforce the principle of non-recognition of territorial changes brought about by force or threats of force, the United Nations occupying forces might set the 1939 boundary as an administrative line, making use of local Rumanian officials in territory which was then Rumanian, and Hungarian officials in the territory of Trianon Hungary. This line would be a starting-point for further deliberation and negotiation.

During the period of occupation, which might last over a considerable period, the competent United Nations authorities would then explore all opportunities for a solution of the Transylvanian question which might be presented by 1) direct negotiations between Hungary and Rumania; 2) local conditions; 3) general developments affecting the whole Danubian or East European area which might fix a pattern into which Transylvania could be fitted.

In the meantime, the alternative solutions of a more permanent character may be given preliminary consideration.

II. *ALTERNATIVE SOLUTIONS*

1. *Return to the Hungarian-Rumanian Boundary of 1939*

Rumania would regain the whole area of 102,787 square kilometers acquired from Hungary after the first World War. The area has a population of approximately five and one-half millions, of whom 3,208,000 are Rumanians 1,353,000 are Hungarians, and 544,000 are Germans (census of 1930). Many of the Hungarians live in the area adjacent to Hungary. The problem of Hungarian irredentism would remain acute.

2. *Cession of all Transylvania to Hungary*

This solution would leave over three million Rumanians in Hungary, a consideration which would probably outweigh any advantages gained by the partial reconstruction of the economic unity of the territory of pre-1918 Hungary.

3. *Maintenance of the Present Boundary, Established in 1940*

The northern part of Transylvania, ceded to Hungary in 1940, has an area of approximately 42,000 square kilometers (about two-fifths of Transylvania), and a total population of some two and one-half millions, of whom 1,200,000 are Rumanians and 900,000 Hungarians. The Hungarian population left in the southern part of Transylvania totals approximately 450,000.

The boundary of 1940 has grave disadvantages from the standpoint of regional economy and communications unless there is to be substantial freedom of trade and of transit between Hungary and Rumania.

In that it satisfies neither party, this boundary tends to heighten and to perpetuate unrest and insecurity.

4. *Rectification of the 1939 Boundary in Hungary's Favor*

The boundary of 1939, from the vicinity of Arad northwards to the border of Czechoslovakia, could be pushed fifteen or twenty miles to the east, adding to Hungary a strip of territory approximately 9,000 square kilometers in area, in which the Magyars outnumber the Rumanians by

300,000 to 200,000. This strip would contain the predominantly Hungarian cities of Szatmárnémeti (Satu Mare), Nagykároly (Carei Mare), Nagyvárad (Oradea Mare), and possibly Arad. At the Peace Conference in 1919, the railway connecting these cities was considered to be such great and strategic importance to Rumania that boundary was drawn to the west of it. The American territorial experts had recommended a line which cut across the railway in several places but was intended to secure a more just ethnic division.

5. *More Drastic Rectification of the 1939 Boundary in Hungary's Favor*

Hungary could be given a larger area at the northern end of the boundary, including the greater part of the counties of Szilágy (Sălaj) and Szatmár (Satu Mare). The Hungarian Government proposed such a line in its negotiations with France in 1920.

The approximate area of this territory is 14,500 square kilometers. Its population is evenly divided between Hungarians and Rumanians, with about 400,000 of each.

This solution might be combined 1) an exchange of populations involving the Rumanians in this area and the 600,000 Hungarians remaining in Transylvania, exclusive of the Szeklers; and 2) a régime of territorial autonomy for the Szeklers. If there were no exchange of populations, cultural autonomy for national minorities on both sides of the boundary would have to be organized on an other than territorial basis.

6. *Creation of an Autonomous or Independent Transylvania within a Federation or Union of East European or Danubian States*

This solution would require effective guarantees or control on the federation and on the part of an outside international authority. If questions of security and of basic economic policy remained in the hands of federal or international bodies, there should be no objection to an autonomous Transylvania on the ground of its small area and population or its vague status in international law.

Autonomy might offer to the people of Transylvania opportunities to work out the problem of getting along together, without pressure from outside. Strong provincial feeling among all the nationalities and the traditions of self-government in historic Transylvania are factors which might increase those opportunities.

Autonomous Transylvania would presumably include not only historic Transylvania but also the other territories ceded by Hungary to Rumania in 1920.

7. *Creation of an Autonomous Transylvania Standing in a Special Relationship to Hungary and Rumania*

If there were no Danubian federation, the terms of Transylvania's autonomy might be defined by agreement between Hungary and Rumania, each recognized the economic and cultural interests of the other in the autonomous area. All three states would probably have to have a common army and foreign policy.

The complicated system of checks and balances which would be needed to give this experiment some chance of success might not be strong or elastic enough to prevent Transylvania from becoming an open battleground between Hungarian and Rumanian nationalists.

PS:JCCampbell:mhp

Box 62

****

§ Document 10 §

Secret

T Document 384
October, 1943

SLOVAKIA: ALTERNATIVE SETTLEMENTS

Four possible settlements may be envisaged for the Slovak problem: union with Poland, union with Hungary, independence, or restoration of Czechoslovakia under some sort of decentralized constitution structure.

I. *UNION WITH POLAND*

For years there have been Polish pretensions to Slovakia, resting on vague historical arguments which in reality apply only to the district of Spiš. There were only 7,000 Poles in Slovakia according to the census of 1930. The Poles assert, for example, that some dialects in northern Slovakia differ very little from the local Polish dialect spoken across the Polish frontier. There is also a Polish contention that Polish Catholicism, strong in its support of the Vatican and never called into question like Czech Hussitism, is more akin to the Slovak spirit than is the Czech spirit.

Back if the Polish pretension, however, has been the desire to establish a common frontier with Hungary, for purposes of alliance and defense, as was demonstrated in the period of the partition of Czechoslovakia from September 1938 to March 1939, when Poland encouraged the separatist movement in Slovakia.

There is no evidence of any real desire whatsoever on the part of the Slovak people for a connection with Poland, though there has been agitation on the part of irresponsible propagandists at times for such a union in order to frighten the Czechoslovak Government into concessions. The economic conditions of Slovakia are unfavorable to its incorporation into Poland. While Poland is an agricultural country with a substantial industrial development, Slovakia is overwhelmingly agricultural in character. Commerce between Poland and Slovakia has never been of significance. Union of Poland and Slovakia, moreover, might serve to stifle the incipient industrial development of Slovakia.

II. *UNION WITH HUNGARY*

Union with Hungary is another possible alternative solution which the Magyars within Slovakia and Hungary have desired ever since the separation in 1918. It is extremely doubtful, however, that more than a very few Magyarone Slovaks have desired to return to Hungary since 1918, after the experience of several centuries of Magyar rule. Before 1918 economic relations between the Slovak region and the central areas of the unitary Hungarian kingdom were close; the possibility has been suggested more than once that more Slovaks would be prepared to accept some kind of federal arrangement with Hungary, under which Slovakia would form an economic unity with Hungary but would enjoy cultural autonomy. On the other hand, it may be pointed out that no responsible Slovak representatives, even those of the Slovak Populist Party, ever advocated reunion with Hungary; even under the "autonomous" and "independent" governments of Slovakia—despite the general orientation of the regime—Slovak troops have twice fought against Hungarian invasions.

III. *AN INDEPENDENT SLOVAKIA*

A third possible alternative envisages complete independence for Slovakia. Complete independence was never on the program of any of the Slovak parties, including the Slovak Populist Party, until it was proclaimed by the extreme elements of the Slovak Populist Party on March 14, 1939. It should be remembered, however, that at the time that "independence" was proclaimed, the state was placed under the "protection" of National Socialist Germany.

The experience of the Slovaks under the "independent" regime of Father Tiso and Dr. Tuka may not be conducive to further developments in that direction. Moreover, there is every evidence that complete independence is quite impracticable. It is extremely doubtful that an independent state would be either politically or economically viable.

IV. *REUNION OF SLOVAKIA AND BOHEMIA-MORAVIA IN A RESTORED CZECHOSLOVAKIA*

A final alternative is the reincorporation of Slovakia in a restored Czechoslovak Republic, under some kind of decentralized administrative and legislative regime.

While the Czechs and Slovaks had their difficulties under the Republic because of mistakes on the part of both these related Slavic peoples, and on account of the impossibility of developing a federal, state structure in the period between 1918 and 1938, the major difficulties appeared to be in process of solution by 1927, when an administrative reform was instituted. Under this reform Slovakia became one of four provinces—the others being Bohemia, Moravia-Silesia, and Ruthenia. Slovakia had a provincial president and vice-president, and an assembly, with a small executive committee. The provincial assembly or diet had authority over economic and administrative affairs, questions of public health, provincial social, educational and communications questions, and the imposition of taxes concerning these matters.

Today, there are four Slovaks in the Czechoslovak Government at London, which is studying various projects for decentralization within the restored Republic. In its first proclamation in 1939, the Czechoslovak National Committee declared: "In the spirit of Masaryk and Štefánik, in the spirit of the founders and the martyrs of our nation, we enter the struggle united. Recognizing no difference of party, class or any other kind, we are determined to fight to the end and to assure a free, democratic Czechoslovak Republic, inspired by the spirit of justice for all its nationalities. We wish to have a republic socially just, founded on equal rights and equal duties for all its citizens. As regards the new organization of the State, the relationship of free Czechs to free Slovaks, the majority of free Czechs and the majority of free Slovaks will decide in democratic form and brotherly understanding, inspired by the principles of equality in rights and duties."

The United States of America, Great Britain and France have never recognized the destruction of Czechoslovakia or the independence of Slovakia. The Soviet Union, however, did recognize the independent State of Slovakia. All the members of the United Nations, including the United States, Great Britain, the Soviet Union and China, have recognized the existence of the Czechoslovak Government in London and are committed to the restoration of Czechoslovakia as a state.

Despite the participation of Slovaks in the Czechoslovak Governmen-t-in-exile, there is some opposition among Slovaks living abroad to the program of the Government. This opposition centers around the personalities of Dr. Milan Hodža, former Prime Minister, and Dr. Štefan Osuský, former Czechoslovak Minister to France. Hodža seems to favor a definite statement from the Government favoring autonomy for Slovakia within a restored Republic of Czechoslovakia. President Beneš and the Government refuse to commit themselves to any specific program on the ground that the internal constitutional structure of the Republic must be decided by the people at home after the war. Some Slovaks fear, however, that the electorate might then be manipulated in favor of a centralist form of Government, even though autonomy might be preferred by a majority in Slovakia.

PS:HNHoward:hmv

Box 65

****

§ Document 11 §

Secret

T Document 388
October 16, 1943

THE PROBLEM OF SUBCARPATHIAN RUTHENIA: ALTERNATIVE SOLUTIONS

I. *REUNION OF SUBCARPATHIAN RUTHENIA WITH CZECHO-SLOVAKIA*

In view of the record of progressive achievement of Subcarpathian Ruthenia within Czechoslovakia, reunion with Czechoslovakia may will be the best possible solution of the problem of Subcarpathian Ruthenia. The reasons for and the conditions of such restoration are similar to those advanced in 1919. Simple restoration, however, might not solve the problem, since it might leave open the door for new revisionism on the part of Hungary, or possibly on the part of the Soviet Union. Granted the development of a genuine Ukrainian national movement, it is possible to conceive of still another angle of this problem.

Restoration has been demanded by the Czechoslovak Government-in-exile in London, which refuses to recognize either the Munich Settlement, the Vienna Award or the Magyar conquest of Ruthenia. The Soviet Union, in the summer of 1942, approved restoration of the Pre-Munich frontiers of Czechoslovakia, and the Czechoslovak Government has interpreted this position to include the restoration of Subcarpathian Ruthenia to Czechoslovakia. The British and American governments did not recognize the Hungarian conquest of Ruthenia, though they are not committed to the restoration of any specific frontiers.

II. *RESTORATION OF SUB-CARPATHIAN RUTHENIA TO CZECHOSLOVAKIA WITH MINOR FRONTIER RECTIFICATIONS IN FAVOR OF HUNGARY*

Restoration of Subcarpathian Ruthenia to Czechoslovakia might be effected with minor frontier rectifications in favor of Hungary particularly in the southwestern portion of Ruthenia. Retention by Hungary, for example, of the line of November 1938, would involve cession to Hungary of about 612 square miles of territory, and a total population of about 172,000 (1930), of whom approximately 36,700 (21 percent) were Ruthenians, 86,600 (50 percent) were Magyars, 25,800 (15 percent) Jews, 17,200 (10 percent) were Czechoslovaks, and 4,900 (2,8 percent) were Germans. The heaviest concentration of Magyars is in the district of Berehovo (Bereg), with 45,277 Magyars out of a total population of 63,143 (1930). The primary difficulty of even the smallest frontier rectification, however, is that it would threaten communications between Užhorod, Mukačevo, and Chust, within Subcarpathian Ruthenia, and would break communications between Subcarpathian Ruthenia and the rest of Czechoslovakia. It would also take from Subcarpathian Ruthenia a portion of its rich land in the valley of the Tisza.

III. *RETENTION OF SUBCARPATHIAN RUTHENIA BY HUNGARY*

Retention of Subcarpathian Ruthenia by Hungary involves the inclusion of more than 430,000 Ruthenians and about 35,000 Czechs and Slovaks in Hungary, in order to "liberate" 115,000 Magyars. Aside from the principle of nationality involved in uniting these Magyars to Hungary, the only genuine argument in support of this solution is the economic one of uniting the Ruthenian mountain and plain in any economic "unity" with the Hungarian plain. There is, however, no evidence at present of any desire for this solution on the part of any important number of Ruthenians. There is also no evidence that the Magyars would permit a free development of the Ruthenian nationality, such as there was in the Czechoslovak Republic. Retention of Ruthenia by Hungary would cut Czechoslovak railway communications to the east, and out off possible communications with the Soviet Union and with Rumania. On the other hand, if Poland regains Eastern Galicia, retention of Subcarpathian Ruthenia by Hungary would make Poland and Hungary neighbors.

IV. *ASSIGNMENT OF SUBCARPATHIAN RUTHENIA TO THE SOVIET UNION*

Subcarpathian Ruthenia might be incorporated in the Union of Soviet Socialist Republics, as part of the Ukrainian S.S.R. (area: 170,978 square miles; population; 40,000,000), with whose people the Ruthenians are related. Union within the U.S.S.R. might take place especially if the Soviet Union retains Northern Bukovina and the portions of Poland occupied in 1939.

This solution would bring the Soviet Union across the Carpathian Mountains into the heart of Central Europe, vastly increasing its influence in the entire Danubian Basin. The Soviet Union, however, has apparently committed itself to the restoration of Subcarpathian Ruthenia to Czechoslovakia, though this does not preclude the possibility of a different policy in the future, in view of the national attraction of the Ruthenians toward union with the Ukrainians.

V. *UNION OF SUBCARPATHIAN RUTHENIA WITH AN INDEPENDENT UKRAINIAN STATE*

Another possibility for Subcarpathian Ruthenia lies in its union with an independent Ukrainian state which would include the present Soviet

Ukraine, Northern Bukovina, Eastern Galicia, Volhynia, and Subcarpathian Ruthenia. The population of this state would be about 47,000,000. A prerequisite to the achievement of this unlikely solution would be the break-up of the Soviet Union.

VI. *UNION WITH A SMALL WEST UKRAINIAN STATE*

Creation of a small West Ukrainian State also represents a possible alternative. This solution would involve the former Austro-Hungarian territories of Eastern Galicia, Northern Bukovina and Subcarpathian Ruthenia. The population is mostly Uniate in religious affiliation, and it has had the experience of living together under the former Dual Monarchy. There is less cultural difference among them than between Ruthenia and the Soviet Ukraine. The area of such a state would be about 29,190 square miles and the population about 6,000,000. The only substantial minorities are Poles and Magyars. It is doubtful, however, that such a state would be strategically, politically or economically viable.

VII. *UNION OF SUBCARPATHIAN RUTHENIA WITH POLAND*

Another possibility lies in the union of Subcarpathian Ruthenia with Poland which some Polish circles have desired. This would mean the union of the 450,000 Ruthenians of Subcarpathian Ruthenia with the 5,000,000 Ruthenians of Eastern Galicia and Volhynia in Poland. The Polish record with respect to the Ruthenian populations of Poland in the period from 1918 to 1939 has been such as to render this solution unlikely of serious consideration. Such a solution, moreover, would involve serious difficulties between Poland and the Soviet Union.

VIII. *SUBCARPATHIAN RUTHENIA AS AN INDEPENDENT STATE*

A final possible solution lies in the establishment of Subcarpathian Ruthenia as an independent state. Such a state would be too weak, politically, strategically and economically, to constitute a genuinely viable community. This solution was rejected in 1919 because of its obvious impossibility. There has been little evidence since 1919, moreover, to indicate that the Ruthenians of Subcarpathian Ruthenia desire an independent state or consider it viable.

PS:HNHoward:mhp Box 65

Chapter III

Summaries and Recommendations

§ Document 1 §

Secret H Document 8
June 1, 1943

CZECHOSLOVAKIA:
HUNGARY

TERRITORIAL PROBLEMS: SLOVAK-HUNGARIAN BOUNDARY

I. *THE PROBLEM*

The problem is the determination of the boundary between Czechoslovakia and Hungary in the region where the latter borders on Slovakia. The problem arises from the conflict of Czechoslovak and Hungarian claims.

The boundary established by the Treaty of Trianon in 1920 was a special target of Hungarian revisionist agitation. By the Vienna Award of November 1938 and by the Slovak-Hungarian Agreement of April 1939, Hungary annexed an area of about 4,000 square miles, with a population (1930) of 1,000,000, of whom 288,903 were Czechoslovaks and 587,692 Magyars. The area borders the Danube River and is devoted to agriculture, forestry, mining and light industry.

The Czechoslovak Government-in-exile desires the return of this territory and has received commitments from the Soviet Government and from the French National Committee (Fighting France) for integral restoration of the pre-Munich frontier. While the American and British Governments do not recognize the legal validity of Hungary's annexation of this territory, they have given no commitments as to specific postwar boundaries.

II. *ALTERNATIVE SOLUTIONS*

(Indicated on Maps 1 and 2, Czechoslovak Series.)

A. *Cession to Hungary of Six Slovak Districts along the Southwestern Frontier (Grosse Schuett and Little Hungarian Plain)*

This solution was preferred by the Territorial Subcommittee. The solution would assign to Hungary six southwestern districts in the Grosse Schuett region and part of the Little Hungarian Plain (Šamorín, Dunajská Streda, Komárno, Stará Ďala, Parkan and Zeliezovce). These districts have an area of about 1,400 square miles and a population of 219,000 Magyars and 40,000 Slovaks. The territory is predominantly agricultural. Its loss would not injure Czechoslovakia's system of railway communications or materially affect its defenses, but it would deprive Czechoslovakia of the river port of Komárno, a center of transshipment of timber.

The American Delegation at the Paris Peace Conference in 1919-20 proposed that the *Grosse Schuett* region be assigned to Hungary.

1. *Discussion of the Territorial Subcommittee*

In view of the apparent willingness of unofficial Czechoslovak circles to discuss limited adjustment of the Slovak-Hungarian frontier, it was suggested that the United States encourage, as part of a general settlement of Czechoslovak-Hungarian difficulties, direct negotiations for a frontier adjustment. If appealed to by the parties directly concerned, the United States might express itself in favor of the transfer of the six districts to Hungary. In view of the uncertainty concerning the future status and tendencies of Hungary, the Territorial Subcommittee did not favor suggesting wider territorial concessions to Hungary.

B. *Restoration of the 1937 Slovak-Hungarian Boundary*

Restoration of the 1937 Slovak-Hungarian boundary would leave about 500,000 Magyars within the Czechoslovak Republic. Czechoslovakia would recover a largely population, together with small mining, forest and industrial areas. Czechoslovakia would also retain a through east-west railway in southern Slovakia. Restoration of the 1937 boundary would give to Czechoslovakia a greater sense of security than would Alternative A or C. Restoration would satisfy the Czechoslovak demand for full legal recognition of Czechoslovakia's territorial integrity. Retention of the 1937 frontiers, however, would again make Czechoslovak-Hungarian reconciliation difficult, if not impossible.

1. *Discussion of the Territorial Subcommittee*

In the discussion of the Territorial Subcommittee one member felt that only the most urgent ethnic and political considerations would justify transfer of any territory to Hungary, since Czechoslovakia had been a victim of German and Hungarian aggression and had pursued more enlightened social and cultural policies than Hungary.

C. *Transfer to Hungary of Ten Southern districts of Slovakia with Certain Adjoining Areas*

This solution would eliminate from Czechoslovakia as large a Hungarian population as is possible without serious economic and strategic injury to Czechoslovakia, and would leave roughly equal minorities on each side of the frontier. To the 1400 square miles involved in Solution A, this proposal would add four additional districts (Feledince, Tornal'a, Moldava nad Bodvou, Král'ovský Chlmec), together with parts of six adjoining districts (Galanta, Nové Zámky, Levice, Rožňava, Šal'á, Vráble). This additional strip of territory contains approximately 1340 square miles. The total area to be transferred to Hungary would amount to about 2740 square miles, with a population of about 310,000 Magyars and 59,000 Slovaks (1930). The remaining minorities, being about equal in number, might then be exchanged, thereby eliminating the ethnic basis for any further irredentism. Czechoslovakia would be fairly well equipped with railways on the southern frontier. The territories acquired by Hungary would have excellent communications with Budapest. Czechoslovakia would retain most of the lumber and minerals of the zone in dispute and part of the rich farm land, while Hungary would hold the richest grain and livestock area. Neither Czechoslovakia nor Hungary would have any substantial advantage of terrain for military operations.

1. *Discussion of the Territorial Subcommittee*

The Territorial Subcommittee, in suggesting direct negotiations between Czechoslovakia and Hungary, gave no detailed consideration to this solution.

D. *Retention of the 1930 Slovak-Hungarian Frontier*

If the existing frontier, established in 1939, is retained, approximately 288,000 Slovaks and a number of districts of Slovak majority would remain in Hungary. Hungary would keep a mining, forest, and agricultural region, whose products would add to its exportable surplus of cereals and animal products. The principal east-west railway of Czechoslovakia in southern Slovakia would be cut. Retention of the present frontier might increase the Hungarian influence in Slovakia to the detriment of Czech-Slovak cooperation.

1. *Discussion of the Territorial Subcommittee*

There was no disposition on the part of the Territorial Subcommittee to favor the retention of the 1939 boundary.

PS:HNHoward:MT Box 152

****

§ Document 2 §

Secret H Document 26
August 6, 1943

HUNGARY:
YUGOSLAVIA

TERRITORIAL PROBLEMS: YUGOSLAV-HUNGARIAN FRONTIER

I. *THE PROBLEM*

The problem is the determination of the boundary between Yugoslavia and Hungary.

The problem arises from the claim of the Yugoslavia government for the restoration of the pre-war boundary and from the Hungarian claim for the retention of the territory acquired in 1941 and for acquisition of the Yugoslav Banat.

The territories in dispute, ceded to Yugoslavia by Hungary in the Treaty of Trianon (1920), are Prekomurje (363 sq. mi.), Medjumurje (307 sq. mi.), and the Baranja, the Bačka and the Banat (7,421 sq. mi.), with a total population of approximately 1.5 million. All these areas were occupied by Hungary in 1941 with the exception of the Banat, which came under German military administration.

In the two western provinces of Prekomurje and Medjumurje, with populations of 92,300 and 96,900 respectively in 1921, the Slavic-speaking inhabitants are in an overwhelming majority.

The complexity of the ethnic problem arises from the mixture of national groups in the Baranja, the Bačka and the Banat. The following table illustrates the proportions of the leading language groups in the three eastern provinces in 1921:

	Baranja	Bačka	Banat	Total
Yugoslavia	15,604	246,598	240,213	502,415
Magyars	16,638	260,998	98,471	376,107
Germans	16,253	173,796	126,530	316,579
Others	957	53,725	96,744	151,426
Total	**49,452**	**735,117**	**561,958**	**1,346,527**

Out of a total of 304 communes in these three territories, the Yugoslavs were in the majority in 100, the Germans in 74, the Magyars in 59, the Rumanians in 24 and the Slovaks in 11, while in 36 communes no language group was in a majority (1921). Of the 24 administrative districts in the three provinces, 6 were predominantly Yugoslav, 3 Magyar and 2 German, while in 13 no language group had a majority. This situation renders impossible the drawing of any clear ethnic line.

These regions, the richest grain-producing lands in Yugoslavia, are of greater economic value to it than to Hungary. Hungary's claim is primarily historical and only secondarily ethnic or economic in character.

II. *ALTERNATIVE SOLUTIONS*

(Yugoslav Series, Map 3)

A. *Restoration of the Disputed Areas to Yugoslavia*

This solution was preferred by the Territorial Subcommittee.

This solution would reestablish the Yugoslav-Hungarian frontier of 1940. The Yugoslav ethnic claim is more valid than the Hungarian, since the Yugoslavs have a clear numerical superiority over the Magyars in Prekomurje, Medjumurje and the Banat, and roughly equal their numbers in Baranja and Bačka.

The agricultural production in the disputed area has held an important place in the Yugoslav economy, providing a substantial surplus of foodstuffs for export and for supplying the cereal-deficient areas of the country. Its processing industries have also been of considerable importance to Yugoslavia.

1. *Discussion of the Territorial Subcommittee*

The Territorial Subcommittee believed that the claims of Yugoslavia were sufficiently strong to give it title to the entire disputed zone. It was agreed that the Yugoslav ethnic claim was decidedly stronger than that of Hungary, and that the region was more important to the former's economy. The fact was stressed that after a United Nations victory Yugoslavia will have a strong political claim to recover its pre-war frontier. The view was generally accepted that whatever possibilities of a compromise settlement may had been destroyed by Hungarian participation in the attack on Yugoslavia in 1941 and by subsequent Hungarian mistreatment of the Yugoslavs in the disputed areas.

B. *Cession of the Disputed Areas to Hungary*

The Magyar minority constitutes only 26 percent of the population of the disputed provinces. However, Magyars and Germans together have a strong numerical preponderance in the Baranja and the Bačka, and the claim has often been advanced that in a free plebiscite the Germans would vote for Hungarian rather than Yugoslav rule. From the economic point of view, these areas contain none of the minerals and industries which Hungary chiefly needs.

1. *Discussion of the Territorial Subcommittee*

It was the consensus of the subcommittee that the ethnic claims of Hungary in the disputed zone were not such as to warrant the cession to it of these areas. Little weight was given to the historical arguments advanced by Hungarian leaders. Hungary's violation of its Treaty of Friendship with Yugoslavia and subsequent adherence to the Axis were cited as further reasons for rejecting the Hungarian claims.

C. *A Compromise Line*

This solution has not been discussed by any of the subcommittee.

This solution would attempt to separate the two leading ethnic groups by a line which would leave under Hungarian sovereignty a number of Yugoslavs approximately equal to the number of Magyars remaining in Yugoslavia. In Prekomurje 25 communes on the eastern frontier, with a Magyar population of some 12,400 and a Yugoslav population of only 2,4550, might be ceded to Hungary. Since this frontier is of no strategic importance, the cession of these communes would constitute no economic or military loss to Yugoslavia. Owing to the small number and dispersed character of the Magyar minority in Medjumurje, no cession is recommended in that province.

Apart from this alteration, the chief concern of a compromise line would be the separation of the Yugoslav and Magyar minorities in the three eastern provinces. In the Baranja Hungary would acquire the greater part of the district of Batina, with a population of some 20,000 including 8,000 Yugoslavs, 7,500 Magyars and 4,600 Germans. In the Bačka, the districts of Senta and Topola and the towns of Subotica, Stara Kanjiža and Senta, and part of the district of Sombor would be transferred to Hungary. This part of the Bačka has a population (1921) of some 307,000, including 172,000 Magyars, 90,000 Yugoslavs and 42,000 Germans. This line would leave in Yugoslavia the town of Sombor, with the Sombor-Stari Bečej railroad and the Danube-Tisza canal system. In the Banat Hungary would receive the districts of Nova Kanjiža and Velika Kikinda and part of the district, but not the town, of Jaša Tomić. Thus in the Banat Hungary would acquire a population of some 108,000, including 49,700 Yugoslavs, 35,900 Magyars and 19,300 Germans. In the three eastern provinces as a whole, approximately one-third of the area and one-third of the population (435,000 inhabitants out of a total of 1,346,500), would be ceded to Hungary by the compromise line. Some 148,000 Yugoslavs would be left on the Hungarian side, and some 160,000 Magyars on the Yugoslav side, of the frontier. The solution of the nationality problem could then be approached either by an exchange of populations or by a reciprocal guarantee of minority rights.

PS:CEBlack:JRB Box 152

§ Document 3 §

Secret

H Document 43
August 25, 1943

HUNGARY:
RUMANIA

TERRITORIAL PROBLEMS: TRANSYLVANIA

I. *THE PROBLEM*

The problem is the disposition of the territory acquired by Rumania from Hungary in 1920 and now in dispute between those two states.

The problem arises because both Hungary and Rumania presumably will be occupied by United Nations forces upon the defeat of the Axis armies in that area. The United Nations will then face the problem of administering the disputed area and ultimately of making a decision as to its final disposition.

In 1940 Germany and Italy drew the present line of partition through Transylvania, forcing Rumania to cede to Hungary the northern sector. Each state has designs on the part now held by the other, and the removal of German domination over both will bring that conflict into the open.

The territory in question, made up of historic Transylvania, the Rumanian Banat, and the Crisana and Maramureş areas, covers 39,686 square miles and has a population of 5,548,000 (1930). Rumanians make up 58 percent of the total, Hungarians 25 percent, and Germans 10 percent. The Rumanians are found throughout the area; the Hungarians are strongest along the western boundary and in the three Szekler counties of southeastern Transylvania; the Germans are settled chiefly in the Banat and in southern Transylvania. The disputed territory has considerable forest and mineral resources; it complements, equally, the agricultural plains of Hungary and those of Old Rumania. The industries of southern Transylvania and the Banat give Rumania a somewhat more balanced agrarian-industrial economy; without them it would be almost wholly agrarian. The economy of Hungary, with or without the disputed area or any part of it, would retain a fairly even balance between agriculture and industry.

II. *ALTERNATIVE SOLUTIONS*

A. *Action to be Taken when the Area is Occupied by the Military Forces of the United Nations*

1. *Maintenance of the Present (1940) Line as an Administrative Boundary during the Period of Occupation, Pending the Final Disposition of the Territory*

Under this solution local Hungarian and Rumanian officials would be utilized by the Allied military government in the respective areas in which they are now functioning. This would be the simplest and probably the most satisfactory solution from the point of view of the occupying authorities. Since no initial boundary change would be involved, this solution would seem least likely to prejudice the ultimate settlement.

2. *Restoration of the Line of 1939 as an Administrative Boundary during the Period of Occupation, Pending the Final Disposition of the Territory*

This solution would require a complete shift from Hungarian to Rumanian administrative personnel in the area now held by Hungary, a change which would complicate and perhaps obstruct the operations of the occupying military authorities. The chances of the emergence of a democratic regime in Hungary favorably disposed towards the United Nations and willing to participate in a negotiated settlement with Rumania would be lessened by the adoption of this solution. In Rumania the restoration of the pre-war boundary, even though for temporary administrative purposes, would be regarded as the restitution of national territory taken by Hungary in 1940. It would increase the difficulties of securing Rumania's acceptance, at some later date, of a final settlement less favorable than the pre-1940 boundary.

Discussion of the Territorial Subcommittee

The Territorial Subcommittee recommended that at the time of the military occupation of Rumania and Hungary by United Nations forces, the boundary of 1939 be restored pro-tempore. West of that line local Hungarian administration would be maintained; east of it local Rumanian administration would be utilized. It was thought that an occupation period of several years, during which the Allied military government would make use of local officials, would give the United Nations an opportunity to take stock of the developing situation and of the possibilities for a final solution and to promote a negotiated settlement. The subcommittee felt that this solution would be in consonance with Point Two of the Atlantic Charter, according to which the signatories "desire to see no territorial changes that do not accord with the freely expressed wishes of the peoples concerned". It was considered that the establishment of the temporary line might influence the ultimate territorial settlement.

Discussion of the Political Subcommittee

In the Political Subcommittee objection was raised to the recommendation of the Territorial Subcommittee on the ground that the fixing of an administrative boundary on the frontier of 1939 during the period of occupation would pre-judge the final settlement.

3. *Immediate Application of a Definitive Boundary Solution Previously Agreed upon by the United Nations*

This solution would have the advantage of avoiding a long period of uncertainty and agitation. Both disputants are Axis states and the United Nations are bound by no commitments to them. This solution makes no provision, however, for a consultation of the population or for new factors which may arise during or after the present war.

Discussion of the Political Subcommittee

Some members of the subcommittee were not in favor of leaving the boundary problem unsettled during a long period of military occupation. They advocated an agreement among the principal United Nations on the main points of the final settlement before the armistice; those decisions could then be applied immediately upon occupation of the area.

4. *Preparation for Holding a Plebiscite or for Establishing Other Machinery for Consulting the Wishes of the Population*

This solution would provide some basis for a rapid settlement which could be justified on the grounds of self-determination. However, it might be difficult to conduct a plebiscite in the confused conditions prevailing at the close of hostilities in this area. In view of the complex ethnic distribution, the results of a plebiscite might be of little assistance in reaching a clearly defined territorial settlement.

Discussion of the Political Subcommittee

Several members stressed the desirability of consulting the wishes of the population if speedy and practical machinery for such consultation could be set up.

B. *Final Solutions*

1. *Rectification of the Boundary of 1939 in Hungary's Favor to Secure a More Accurate Ethnic Division between Hungarians and Rumanians*

The boundary of 1939, from the vicinity of Arad northwards to the border of Czechoslovakia, could be moved from ten to twenty miles to the east in the Arad area, in the vicinity of Szalonta, and in a continuous strip from Nagyvárad (Oradea Mare) to a point north of Szatmár (Satu Mare). The irregular strip which would be ceded to Hungary, approximately 3,475 square miles in area, had a population, in 1930, of some 298,000 Hungarians, 167,000 Rumanians, and 50,000 Jews. Since over one million Hungarians would remain in Rumania, this solution would not represent a genuine ethnic solution.

The three cities of Arad, Nagyvárad and Szatmár, which would be returned to Hungary, were assigned to Rumania in 1919 largely because the railway connecting them was considered to be of vital economic and strategic importance to Rumania. An ethnic line would cut this railway in several places between Arad and Nagyvárad.

Discussion of the Territorial Subcommittee

The Territorial Subcommittee did not agree on any recommendation for the ultimate disposition of the disputed territory. Some members were of the opinion that a residue of injustice had been left by the settlement of 1919-1920. It was thought that, even though Hungary's conduct since that time gave that country no claim to leniency, the boundary of 1939 might be modified in Hungary's favor along an ethnic line, if it should be apparent that such modifications would contribute to peace and stability.

2. *Cession to Hungary of a Broader Strip of Territory East of the Boundary of 1939, including the Greater Part of the Counties of Szilágy (Sălaj) and Szatmár (Satu Mare)*

This solution represents an attempt to make a generous revision of the boundary of 1939 in favor of Hungary in the northwestern area, where Hungarians and Rumanians are about equal in numbers. The Szekler districts which are over 85 percent Hungarian in population, would be returned to Rumania. The other Hungarians left in Rumania would be slightly more numerous than the Rumanians remaining under Hungarian jurisdiction. The boundary envisaged by this solution would run to the east of the cities of Arad, Nagyvárad and Szatmár, leaving the railway connecting them entirely within Hungarian territory. It would give to Hungary an area of approximately 5,600 square miles, with about 450,000 Rumanians, 390,000 Hungarians, 138,000 Germans, and 60,000 Jews. Rumania would have 34,000 square miles of the disputed territory, with a population of 2,768,000 Rumanians, 963,000 Hungarians, and 406,000 Germans. Any further enlargement of the area, ceded to Hungary, short of extending it all the way to the Szekler districts, would increase greatly the number of Rumanians, as compared to Hungarians, left in the Hungarian share of the disputed area.

This solution might be combined with an exchange of populations involving the nearly 500,000 Rumanians left in Hungary and the approximately 600,000 Hungarians remaining in Rumanian Transylvania (not including the Szeklers) and with the establishment of a régime of territorial autonomy for the approximately 400,000 Szeklers.

Discussion of the Territorial Subcommittee

This solution was suggested by the chairman as suitable for further discussion pending research. The subcommittee felt that transfers of population should be held to a minimum. The transfer of the Szeklers to Hungary proper or to western Transylvania was considered impracticable. It was thought that the Szeklers, if left within Rumania, should have some form of administrative and cultural autonomy.

3. *Restoration of the Boundary of 1939*

This solution represents a return to a boundary which was changed by fiat of the Axis Powers and was accepted under duress by Rumania, without consultation of the wishes of the population transferred to Hungary. That boundary, however, represented nearly the maximum Rumanian claims and has been considered unjust even by moderate and conciliatory Hungarian opinion. This solution would resurrect the unsolved problem of the large Hungarian minority of one and one-half millions in Rumania.

Discussion of the Territorial Subcommittee

The subcommittee considered the boundary of 1939 unsatisfactory, since it had extended Rumanian territory in the west to include some purely Hungarian-speaking districts. It was agreed, however, that at least a temporary restoration of that boundary should be effected, as a basis of negotiations for a final settlement.

4. *Maintenance of the Present Boundary Established by the Axis Powers in 1940*

This solution includes the solidly Hungarian-speaking Szekler region within Hungary, but this is made possible only by the inclusion of a wide stretch of intervening territory inhabited chiefly by Rumanians. Rumanian irredentism directed against this solution would be persistent. The northern part of Transylvania ceded to Hungary in 1940 is approximately 16,000 square miles in area and has about 909,000 Hungarian and 1,149,000 Rumanian inhabitants. In the part of Transylvania left to Rumania, 23,686 square miles in area, there are approximately 445,000 Hungarians and 2,059,000 Rumanians. This solution would have economic disadvantages unless provision were made for substantial freedom of trade and transit between Hungary and Rumania.

Discussion of the Territorial Subcommittee

Although it was admitted that the present boundary had some validity as a compromise line, no member of the Territorial Subcommittee favored its retention. It was considered an artificial solution which Germany had imposed partly with a view to perpetuating Rumanian-Hungarian antagonism.

5. *Cession of all Transylvania to Hungary*

This solution, the maximum satisfaction of Hungarian claims, would place over three million Rumanians under Hungarian sovereignty, reviving in more acute form the minority problem of the pre-1918 period. Possession of Transylvania's forest and mineral resources would give definite economic advantages to Hungary. Transylvania itself might derive some benefits from this partial re-constitution of the economic unity of pre-1918 Hungary, but its industrial and agricultural products would compete on unfavorable terms with those of Hungary proper.

Discussion of the Territorial Subcommittee

No member of the Territorial Subcommittee specifically favored this solution. Two members suggested that, in view of the uncertain future of Rumania and the apparent impossibility of reaching any solution of the Transylvanian problem by attempting to disentangle the nationalities, the re-constitution of a large political and economic unit including both Transylvania and Hungary might be envisaged as a possible basis of settlement.

6. *Creation of an Autonomous or Independent Transylvania within a Federation or Union of East European or Danubian States*

This solution represents an attempt to avoid the irredentist movements which almost certainly will appear if Transylvania is assigned either to Hungary or to Rumania or is partitioned between them. There is an historic basis for autonomy in the special status and privileges of self-government which certain elements in Transylvania enjoyed during long periods of its history, but there has been little evidence in recent years that either the Rumanians or the Hungarians in the province would regard autonomy as a final or even as a workable solution. If questions of security and of basic economic policy remained in the hands of federal or international bodies, objections to the creation of an autonomous Transylvania, on grounds of its small area and population and its uncertain status in international law, might be disregarded.

Discussion of the Territorial Subcommittee

Some members of the Territorial Subcommittee regarded the creation of an autonomous Transylvania with equal rights for all citizens as the least unsatisfactory of the alternative solutions. It was believed that this solution would be possible only if an Eastern European or Danubian federation, of which it would be a member, was a going concern. The argument was advanced that an autonomous Transylvania would serve merely as a field of conflict between Hungarians and Rumanians both inside and outside the province. It was agreed that a strong pressure from outside, from a regional or world authority or from the interested great powers, would be needed to maintain respect for this settlement.

7. *Creation of an Autonomous Transylvania Standing in a Special Relationship to Hungary and Rumania*

If there were no Danubian or Eastern European federation, the terms of Transylvania's autonomy might be defined by agreement between Hungary and Rumania, each recognizing the economic and cultural interests of the other in the autonomous province. Probably there would need to be a common security and foreign policy for all three territorial units. Transylvania would be expected to work out its own local problems without interference from the governments of Hungary and Rumania. The practical prospects of such a solution would depend largely on whether Russian pressures on both Hungary and Rumania had the result of forcing them into agreement on Transylvania.

Discussion of the Territorial Subcommittee

The member of the Territorial Subcommittee suggesting this solution pointed out that it would obviate the necessity of segregating different ethnic elements and that Transylvania might form a bridge between Hungary and Rumania, leading toward a federation of the lower Danube. It was not made clear whether Transylvania should have the attributes of sovereignty or, while autonomous in relation to Hungary and Rumania, would act jointly with them in matters of foreign and military policy. This solution was considered possible only if applied also to other areas of mixed population in eastern Europe, thus forming a number of small federations.

PS:JCC Campbell:MHP Box 153

****

§ Document 4 §

Secret
Preliminary

H Document 86
November 8, 1943

AUSTRIA:
HUNGARY

TERRITORIAL PROBLEMS: THE BURGENLAND

I. *THE PROBLEM*

The problem is the disposition of that part of the Burgenland ("German West Hungary") which was ceded to Austria through the decision of the Paris Peace Conference and through the Protocol of Venice in 1921.*

The problem arises from Hungary's long-standing desire for the restoration of all territory of historic Hungary, of which the Burgenland was a part, and from the almost certain desire of Austria, if restored to independence, to retain it. Although no question has yet arisen with respect to the Burgenland the issue may develop after the war.

The Burgenland is a narrow strip of territory, 1,532 square miles in area, running the entire length of the Austro-Hungarian frontier from

* The Conference of Versailles gave 4,312 sq.km of theretofore Hungarian land to Austria. At the October 11-13, 1921 conference in Venice, however, due to armed Hungarian resistance and to Italian pressure, Austria agreed that a referendum be held to decide the fate of the smaller part of the territory in dispute (Sopron, and 8 villages of the Sopron area).

the Czechoslovak boundary in the north to the Yugoslav frontier in the south and is made up of two distinct parts, almost entirely separated by a salient containing the city of Sopron (Ödenburg) which was left to Hungary by the Venice Protocol (1921). For several centuries in dispute between the Habsburgs and Hungary, the Burgenland since 1647 had been a part of Hungary, whose possession of it was confirmed by the Compromise of 1867. The entire Burgenland was claimed on ethnic grounds by the Austrian Republic in 1918 and assigned to it by the Peace Conference in 1919. After a plebiscite held in the city of Sopron and its vicinity in 1921, that area was allowed to remain in Hungary.

Ethnographically the region has been German for some time and the line of demarcation between Germans and Magyars had remained unchanged for centuries. The rural population has remained consistently German. The towns were German until well past the middle of the nineteenth century but then began to acquire a Hungarian character owing largely to the success of the minority was greatly reduced by the transfer of Sopron to Hungary after the plebiscite of December 1921, in which the total vote was 65 percent for Hungary and 35 percent for Austria. In the city of Sopron the vote went heavily in favor of Hungary and in the surrounding rural communes slightly in favor of Austria. According to the 1934 Austrian census the population was 299,447, of whom 241,326 were Germans (80 percent), 40,500 were Croats (14 percent) and 10,442 were Magyars (4 percent). Only four communities in the Burgenland had a Magyar majority but forty-four had a Croat majority. These communities, most of them in the northern and central districts, are so scattered that no ethnic ground can be found for transferring any part of the Burgenland to Yugoslavia. These Croats provided the ethnic basis for a "Slavic corridor" between Czechoslovakia and Yugoslavia, proposed but not seriously considered in 1919. The Croat inhabitants might be given the opportunity to opt for Yugoslav citizenship and for emigration to Yugoslavia.

The economic interests of the region lie with Austria rather than with Hungary. Although communications are easier with Hungary, the natural markets for the food products produced in the Burgenland are situated in Austrian territory, hence means of transportation are essential to its economic welfare. The cession of Sopron to Hungary severed the arterial communications of the region and further intensified the difficulties of transportation. A transportation agreement (1922) setting up a system of privileged traffic partially compensated for the loss of the Sopron junction. Although Austria constructed one secondary railway connecting the Central Burgenland with Vienna and built a better system of roads, good transverse rail communications, especially in the Central and Southern Burgenland, are still lacking.

II. *ALTERNATIVE SOLUTIONS*

A. *Retention of the Boundary of 1921.*

The area is inhabited by a predominantly German population which benefited economically by inclusion within Austria. The economic interests of the Burgenland would profit from the establishment of a customs union between Austria and Hungary, which would enable its timber to move freely to Hungary and its agricultural products to Styria and to the Wiener Neustadt region of Austria. The situation of Sopron might readily be improved if a customs union were set up, as most of the traffic passing through that city before 1918 was destined for Austria.

B. *Retrocession of the Burgenland to Hungary*

This solution can be justified on historical but not upon economic or ethnic grounds. Hungary has not pushed its claim to the Burgenland rigorously. its loss has not been of great economic importance, although Hungary still needs timber which the Central Burgenland formerly supplied and could easily transport it to central Hungary.

PS: M.E. Bradshaw:DFN

Box 153

****

§ Document 5 §

Secret
Preliminary

H Document 122
January 21, 1944

CZECHOSLOVAKIA:
HUNGARY

TERRITORIAL PROBLEMS: THE FRONTIER BETWEEN HUNGARY AND SUBCARPATHIAN RUTHENIA

I. *THE PROBLEM*

The problem is the determination of the frontier between Subcarpathian Ruthenia and Hungary.

Although the primary issue is the disposition of Subcarpathian Ruthenia as a whole, the problem of the frontier as such may arise if an attempt is made to reach a compromise between the Hungarian demand for a just ethnic frontier and the Czechoslovak claims for restoration of the 1937 frontiers. With an area of about 4,886 square miles, Subcarpathian Ruthenia includes parts of the Hungarian counties of Ung (Užhorod), Bereg (Berehovo), Ugocsa (Sevluš) and Máramaros.

Subcarpathian Ruthenia became a part of Czechoslovakia in 1919, after having been a part of Hungary since the eleventh century. Hungary annexed a portion of southwestern Subcarpathian Ruthenia in November 1938, as a result of the Vienna Award, and occupied the rest of the country in March 1939. Czechoslovakia demands the integral restoration of all former Czechoslovak territories, including Subcarpathian Ruthenia. While Great Britain and the United States do not recognize the legal validity of Hungary's annexations, neither is committed to specific boundary restoration. Both the Soviet Union and the French Committee of National Liberation have announced their recognition of Czechoslovakia's pre-Munich frontiers, including those of Subcarpathian Ruthenia, and the former is now allied with the Czechoslovak Republic for post-war collaboration.

II. *ALTERNATIVE SOLUTIONS*

A. *Restoration of the Pre-Munich Frontiers*

This solution would mean the restoration of Subcarpathian Ruthenia as a whole to Czechoslovakia. It would give Czechoslovakia common frontiers with Rumania and the Soviet Union, if the latter regains Eastern Galicia and the former regains Transylvania. Restoration of the pre-Munich frontiers would leave the farm lands of the upper Tisza River valley within Subcarpathian Ruthenia and preserve the unity of the railway system of the country. This solution might be the most beneficial to the Ruthenian population, since the Ruthenians made considerable progress, especially in the political and cultural fields, when the province was a part of Czechoslovakia. Restoration of the pre-Munich frontiers would be in agreement with the principle of minimum boundary change, and with that of non-recognition of territorial changes achieved by the threat or use of force. It would also be in accord with the American position at the Paris Peace Conference in 1919.

According to the Czechoslovak census of 1930, restoration of Subcarpathian Ruthenia to Czechoslovakia would place approximately 115,800 Magyars (16 percent) under Czechoslovak rule, the total population being 725,350, of whom about 450,900 (62 percent) are Ruthenian. The Hungarian census of 1910, however, listed about 338,500 Ruthenians (54 percent) and 176,500 (28 percent) Magyars, out of a total population of approximately 625,900. Although it is not a rich region, restoration of Subcarpathian Ruthenia to Czechoslovakia would involve a loss to Hungary of some timber and farm land, as well as a source of farm labor. Hungarians have also contended that possession of the Upper Tisza River is necessary for purposes of flood control and irrigation in the Central Hungarian Plain (Alföld).

B. *Cession of Territory Acquired by Hungary through the Vienna Award (1938)*

This solution would assign to Hungary, according to Czechoslovak estimates, about 612 square miles of territory in the southwestern part of Subcarpathian Ruthenia, in the districts of Užhorod (Ung), Mukačevo (Munkács), Berehovo (Bereg), and Sevluš (Ugocsa). This territory had a population, according to the Czechoslovak census of 1930, of approximately 172,000 of whom about 86,600 (50 percent) were Magyars, 37,700 (21 percent) were Ruthenians, 25,800 (15 percent) were Jews, 17,200 (10 percent) were Czechoslovaks, and 4,900 (2.8 percent) were Germans.

According to Hungarian estimates, however, the Vienna Award involved an area of about 731 square miles, with a total population of approximately 207,000. The Hungarian estimates were not broken down as to nationality, although they indicated that about 178,100 (86 percent) used Hungarian as their maternal language or had a "knowledge of Hungarian," while only 19,000 (9.2 percent) were listed as Ruthenian-speaking elements. In addition there were 3,700 Germans and 2,260 Slovaks.

If this solution were adopted, it would leave within Subcarpathian Ruthenia, according to Czechoslovak estimates, about 26,000 Magyars, or according to Hungarian calculations, about 59,000. While it would assign to Hungary valuable farm lands and enable that country to control the waters of the Upper Tisza River, it would deprive Subcarpathian Ruthenia of its most valuable lowlands. It would also take from Subcarpathian Ruthenia the important cities of Užhorod (Ungvár), Mukačevo (Munkács), and Berehovo (Beregszász). Moreover, Czechoslovak communications would be severed in Subcarpathian Ruthenia along the principal east-west railway line from Čop to Chust near Fancikovo, and along the north-south lines from Čop to Užhorod and Uzok on the Polish frontier, from Batovo to Lawoczne, also on the Polish border, and between Berehovo and Kuánice. Since this solution would deprive Subcarpathian Ruthenia of its most valuable lowlands and place its most important market towns and railway connections in foreign hands, it is probable that Subcarpathian Ruthenia would cease to be viable as a part of Czechoslovakia.

C. *A Compromise Solution Based Primarily on Ethnic Considerations According to the Hungarian Census of 1910*

This solution would assign to Hungary a small portion of the district of Užhorod, practically all of Berehovo, and a small part of Sevluš. The total area would be about 535 square miles. It would involve the cession to Hungary of the cities of Beregszász (Berehovo) and Nagyszőllős (Sevluš) but not Užhorod or Mukačevo. This territory, like that involved in the Vienna Award, is in the southwestern part of Subcarpathian Ruthenia, in the upper Tisza River valley. According to the Hungarian census of 1910, this solution would involve a total population of about 89,200, of whom approximately 78,400 (87.6 percent) were Magyar-speaking, and about 9,150 (10.2 percent) Ruthenians. Estimates based on the Czechoslovak census of 1930, which are somewhat more generous to the Ruthenians partly because they include territory extending beyond the ethnic line, gave a total of about 90,350 for the area, of whom about 52,800 were Magyars (58.58 percent), 29,900 (33.11 percent) Ruthenians, 7,700 (8 percent) Jews, 4,300 (4.7 percent) Czechoslovaks, and 2,200 (2.4 percent) Germans. It is possible that the Hungarian figures are substantially accurate, if the necessary deductions of Jews from the Magyar total are made, since they are broken down as to communes, and that specific Czechoslovak figures for communes in the area would show a Magyar population of about seventy-five percent.

This solution would have the distinct advantage of removing from Subcarpathian Ruthenia the largest single block of Magyar districts. Nevertheless, if the Hungarian census is taken as the basis, about 98,100 Magyars would remain in Subcarpathian Ruthenia; if the Czechoslovak census is taken as the basis, about 63,000 Magyars would remain in Subcarpathian Ruthenia. This solution, however, offers the nearest approach to ethnic justice, and might lay a basis for an exchange of minority populations.

Economically, this solution would have substantially the same effect on Subcarpathian Ruthenia as cession of the territory involved in the Vienna Award, although it would not involve the cities of Užhorod and Mukačevo. It would deprive Subcarpathian Ruthenia of the rich farmlands of the upper Tisza River Valley. It would also out the principal east-west railway line between Čop, Sevluš and Chust near Fancikovo, and between Batovo and Mukačevo and Berehovo and Kusnice on the north-south railway lines. In view of the serious injury thus inflicted on Ruthenian railway communications, this solution might be accompanied by provision for the construction of an east-west railway between Užhorod, Mukačevo and Chust, connected with the Košice railway network in Slovakia through the center of Čop. Since the existing east-west railways were built primarily to serve Hungarian interests and since Hungary would be the beneficiary of this solution, Hungary might be required to make provision for the construction of the new railway as a condition of the cession of this territory.

D. *Cession of territory South of the Primary East-West Railway between Čop and Novo Selo*

Cession of this territory to Hungary would involve an area south of the principal east-west railway between Čop and Novo Selo, in the southwestern border region of Subcarpathian Ruthenia, in the districts of Užhorod, Berehovo and Sevluš. The region is about 125 square miles in area. According to the Hungarian census of 1910 this area would have a total population of approximately 18,600, of whom about 17,300 (93 percent) are Magyars and about 1,200 (6.6 percent) Ruthenians.

According to the Czechoslovak census of 1930 about 15,000 Magyars, out of a total of 21,000, live in this border strip.

This solution would be in the nature of a boundary adjustment and would provide no real basis for a solution of the ethnic problem. Although it would involve cession of rich agricultural lands in the upper valley of the Tisza River, the area is so small that it is doubtful that its cession would be of much benefit to Hungary or of injury to Subcarpathian Ruthenia. Since this solution involves territory south of the principal east-west railway, it would not cut the primary railway system of Subcarpathian railway communications with the rest of Czechoslovakia. It would, however, place the boundary with Hungary somewhat nearer this important railway than it was in 1937. In the negotiations immediately preceding the making of the Vienna Award, the Czechoslovak Government proposed an adjustment of the boundary similar to that involved in this solution.[*]

TS:HNHoward:AHA Box 154

---

[*] The Czechoslovak-Hungarian negotiations preceding the First Vienna Award, and the proposals for boundary revision made, are covered in accurate detail in András Rónai, *Térképezett történelem* (Budapest, 1989), 137-192.

Part Three:

Political Reorganization of Hungary

§ Document 1 §

Secret
Preliminary B

H Document 104
January 22, 1944

HUNGARY. POLITICAL RECONSTRUCTION: NATURE OF A PERMANENT GOVERNMENT.

I. *THE PROBLEM*

The problem is the form of government in post-war Hungary which the United States should favor.

The problem arises by virtue of the fact that the United Nations have made common commitments at Moscow in November 1943, to continue hostilities against the Axis powers until such powers have surrendered unconditionally.* If the declaration regarding Italy is used as a precedent the Hungarian people as the Italian people "shall be given every opportunity to establish governmental and other institutions based upon democratic principles." While Hungary for many years has maintained the form and structure of a parliamentary system, since 1920 the regime has been authoritarian in many of its practices. Furthermore, the extreme revisionist foreign policy of Hungary has contributed to the instability of Central and Eastern Europe. Moreover, President Roosevelt has stated that no vestige of fascism "in any of its malignant forms" shall be permitted to survive anywhere in the world and stipulated that the right of self-determination recognized in the Atlantic Charter does not include the right of any government "to make slaves of its own people."

In 1920, after a brief period of republican government and a soviet regime, the National Assembly made Admiral Nicholas Horthy head of the state. Although the Allied Powers refused to sanction the return of the Habsburgs, Hungary remained a monarchy with Admiral Horthy as Regent. The powers accorded to Admiral Horthy in 1920 were

* Halmosy, *op. cit.*, 559.

extensive, including the command of the army, the power to initiate legislation and the right to prorogue and dissolve Parliament. Additional authority was bestowed upon the Regent under laws passed in 1937; he was empowered to make recommendations as to his successor and he was freed from his formal responsibility to Parliament. In the period prior to 1937 the Government restricted the right of political groups to advocate fundamental economic and political reforms, a reform of land tenure and a modification of the electoral system. In some instances the Government interfered with the independence of the courts.

Governmental opposition, insofar as it was possible, grew in volume from 1938 to 1943, which was the period of outward Nazi orientation. If political interrogations became too embarrassing, as for example in May 1943, the Government could prorogue Parliament. With the resumption of parliamentary sessions, in October 1943, there seems to exist a greater degree of leniency in political debate, to make a better impression upon the United Nations. Late in 1942, on the ground of wartime expediency, the autonomous municipalities and the counties were deprived of their powers of nomination and election to local government offices, thus losing the last vestiges of local autonomy; no guarantee of restoration at the end of the emergency was given.

Trianon Hungary was an agricultural country with some manufacturing establishments, which suffered by being cut off from their essential raw materials—timber, iron ore, copper, lead, zinc, manganese, and salt. These raw materials were located in the succession states which had been complementary parts of the Hungarian economic system prior to 1918; these succession states were compelled to rely upon Hungary for a large part of their agricultural produce so that the former markets remained open to Hungary even after 1920. With the aid of foreign capital which poured into the country between 1920 and 1930 Hungary underwent a rationalization of industry and an adjustment to new economic conditions. The world depression, the tariff war with Czechoslovakia, the failure of the Österreichische Credit-Anstalt in May 1931, and the collapse of the German banking system in July 1931 led to an economic crisis in Hungary, but by 1933 a gradual recovery had taken place. After several years of more nearly normal foreign trade and average agricultural prices Hungary began sending its agricultural produce to Nazi Germany, which ultimately absorbed fifty percent of Hungarian exports. The Hungarian peasant with insufficient land to meet his family needs, or with no land whatsoever, had no share in this prosperity, as political and economic power was concentrated in the hands of those who supported the régime.

The lack of an extensive land reform such as the other succession states adopted, the continued control of the government by the "magnates", the fear of Habsburg restoration and official Hungarian preoccupation with the revision of the Treaty of Trianon, whereby the Magyars hoped to recover the lands ceded to the other succession states, made the neighboring states suspicious of Hungarian policies. As a counter-weight to the organization of the Little Entente, Hungary established close ties with Italy and Germany and friendly relations with Poland. Hungary's territorial gains at the expense of Czechoslovakia, Rumania and Yugoslavia in the 1938-1941 period were acquired with the support of Germany and Italy. The present Hungarian régime, while endeavoring to preserve some freedom of action, has identified itself with the foreign policy of Nazi Germany. The Czechoslovak and Yugoslav Governments-in-exile have expressed the view that no genuine understanding could be established with Hungary unless there were serious political, social and economic reforms. The Polish Government-in-exile, which is not at war with Hungary, has made no such expression of opinion.

II. *ALTERNATIVE SOLUTIONS*

A. *Authoritarian Régime*

The acceptance of the present régime, the Regency, would mean the continuation of a government legally established. It would be in line with a traditional American non-intervention in the internal affairs of other states. It might be the logical solution in case the Regency was able to maintain itself and no intervention by the United Nations took place.

The retention of the Horthy Regency or of its successor, with the same group in power, would mean the continuation of an authoritarian regime. In all probability Hungary would again be a factor of instability in the Balkan-Danubian region, unless a satisfactory solution of regional economic and territorial problems was reached. The Russians have expressed their objection to retention of the Regency and of the regime of the landlords.

If the throne were filled by a Habsburg in the event of Horthy's resignation or death, it is not unlikely that a similar group no less objectionable, would gain power.

B. *Democratic Constitutional Monarchy*

The development of a truly democratic government within the framework of a parliamentary system would involve the replacement of the present régime by one which would establish a democratic electoral system, guarantee and protect the exercise of civil and political rights, and pressure an adequate land reform. It might be prepared to recognize equitable boundary settlements with the succession states and to collaborate with them in the interests of peace and stability.

The revival of constitutional monarchy might result in the constitution of the kingless monarchy which has legally existed for twenty-three years. It is legally possible to designate a successor to the Regent should the Regency become vacant. In that event the Upper and Lower Houses must meet in joint session within eight days to elect a Regent. Until the election is completed the Houses cannot adjourn. In the interval prior to the election a Council of State, composed of seven members, leading personalities of the two Houses, becomes the executive power. On the other hand the Regent can recommend his successor; he then recommends three persons of his own choice to Parliament. Parliament, however, is in no way bound by the Regent's recommendations. The chief objection to the kingless monarchy is its record of non-parliamentary and anti-constitutional exercise of powers during the two decades of its existence. It is not clear to what extent the Hungarian electorate would favor the continuation of the Regency or the election of a king. The restoration of a Habsburg as King of Hungary would be inacceptable to the neighboring states and unfortunate for the cause of democratic government.

C. *Centralized Democratic Republic*

A democratic republic might take the form of a government similar to the one which existed for a brief period in 1918-1919. Some republicans claim that the chances of a republican government coming into power through a mandate from the electorate seem greater than those of any monarchial régime. Certainly without the encumbrances of the monarchical record of inaction prior to 1938 or of reliance on the landed gentry the republican government could give its attention to a land reform. It is now rather generally conceded that only with a program of adequate land reform can a republican group win power in Hungary.

At the present there are indications of the emergence of a "people's front" in Hungary. The "people's front" has active and passive members among factory and farm workers, university professors, actors, writers and people of liberal thought. These Socialist-Agrarian-Liberal groups include the organized Trade Union of Landowners, founded on May 9, 1943, the Small-holders Party and representatives of the Peasants' Association, the Social Democratic Party and Liberal Party. If this coalition were to take the form of a democratic republican government favoring electoral and land reforms, it would be opposed by the feudal landlords, the bureaucracy, the ruling army cliques and possibly the Roman Catholic Church.

D. *A Decentralized Republic*

A federation within Hungary on the Swiss model has been suggested in certain Hungarian circles.* They propose a federal structure for the states of the Danubian area including Hungary and regard the question of boundaries as administrative problems of secondary importance. The proposal implies the adoption of the Swiss cantonal system in which sovereignty is lodged with the canton and not with the federal or central governments as is the case in Hungary. The cantonal system, as applied to Hungary, would accord to such minorities as remain in Hungary a degree of cultural and political autonomy. Under a decentralized régime the Hungarian county and municipality might recapture some of their very wide and real autonomy enjoyed until 1942. This alternative would encourage an old trend in Hungarian politics, autonomy on a local governmental level.

Decentralization might be impractical in that it could lead to disorder, especially if adequate resources and personnel for cantonal administration were lacking, as might be the case in the northeast part of Hungary. Decentralization might provide the Hungarian Government with the means of escaping the realization of democratic, constitutional and agrarian reforms which many Hungarians are demanding.

Decentralization which runs counter to economic trends of the last two decades, would be practical only if Hungary were a member of a multinational Federal State or of a democratic Danubian or East European Federation. At the present such regional units are viewed with disfavor in official quarters.

---

* The reference is to Oszkár Jászi, Rusztem Vámbéry, and the democratic wing of the Hungarian exiles, which they headed.

E. *A Soviet Régime*

If Russian forces occupy Hungary previous to the creation of a permanent national government a soviet régime may come into being as a result of the Red Army's occupation of Hungarian territory. In this event, it is possible that the Communist elements within the present "people's front" would grow in strength and gain control of the whole left-wing movement. In that case a social revolution would probably follow the overthrow of the present régime of landlords followed by the nationalization of the land, and perhaps by the establishment of collective farming along Soviet lines and of other institutions characteristic of socialized (Sovietized) economy.

While this solution would represent a complete break with the feudal past of Hungary, it is possible that the peasants with their love of land would oppose collectivized agriculture. The propertied elements would be completely opposed to this solution, and recollections of the Béla Kun Soviet Republic of 1919 might serve to dampen enthusiasm among all classes for the establishment of a Soviet régime.

A Hungarian Soviet régime would probably be federated with, or in any event would be greatly influenced by the U.S.S.R., and its foreign policy would have an eastern, not western, orientation.

III. *DOCUMENTATION*

A. *Available Memoranda*

Land Distribution in Hungary (T-236; Feb. 8, 1943).
Hungarian Land Reform Since 1918 (T-430; Dec. 29, 1943).
Hungarian Agriculture (T-431; Jan. 7, 1944).
Treatment of European Enemy States (P-176; Jan 15, 1943).
Soviet War Aims (T-200; Dec. 19, 1942).

B. *Other Studies*

Rustem Vambéry, *The Hungarian Problem* (Published by the Nation, 1942).
Oscar Jászi, *The Dissolution of the Habsburg Monarchy* (Chicago, 1929).
C. A. Macartney, *Hungary and Her Successors* (London, 1937).
A.J.P. Taylor, *The Habsburg Monarchy, 1815-1918* (London, 1941).

Cahiers d'informations francaises, no. 7, Un état dans "l'espace vital;" *Le pangermanisme at la conquête de la Hongrie.* Preface de M. Henri Hauser (Paris, 1940).

IV. *PLANS FOR FURTHER RESEARCH*

The Horthy Régime.
Political Forces in Hungary.
The Hungarian Movement outside Hungary: Free Movements.
Problem of Minorities within Hungary.

PS:MEBradshaw:AHA:JRB Box 153

****

§ Document 2 §

Secret H Document 104
Supplement Preliminary A January 27, 1944

NATURE OF A PERMANENT GOVERNMENT IN HUNGARY

Views of the Inter-Divisional Committee on the Balkan-Danubian Region

The Inter-Divisional Committee on the Balkan-Danubian Region, considering the problem of Hungary's post-war government, does not believe the retention of the present regime in view of its participation in the war against the United Nations and its record as one of the disturbing influences in the Balkan and Danubian area (Solution A) would be acceptable to the United Nations or contributory to stability in the area. The Committee also holds the view that the restoration of the Habsburgs to the throne of Hungary would prove a disturbing influence in Central and Southeastern Europe.

The Committee favors, in principle, a stable democratic regime whether it takes the form of a monarchy or a republic (Solutions B and C). The Committee is of the opinion that the protection of civil liberties, the extension of the franchise, the enactment of an adequate land reform and some adjustment of the pre-war frontiers based on ethnic considerations are necessary prerequisites to the success of that regime.

It considers the idea of a decentralized republic (Solution D), at least for the immediate future, as impractical, both politically and economically. The Committee does not favor the establishment of a Soviet regime (Solution E) unless, as is extremely unlikely, it should receive the support of the Hungarian people.

Prepared and reviewed by:

TS:	MEBradshaw (Drafting officer)	SE: Cloyce K. Huston
	CEBlack	FTMerrill
	JCCampbell	
	HNHoward	VD:HKTravers
	TFPower	

Box 153

****

§ Document 3 §

Secret

H Document 135
February 26, 1944

HUNGARY. TRANSITION TO PERMANENT GOVERNMENT: ESTABLISHMENT OF A PROVISIONAL GOVERNMENT

I. *THE PROBLEM*

The problem is the form of provisional government best suited to Hungary for the period between its surrender to the United Nations and the establishment of a permanent government.

The principal United Nations are committed to the imposition of unconditional surrender on Hungary and to joint action in all matters relating to its surrender and disarmament. The United States Government, as well as the U.S.S.R., has warned the Hungarian Government that it will have to share the responsibility for and the consequences of the defeat which United Nations arms will inflict on Nazi Germany.

Acceptance of any provisional government should depend upon that government's ability to preserve order in Hungary and to stabilize conditions in the Balkan-Danubian area in conjunction with the other states of the region, its willingness to cooperate with the United

Nations, of which the U.S.S.R. is their closest neighbor and against which Hungarian troops have been used, and its desire to help bring about on the consent of the Hungarian people.

The personnel for the provisional government could be drawn from a number of sources: (1) MÉP, the party in power; (2) anti-German groups such as the Industrialists of the M.E.P.; (3) the Imrédyist Party of Regeneration and the National Socialists; (4) the Clerical elements such as the Christian Peoples Party; (5) the Smallholders and Liberals; (6) the Social Democrats; (7) Peasant elements; (8) the Communists.

The Party of Hungarian Life (M.É.P.) which now controls 220 seats out of 375 in the Chamber of Deputies, has been in power since 1920.* It obtained 80 percent of those seats in the 1939 election and bears responsibility for Hungary's adherence to the Anti-Comintern Pact signed several months later.** The Hungarian Government, at that time under the M.É.P.,*** established friendly relations with Fascist Italy as early as 1927 and with Nazi Germany during the Gömbös Ministry (1932-1936) and subscribed to the Rome Protocols in 1934 as a counter-weight to the Little Entente.**** Since 1939 pro-Nazi and Fascist Hungarians within the Party have become the leading collaborationists. A cleavage, which has not developed into a formal rift within the party, became apparent in the spring of 1943. At that time the M.E.P. split into two groups, the Agrarians and Industrialists. The Agrarian Group led by Béla Lukács, is pro-German and is reported to number among its adherents Antal, Minister of Propaganda, Szász, Minister of Foods, Zsindely, minister of Commerce, Reményi-Schneller, Minister of Finance, and all political under-secretaries with the exception of Gargeliffe. The majority of the M.E.P. deputies are collaborationists in the sense that they tacitly favored or, at least did not rigorously oppose, the Government's participation in the Axis. The

---

* An inaccurate statement. The Party of Hungarian Life was formed on February 22, 1939, and formed the government until October 16, 1944. Its predecessors in power were the Party of National Unity (1932-1939), and the Unified Party before that. For the latter's political structure and activities, see: William M. Batkay, *Authoritarian Politics in a Transitional State. István Bethlen and the Unified Party in Hungary 1919-1926* (New York, 1982).

** Hungary joined the Anti-Comintern Pact on February 24, 1939. Parliamentary elections, however, were held only on May 28-29, 1939.

*** Properly: Unified Party.

**** The Italian-Austrian-Hungarian cooperation agreed upon in Rome, on May 17, 1934, was to safeguard not only against the Little Entente, but also against the German penetration of Southeastern Europe, which was already under way.

hope of regaining lost territory brought many within the Party to the side of the Axis.

Since the anti-German Industrial Group of the M.E.P. fears a German occupation of Hungary it is unwilling to break with the pro-German Agrarians. The Industrialists, led by Professor Zaky, are reported to control 100 out of 220 members of the M.É.P. Only 15 to 20 individuals are considered to be favorable to the United Nations, and they are anti-Soviet in attitude. Count Bethlen, a member of the M.É.P.* and a premier of Hungary from 1921 to 1931, is considered in some English and American circles as a Hungarian of great possibilities, despite his somewhat advanced ago. Although he restored order and to a certain extent economic stability in Hungary, he reduced the electorate, effectively opposed any adequate land reform, tolerated the Awakening Magyar scandal,** adopted an extremely revisionist foreign policy and permitted anti-Semitic practices.*** During his premiership occurred the Treaty of Friendship with Italy and the first of the subsequent shipment of arms from Italy to Hungary and the counterfeiting of French Francs.**** Keresztes-Fischer, the present Minister of the Interior, may be of assistance to the United Nations, although he like Bethlen, has a record that is open to question. He has been minister of the Interior almost continuously since 1931 and as such has been acceptable to even the pro-Nazi cabinets. On the other hand he recently attempted to protect the Left Opposition from attack by the pro-Nazi parties.

The Hungarian Right Opposition, the Nyilasok, is more pro-Nazi than the Agrarian wing of the M.É.P. Imrédy, once a member of the M.É.P., is now allied with a group of Nyilas which calls itself the Party

---

* Count Bethlen was not a member of the Party of Hungarian Life. He resigned from the ruling party already in 1935, and he continued his political activities as an independent member of Parliament.

** Bethlen did not "tolerate" the terrorist activities of the Association of Awakening Magyars; on the contrary, he unrelentingly castigated them at every turn. See Ignác Romsics, *Bethlen István* (Budapest, 1991), 124-125.

*** What was characteristic of the Bethlen government's policies (1921 to 1931) was not a permissive attitude toward Anti-Semitic practices, but their condemnation and repression. Romiscs, *ibid.*, 126, 156.

**** The 1925 counterfeiting of the French franc was an action of various extreme rightist organizations. Their aim was a rather naive one. They expected to create a monetary crisis in France, which they held responsible for Peace Treaty Trianon, and, at the same time, to create funding for their irredentist activities. The Italian-Hungarian Treaty of Friendship was signed on April 5, 1927.

of Regeneration.* The express aim of this group is to bring Hungary into closer alignment with Germany. In December 1943, Imrédy, until than a violent critic of the Government, declared a truce with the Government. According to one source, Imrédy may become the head of a Hungarian puppet state under German aegis.

The clerical Center group is a political force of some importance since it is in a position to hold the balance of power between Right and Left. At the present the Christian People's Party is taking no definite stand in either direction. Conceivably the Center may move toward the Right because of its legitimist sympathies. It is possible that from this group may emerge some trustworthy personnel satisfactory both to the M.E.P. and the Left Opposition. The Prince Primate, Cardinal Serédi, might be acceptable as head of the government in the interim period. He has stated that the Church does not oppose necessary land reforms.

Until recently there was no outward expression of monarchist sentiment in Hungary except from the German Nazis who have publicly proclaimed the candidacy of Archduke Albrecht. Abroad Archduke Otto has continued to reassert his claim to the throne from Count Sigray and Marquis Pallavicini, of the Upper House, Tibor Eckhardt, the Albert Apponyi Society, the Catholic hierarchy, high army circles and many elements of the nobility. The Christian People's Party is pro-Legitimist. The Smallholders, now under the leadership of Zoltán Tildy, have twelve deputies in the Lower House and a considerable following in the country. The departure from Hungary of their former leader, Tibor Eckhardt, and the alleged loss of his citizenship brought political reverses to the Smallholders. According to the latest report the Smallholders have recovered from that political set-back and are now willing to accept Eckhardt as one of them. He is a Hungarian of undoubted political ability who was associated with the Awakening Magyars in the early years of the Bethlen Ministry. In the late thirties he demanded some changes in the electoral law and land reforms of a somewhat limited nature. He left Hungary for America in 1941 on a mission for the Teleki Government. Since his Independent Hungary Movement collapsed in the summer of 1942 he has been reported as moving in Habsburg circles in the United States. As a consequence he would not be acceptable to the Social Democrats with which his party, the Smallholders, is now cooperating. He might, on the other hand, have the backing of the Legitimists, in addition to support from his own

---

* As of October 3, 1940, Imrédy was no longer a member of the ruling party. From October 21, he led the fascistic Party of Hungarian Regeneration, fighting and criticizing the ruling party's actions.

ranks. Bajcsy-Zsilinszky, an influential member of the Smallholders somewhat to the left of Zoltán Tildy, might be acceptable to the Social Democrats.

The Social Democrats have been the most outspoken of all Left Opposition elements, in their criticism of the Government and their leader, Károly Peyer, so audacious in his attacks upon the Government that he has aroused the wrath of Imrédy, Count Bethlen and the General Staff. It is possible that the charge of treason recently brought against him, will so affect Peyer's political career that he may lose caste in Hungary. It is doubtful that his standing outside the country will be altered to any extent.

To date there are no real peasant groups emerging as distinctly peasant in character. The government sponsored Peasant Union is not a political party, although some of its members have acting as unofficial observers at political meetings arranged by the Social Democrats, Smallholders and Liberals. Ferenc Nagy, former president of the Peasant Union, just recently was removed from his post because of political activity. At the present there are indications of the emergence of a "People's Front" in Hungary, with backing from the Social Democrats, Smallholders and Liberals. This coalition, however, has a parliamentary representation of only twenty-two deputies, but a following of possibly four millions. The Liberals, led by Rassay, represent a caste that is unpopular, hence they are more a group of individuals than a political force of size and importance such as the Social Democrats and Smallholders. Professor Gyula Szekfű, who enjoys the confidence of the Liberals, is striving to effect cooperation of the Hungarian middle class with the workers. His interest in the political role of the middle class and his concern with the nationality question have attracted attention but produced no political results of consequence. Professor Szekfű is a Hungarian historian well known in and outside of Hungary; he is not, unfortunately, a man of political experience, yet it is expected that both Szekfű and Peyer would be prominent leaders of a "People's Front" should such develop. Szekfű, unlike Peyer, is acceptable to clerical circles being a spokesman for the Catholic point of view in the academic world.

There is no reliable information concerning the Communists who are regarded as an unknown quantity in Hungary. Secret calls in the Socialist trade unions do exist and radical-elements which went Nyilas in 1939 may become Communistic. Memories of the Béla Kun Soviet, traditional fear of Bolshevism so constantly expressed in the Hungarian press, and dislike of the Czechs, now regarded as protégés of the U.S.S.R., are obstacles to the growth of a Soviet movement within

Hungary. Soviet policies and the progress of their armies may be a determining factor as to whether Hungary will be Sovietized.

II. *ALTERNATIVE POSSIBILITIES*

A. *Acceptance of the Anti-German Groups within the MEP.*

This solution would mean the continuation in power of experienced men of anti-German views, such as the Industrialists of Count Stephen Bethlen and his following. These men, however, are partly responsible for Hungary's membership in the Axis and its participation in the war against the United Nations and for Hungary's contribution of men and material resources to the Nazi war machine.

Their governmental experience might be useful for the preservation of order, but by the mere act of retention, the principal United Nations would be open to the charge of favoring a government tainted with collaboration and unrepresentative of the Hungarian people. The U.S.S.R. would look with disfavor upon the retention of the present regime which from 1920 to the present, has been violently anti-Soviet. Yugoslavia and Czechoslovakia would view with distrust the continuation in power of the M.E.P., which waged war upon them.

B. *Acceptance of a Clerical Provisional Government with or without Legitimist Backing*

This solution would imply the creation of a clerical government with personnel drawn from the Center and conservative groups favorable to the Catholic Church, and the Protestant leaders. Cardinal Serédi, the Prince Primate of Hungary, might head this government. It is possible that the Legitimists would be willing to unite with the clericals in a Clerical-Legitimist Provisional Government; under such auspices it would be easier for the Legitimists to submit to the Hungarian nation the question of the monarchial restoration. It is probable that the M.E.P. would furnish some support to a purely ecclesiastical provisional regime.

A clerical provisional government might satisfy the Catholic majority, 65 percent of the Hungarian nation and a very stable element. The other religious groups and the liberal elements might oppose this solution, the latter on the grounds of the Church's reactionary policies. Yugoslavia, Czechoslovakia and Rumania would look with disfavor upon any coalition which might open the way for the return of the Habsburgs.

C. *Formation of a "People's Front"*

A coalition government supported by Smallholders, Social Democrats, Liberals and other political forces may develop in Hungary in opposition to the Government. It is possible that this coalition would be a transitory one, dissolving once conditions in Hungary were more normal.

Two of the group, the Smallholders and the Social Democrats, have concluded a formal working agreement.* Although their parliamentary representation is small (seventeen seats) their potential backing might be the greatest in Hungary, especially if the peasants, attracted by the program of land reforms, join in large numbers. This group might contribute a large reservoir of untrained personnel with a democratic point of view and program. Parliamentarians of the Opposition now associated with the coalition are Bajcsy-Zsilinszky, Peyer and Rassay. These men and Professor Szekfű may become leaders of the "People's Front." Its program is perhaps overambitious and the coalition is composed of such diversified elements that it may not survive the period of the crisis.

D. *Emergence of A Peasant Government*

This solution presupposes the creation of a peasant government unlike any which has existed in Hungary. Rigid electoral requirements have disfranchised many individuals among the peasants who, therefore, have not been courted by any particular party.

The peasant group, including the landless peasant is a large aggregation and given the vote might become a political force of great importance strong enough to carry on adequate land reform. It would be a stable force interested in the protection of the rights and property of the peasant and in the maintenance of order. Given some economic and technical assistance in the early period this group might be expected to furnish competent personnel for the management of land problems. On the other hand it might encounter great difficulties for lack of personnel qualified to handle the complicated questions of government, such as foreign relations, banking, industry and education.

---

* The Smallholders' Party and the Social Democratic Party formed a political alliance at the end of July, 1943.

E. *Acceptance of a Soviet Regime*

If a revolution takes place in Hungary with or without the support of invading Red armies a Soviet regime may emerge.

This solution would presumably bring Hungary into closer alignment with the neighboring states, particularly if these states maintained friendly relations with the U.S.S.R. The propertied classes, the strongest workers' party (the Social Democrats) and probably the peasants, who do not desire collectivized agriculture, would oppose this solution.

F. *Acceptance of a Non-Party Regime*

There is a possibility of an obviously transitory non-Party regime arising in Hungary. It might be headed by a personality of integrity and prestige who would agree to assume office on behalf of the Hungarian nation. A college professor like Elemér Hantos or the former head of the National Bank, Lipót Baranyai, might be acceptable to Hungary and to the United Nations. Presumably government functionaries would carry on under this regime as under any regularly selected political head.

One advantage of this solution is the transitory character of the regime which could give its entire attention to the protection of Hungarian interests and to the preservation of order in a period of highly probable confusion. The character and standing of the head would be sufficient pledge of the regime's willingness to cooperate with the United Nations and at the same time an indication of its desire to bring about the establishment of a permanent regime based on the consent of the Hungarian people.

TS:MEBradshaw:LB Box 154

****

§ Document 4 §

Secret H Document 135
Supplement March 18, 1944

NATURE OF A PROVISIONAL GOVERNMENT IN HUNGARY

Views of the Inter-Divisional Committee on the Balkan-Danubian Region

The Inter-Divisional Committee on the Balkan-Danubian Region, considering the problem of Hungary's provisional government, regards a "People's Front" coalition (Solution C), composed of Social Democrats, Smallholders, Liberals and similar elements, as the preferred solution. It favors this coalition because: (1) there appears to be a good possibility that such a government may emerge from the probable confusion after the time of surrender; (2) it offers the most favorable opportunity for varied political elements to formulate a future program in consonance with the war aims of the United Nations; (3) and presents the best likelihood for the construction of a peaceful, more democratic Hungarian state.

The Committee does not favor the continuation in power of the present regime (Solution A) or a clerical provisional regime (Solution B). It considers the emergence of a purely peasant provisional government (Solution D) as unlikely. It is of the opinion that the creation of a Soviet provisional government (Solution E) is inconsistent with the desires of the Hungarian people.

In case no political group, emerges the Committee believes that there is a definite possibility of the creation of a non-political regime (Solution F), composed of persons widely respected in Hungary.

Prepared and reviewed by:

TS: CEBlack
MEBradshaw (Drafting Officer)
JCCampbell
HNHoward
TFPower
REldridge
JSChapin

SE: CWCannon
KHuston
FTMerrill
CEHulick

VD:HKTravers
TA:HBalabanis

Box 154

Part Four:

Final Summaries and Recommendations

§ Document 1 §

Secret PWC-151, CAC-142b
May 1, 1944

TREATMENT OF ENEMY STATES: HUNGARY

Although Hungary preserved the forms of a parliamentary government under the Horthy régime, its government since 1920 has been semi-authoritarian in character, with the Party of Hungarian Life in firm control. The fundamental political struggles in the country during the postwar era centered about the successful efforts of the Magyar landholding groups to retain control of the state by preventing genuine measures of electoral and land reform. In foreign policy their basic idea was to obtain revision of the Treaty of Trianon in the ultimate interest of the restoration of the historic lands of the Crown of St. Stephen.

Hungary became associated with Fascist Italy as early as 1927, and became, together with Italy and Germany, a member of the Anti-Communist Pact in 1939. As an associate of the Axis, Hungary shared in the partition of Czechoslovakia in 1938-1939, received Northern Transylvania in 1940 as a beneficiary of the German-Italian ultimatum to Rumania, and seized Yugoslav territory in 1941, following the German attack on Yugoslavia. The Hungarian Government declared war on the Soviet Union on June 27, 1941, a few days after the German invasion of the U.S.S.R., and declared war on the United States and Great Britain in December 1941.

About 250,000 Hungarian troops have fought on the Eastern front against the Soviet Union, and, in general, Hungarian resources have been placed at the disposal of Germany. On December 11, 1943, the United States Government, warned the Hungarian Government which had recklessly carried on the war against the United Nations, that it would have to share the responsibility for and the consequences of the defeat of Nazi Germany. After the occupation of Hungary by Nazi Germany in March 1944 and the establishment of a puppet government, with Admiral Horthy remaining as Regent, the United States Government advised the Hungarian people that only by firm resistance to the

Nazi invaders could Hungary hope "to regain the respect and friendship of free nations and demonstrate its right to independence."

In the analysis which follows, a clear distinction is made between the objectives of the United States with respect to Hungary during the period immediately following surrender and the long-range objectives. During the first period the United Nations may be able to deal with a friendly government in Hungary which is encouraging resistance to the Germans. On the other hand, it may be necessary to occupy Hungary and to set up strict military government. In this case, Hungary should nevertheless have an opportunity to demonstrate a capacity for genuine self-government and orderly domestic progress and a disposition toward friendly cooperation with its neighbors. During the second period the Hungarian people should have a genuine opportunity freely to choose their own form of government, to develop their economic resources and improve their standard of living, and to participate in general political and economic arrangements.

I. *PERMANENT AMERICAN INTERESTS*

A. *Frontiers*

By the Treaty of Trianon (1920) Hungary was reduced from a state with an area of more than 125,000 square miles and a population of approximately 20,000,000 to a land-locked state with an area of 35,000 square miles and a population of about 8,000,000. About 3,000,000 Magyars lived beyond the new frontiers of Hungary, in Czechoslovakia, Rumania and Yugoslavia. Against these losses Hungarians never ceased to complain. Nevertheless, it should be borne in mind that the population of pre-1918 Hungary was only about fifty percent Magyar in ethnic composition, and that Trianon Hungary was essentially an ethnically homogeneous state.

In the dismemberment of Czechoslovakia Hungary received by virtue of the Vienna Award (November 2, 1938), a predominantly Magyar-populated southeastern strip of Slovakia and a part of Subcarpathian Ruthenia. In March 1939 Hungary occupied by force the rest of Subcarpathian Ruthenia and an additional strip of Eastern Slovakia. As a result of these various annexations from Czechoslovakia Hungary added 9,261 square miles of territory with a population of approximately 1,728,000. In 1940 Hungary acquired Northern Transylvania from Rumania, with an area of about 16,642 square miles and a population of approximately 2,633,000. In 1941 Hungary occupied the Yugoslav districts of Prekomurje, Medjumurje, Baranja and Bačka, with an area of 4,520 square miles and a population of about 1,000,000.

Since 1941 Hungary has had an area of 66,400 square miles and a population of about 14,733,000, about 77.5 percent Magyar by nationality according to the Hungarian census, and including more than 1,000,000 Rumanians, about 550,000 Ruthenians, 269,000 Slovaks and 370,000 Serbs and Croats.

The United States is not committed to any specific boundaries in this area, although it has denounced territorial changes effected by force. It would look with favor upon territorial adjustments which would contribute to the development of more friendly relations among the peoples of Central and Southeastern Europe and which would thereby contribute to the peace and stability of Europe as a whole. Hungary's claims for frontier adjustment, in so far as they are based on ethnic considerations, should receive sympathetic consideration, although care should be taken to avoid the appearance of rewarding Hungary for acts of aggression against its neighbors.

1. *The Slovak-Hungarian Frontier.*—In the case of the Slovak-Hungarian frontier, the United States should favor the restoration, in principle, of the 1937 frontiers, although it might use its influence to encourage Czechoslovakia and Hungary to work out such adjustments as would foster better relations between them and would take into account the desires of the local population.

One such solution, which was favored by the American Delegation at the Paris Peace Conference, would be to cede to Hungary the *Grosse Schuett* and a strip of the Little Hungarian Plain, involving an area of about 1,400 square miles, with a population (in 1930) of approximately 219,000 Magyars and 40,000 Slovaks. The territory is primarily agricultural in character; its loss would not injure the communications of Czechoslovakia or materially affect its defenses, Although the Czechoslovak Government has repeatedly demanded the integral restoration of the pre-Munich frontiers, in principle, it has indicated a willingness to make some adjustments with a "democratic Hungary," provided a "common ethnical and political denominator" could be found.

A more drastic solution would involve the transfer to Hungary of an additional 2,740 square miles, with a population (in 1930) of 310,000 Magyars and 59,000 Slovaks; this solution would offer the possibility of a generally equitable exchange of population between Hungary and Czechoslovakia. It is doubtful, nevertheless, that the Czechoslovak Government would be willing to consider the larger cession to Hungary. The United States should support cession of the *Grosse Schuett* and the

Little Hungarian Plain because of its probable feasibility, without rejecting the latter solution, if Czechoslovakia should be willing to make such a territorial adjustment as a part of a broader settlement of the issues in dispute between it any Hungary.

Restoration of the 1937 Slovak-Hungarian frontier without modification would leave about 500,000 Magyars within the Czechoslovak Republic. Although restoration would satisfy the Czechoslovak demand for full legal recognition of Czechoslovakia's territorial integrity, as well as the desire of the United States to avoid penalizing victims of aggression, it would again make Czechoslovak-Hungarian cooperation difficult, if not impossible. On the other hand, retention of the 1939 frontier should be rejected not only because it would mean rewarding Hungary for its acts of aggression against Czechoslovakia but because that frontier cannot be justified on ethnic grounds.

2. *Subcarpathian Ruthenia.*—The essential solution of the problem of Subcarpathian Ruthenia is to treat the region as a whole, since any major adjustment on ethnic lines in behalf of Hungary would threaten the economic viability of the region. Czechoslovakia, Hungary and the Soviet Union are all concerned with the disposition of Subcarpathian Ruthenia. Incorporation of Ruthenia into the Soviet Union would cut Ruthenia off from its normal economic connections to the south and west and would result in extending Soviet rule across the Carpathian barrier to the northern edge of the Danubian plain. Although the Ruthenians are ethnically related to the Ukrainians, the Soviet Union apparently favors the restoration of Ruthenia to Czechoslovakia. The Czechoslovak claim to Ruthenia is strengthened by the rapid progress made under Czech rule in modernizing and developing the backward region, while the oppressive policy of Hungary prior to 1918 and since 1939 alienated the sympathies of the great mass of Ruthenians.

Although there is still a possibility that Subcarpathian Ruthenia might be annexed by the Soviet Union, in the American view the interest of European stability would best be served by its restoration to Czechoslovakia. In principle, the 1937 frontiers should be restored, although the United States might well support any compromise worked out in an amicable manner by Czechoslovakia and Hungary. Any compromise solution which would aim to leave predominantly Magyar districts in Hungary should take into consideration railway communications between Subcarpathian Ruthenia and the rest of Czechoslovakia.

However, if the Soviet Union should annex Subcarpathian Ruthenia, the United States should, in the interests of the peace and stability of the Danubian region, favor the establishment of an ethnic line which would leave the compact body of Magyars, in the valley of the Upper Tisza River, to Hungary. This would be possible because Subcarpathian Ruthenia would then be a part of the Soviet economy, and its communications with the west would be less important.

3. *The Hungarian-Rumanian Frontier.*—The United States has not recognized the acquisition of Norther Transylvania by Hungary and holds the view that the problem of Transylvania, territory in dispute between two enemy states, should be considered at the time of the general peace settlement. Transylvania contains a slight absolute majority of Rumanians and has a large bloc (400,000) of Hungarians (the Szeklers) in the extreme southeastern corner, remote from the bulk of Magyar population. No simple or satisfactory territorial division of its western boundary along ethnic lines would result in transferring to Hungary a small strip from north of Arad to Szatmár; to include the Szekler region within Hungary, as was done in 1940, is impossible without transferring an even larger bloc of mainly Rumanian-inhabited territory to Magyar rule. The possibility that an autonomous territory of Transylvania might participate in a Balkan or Danubian union of some sort should not be excluded from consideration, although the idea of autonomy has little support among either Hungarians or Rumanians within Transylvania or outside it, and the idea of federation in this area has been discouraged by the Soviet Union.

4. *The Hungarian-Yugoslav Frontier.*—The territories in dispute between Hungary and Yugoslavia, part of which were acquired by Hungary in 1941, have a total population of approximately 1,500,000, about 40 percent of which is Slavic, 26 percent Magyar and 21 percent German. The United States should favor return to the 1940 frontier between Hungary and Yugoslavia, without prejudice to any compromise reached between Hungary and Yugoslavia. While a considerable part of the Magyar minority in the Voivodina is in the northern districts adjacent to Hungary, those districts are also settled by a substantial number of Slavs. In general, the ethnic fragmentation is so great that in only eleven of the twenty-four administrative districts into which this region is divided, does any one of the national groups have a majority.

5. *The Austro-Hungarian Frontier.*—In 1922, after a plebiscite, Austria acquired the Burgenland, previously a part of Hungary. The Burgenland covers an area of about 1,532 square miles with a population (1934) of about 299,247, of whom approximately 80 percent (241,300) are German Austrians, 14 percent (40,500) are Croats and 4

percent (10,400) are Magyars. Hungary has not asserted its claim to the Burgenland vigorously, and there is no compelling reason why this territorial question should be reopened.

B. *Internal Political and Economic Conditions within Hungary*

Despite the rapid expansion of industry since 1924, Hungary has remained a predominantly agricultural country, with control of the greater part of the land concentrated in the hands of the nobility and gentry. The basic political struggles of Hungary since 1918 have been concerned with the successful efforts of the landholding groups to retain control and with agitation for revision of the Treaty of Trianon. Hungary is the only country in the Danube basin where the big estates were not broken up after 1918. The persistence of an antiquated political and economic system within Hungary prevented the development of a democratic order and contributed to the disturbance of peace and security in Central and Southeastern Europe.

The United States is concerned with the elimination of aggressive and war-minded elements in Hungary and with those political and economic developments which affect the strengthening of peace and of orderly progress in Central and Southeastern Europe. For this reason the United States should encourage the establishment in Hungary of a government representing the desires of the Hungarian people and capable of providing greater equality of opportunity and better living standards for all its people. Electoral reform and land reform are requisites to the achievement of a democratic Hungary. Land reform, which will probably be the primary demand of the Hungarian people at the close of the war, may be effected by the division of large estates either by revolutionary means or in planned and gradual manner. Planned resettlement would require a considerable period of time, but it would improve the standard of living and the national wealth of Hungary if units of sufficient size to insure efficient production could be established and if the new peasant owners were assisted with capital and with educational and managerial advice.

A thorough-going land reform would open the way for peaceful development of social and political democracy and would eliminate the control of a reactionary minority which has in the past monopolized political power at home and threatened the peaceful development of the Danubian region through its cooperation with an aggressive Germany.

C. *The Foreign Policy of Hungary*

Hungary became closely associated with Fascist Italy as early as 1927, when Mussolini openly championed the revisionist aims of Hungarian foreign policy. In 1934 Hungary, Austria and Italy signed the Rome Protocols establishing close political and economic ties and forming a bloc against the Little Entente. In 1939 Hungary joined with Germany, Italy and Japan in the so-called Anti-Comintern Pact, and logically took the side of the Axis Powers during the present war.

It is possible that democratic reform within Hungary and some adjustment of Hungary's frontiers might orient Hungary's foreign policy in other directions and enable it to fulfill a constructive role in a peaceful world. In line with its general policy, the United States should favor the participation of Hungary in such general international arrangements as may be established after the war, as soon as Hungary gives convincing proof that it has embraced loyally the basic principles of peaceful processes in international relations.

D. *Regional Policy*

Although the United States is not directly interested in the regional political and economic arrangements which might be entered into by Hungary in so far as such arrangements are not discriminatory in character, it is concerned with such arrangements as might affect European security and stability, and the welfare of the Danubian region as a whole. The United States should, therefore, be willing to examine any proposals for regional arrangements which would meet these criteria, provided that they are freely adopted by the peoples concerned and have the support of Great Britain and the Soviet Union.

In the inter-war period there was constant antagonism between Hungary, on the one hand, and Czechoslovakia, Yugoslavia and Rumania, on the other. The latter states organized the Little Entente, in order to prevent restoration of the Habsburgs to the throne of Hungary and to forestall revision of the Treaty of Trianon by force of arms.

On the other hand, the Hungarian Government rejected any kind of association whether with the Little Entente or the Balkan Entente unless the member states would agree to give prior consideration to frontier revision. Official circles of the Czechoslovak Government-in-exile have expressed the view that basic reforms within Hungary would be prerequisites to any closer regional association with Hungary. Although the Soviet Union has expressed strong opposition to any political grouping in the Danubian area which might become a cordon sanitaire against the Soviet Union, it might take a different view of some regional association which offered prospects of reducing political and economic frictions among the states of the region without constituting a threat to any outside power. Any agreement which reduces friction between Hungary and its neighbors would be a valuable contribution to the construction of a peaceful post-war world, although such a regional union should take its place within a general security system.

II. *AMERICAN POLICY DURING THE PERIOD IMMEDIATELY FOLLOWING HOSTILITIES*

A. *Armistice Terms*

The surrender of Hungary may come prior to military occupation of the country or during the course of military operations. The Hungarian people may remain passive after surrender or they may desire to cooperate with the forces of the United Nations in the final defeat of Germany. If Hungary should participate actively in the war against Germany, it might possibly receive the status cobelligerency.

The armistice terms for Hungary proposed as a guide for the American representative on the European Advisory Commission, called for unconditional surrender. The surrender provisions envisage the demobilization of the Hungarian Army and the complete control by the occupation authorities of the administration, political activity and productive facilities. In view of the changed circumstances, the terms to be applied might well be affected by the degree of resistance which the Hungarian people offer to the German invaders.

In negotiating for Hungarian surrender the principal United Nations would presumably be willing to deal with any Hungarian group which is in a position to offer surrender. They should bear in mind, nevertheless, the political desirably of accepting surrender from the groups responsible for Hungarian participation in the war against the United Nations.

Hungary suffered the consequences of its policy of collaboration with Nazi Germany when the country was occupied by German forces in March 1944 and a puppet government subservient to Hitler was established, with Admiral Horthy continuing as Regent. The United States condemns the policy by which the leaders of Hungary aligned their country with Nazi Germany and plunged it into war against the United Nations. Nevertheless, this Government might well point out to the Hungarian people that provided they demonstrate their right to independence by active resistance to the Germans:

1. Hungary should exist as an independent state;
2. The people of Hungary should ultimately have the right to choose their own form of government;
3. Hungary should have a territorial and economic status which would enable it to fulfill a constructive role in a peaceful world.

Any declaration of policy regarding Hungary, should, of course, be concerted with the British and Soviet Governments.

B. *Occupation and Controls*

1. *No Military Government.*—The armistice with Hungary may or may not be followed by a period of occupation and military government. If the Hungarian people break with their Nazi masters, actively resist the invader, and establish a more democratic government friendly toward and acceptable to the United Nations, military government might not be regarded as necessary by the United States. It is even conceivable that Hungary might be accorded the status of a co-belligerent. Even if no military government is set up, the United States may desire to see established in Hungary some kind of control over such matters as disarmament, reparation and the punishment of war criminals. If the Italian pattern is followed, this control might take the form of a commission in which the United States, Great Britain and Soviet Russia, and possibly Czechoslovakia and Yugoslavia, would be represented.

2. *Military Government.*—If a military government is established, the supreme authority will rest with the commander-in-chief of the armed forces of the United Nations in Hungary, acting in the interest of the United Nations as a whole and in accordance with the broad instructions agreed upon by the Governments of the United States, Great Britain and the Soviet Union, presumably thought the instrumentality of the European Advisory Commission. The Czechoslovak and Yugoslav Governments should receive adequate opportunity to present their views concerning the surrender terms.

Whether the commander-in-chief in this area is Soviet or Anglo-American would presumably depend on the course of military operations prior to Germany's final surrender. In such a period of military government, the United States should participate either directly or through membership in a tripartite control commission or in a United

Nations Political Advisory Council for Hungary. The controls established over Hungary, as one of the aggressor nations, should last until such time as Hungary demonstrates its willingness and ability to live at peace with its neighbors.

If a military government is established in Hungary, the United States should encourage the development of a provisional government which would lay the foundations for a more democratic constitutional and political structure than Hungary has had in the past.

3. *Territorial Policy.*—Whether or not a military government is established, the territories which Hungary acquired from Czechoslovakia in 1938-1939 and from Yugoslavia in 1941 should be returned to these countries immediately following Hungary's surrender, without prejudice, however, to any mutually satisfactory adjustments which might be arranged between the parties concerned. The disputed area between Hungary and Rumania, two enemy countries, constitutes a special problem. A preliminary determination of the Hungarian-Rumanian frontier in Transylvania may be made prior to the end of the war, as the Soviet Union has suggested, as an inducement to encourage Rumanian surrender. If no settlement is reached prior to the end of the war, provisional control of the administration over Transylvania or any part of it might be vested in the principal United Nations.

C. *Relief and Reconstruction*

At its organization meeting in November 1943, the United Nations Relief and Rehabilitation Administration agreed to general principles and conditions governing the extension of relief to enemy states, such as Hungary. In the period immediately following surrender the administration of relief in Hungary will be a matter for the period of occupation, relief and rehabilitation operations will be undertaken by the United Nations Relief and Rehabilitation Administration at such time and for such purposes as may be agreed upon by the military command, the established control authorities or duly recognized administration on the one hand, and the UNRRA on the other. In any case, Hungary, like other enemy states, will be required to bear the expense of such relief as it may receive, and may be required to make available to the occupying authorities Hungarian supplies, particularly foodstuffs, for the relief of states which are members of the United Nations.

Despite uncertainties concerning internal developments in post-war Hungary and in Europe as a whole, among primary problems in the reconstruction of its economy are likely to be the laying of foundations for a long-range program of land reform; conversion of Hungarian industry to peacetime production and its emancipation from German domination; control measures to avoid domestic inflation; access to foreign supplies needed for industrial and agricultural rehabilitation and outlets for Hungarian exports, particularly for agricultural products.

The United States may assist in the economic reconstruction of Hungary through its participation in such programs of the UNRRA or other international organizations of which it is a member as are undertaken in Hungary. It may also desire to participate in loans and in arrangements for supplying technical assistance to Hungary, as part of the process of economic reconstruction in Europe as a whole. It would also be prepared to open its markets to Hungarian trade and to supply such commodities as Hungary may need. Hungary may be expected to carry through its reconstruction with a minimum of direct assistance from other nations, if world markets are reopened and exchanges are stabilized.

If Hungary emerges from the war with its productive capacity relatively intact, it will be in a position to contribute substantial reparation in kind for European reconstruction. Foodstuffs presumably would be available in considerable quantities, and there are important deposits of bauxite and of coal. Hungarian iron and steel, as well as its manufacture of sugar, hemp and flax should also contribute to reparations requirements. It is improbable that the United States Government will have any direct interest in receiving Hungarian reparations in kind, but in view of the American interest in an orderly reconstruction of European economy, this Government should favor the treatment of the problem of Hungarian reparation on the basis of an agreed policy towards reparation in general, rather than by unilateral action by any one of the United Nations.

The United States would also be prepared to conclude trade agreements with Hungary for the reduction of trade barriers between the two countries, with a view to expanding mutual trade relationships. However, in view of the fact that in the inter-war period, direct trade between the two countries was relatively unimportant, and that Hungarian exports are chiefly agricultural, the country's foreign trade would best be developed by arrangements for the expansion of trade relationships between Hungary and western Europe on a non-discriminatory basis.

D. *Establishment of a Permanent Government in Hungary*

In accordance with its general policy, the United States desires to see Hungary ultimately restored to independence, with political and economic foundations which will enable the Hungarian people with their neighbors, in the Danubian region.

The Hungarian people should ultimately be free to decide for themselves the forms and details of their governmental organization, so long as Hungary conducts its affairs in such a way as not to menace the peace and security of its neighbors. Therefore, the United States should not look with favor on projects designed to restore the Habsburgs to the throne of Hungary or upon the continuance in power of those Hungarian political forces which were fundamentally instrumental in bringing Hungary into alliance with the Axis Powers and into the war with the United Nations. Probably the most significant contributions which the United States could make toward the development of an independent and democratic Hungary would be to use its influence to facilitate more equitable frontier adjustments between Hungary and its neighbors and to encourage the efforts of the Hungarian people to advance toward greater social and political democracy.

Prepared and Reviewed by the Inter-Divisional Committee on the Balkan-Danubian Region.

TS: HNHoward (drafting officier)
PEMosely
CEBlack
MEBradshaw
JCCampbell

SE: CWCannon
CKHuston
CEHulick
FMerrill
CE:JWRiddleberger
TA:HPBalabanis
WEA:DDort

Box 109

****

§ Document 2 §

Secret

PWC - 150b
July 26, 1944

SUMMARY OF RECOMMENDATIONS. TREATMENT OF ENEMY STATES: HUNGARY

I. *LONG-RANGE INTERESTS AND OBJECTIVES OF THE UNITED STATES*

1. The United States favors the independence of Hungary following its surrender, subject to such temporary controls as may be necessary.

2. The United States should favor the participation of Hungary in the general international organization with Hungary has demonstrated its intention and capacity to live at peace with its neighbors.

3. In accordance with its general policy of not recognizing territorial changes made by force, the United States should in principle, favor the restoration of the 1937- Slovak-Hungarian frontier. In the interest of the peace and stability of the Danubian region, however, consideration should be given to the ethnic claims of Hungary in the area of the *Grosse Schuett* and the Little Hungarian Plain. The United States should be prepared to look with favor upon any settlement of these claims reached through free and direct negotiations between Czechoslovakia and Hungary or through other peaceful procedures.

4. The United States should, in principle, favor the restoration of to Czechoslovakia with the frontier established in 1920. The United States should be prepared to look with favor upon any minor rectifications in the frontier reached through free and direct negotiations between Czechoslovakia and Hungary or through other peaceful procedures.

6. The United States favors preservation of the existing frontier between Austria and Hungary.

7. The United States favors an adjustment of the Hungarian-Rumanian frontier in Transylvania along from north of Arad to Szatmár to Hungary. Provided the two countries are not occupied by forces of the United Nations, the territory in dispute between Hungary and Rumania

may be placed under United Nations control pending subsequent adjustment.

8. Full encouragement should be given to the democratic forces within Hungary. In order to achieve this, the United States should lend encouragement to electoral and land reform which would open the way for peaceful development of social and political democracy and would eliminate the control of the reactionary minority which has monopolized political power at home and threatened the peace of the Danubian region.

9. In order to reorient the Hungarian economy and to overcome Hungary's excessive dependence upon German markets, Hungary should be encouraged to expand its world trade on a non-discriminatory basis and within the framework of such international economic organizations as may be established.

10. The United States should be prepared to conclude a trade agreement with Hungary after the war, with a view to reducing trade barriers between the two countries and to expanding mutual trade relationships.

11. The United States should favor the participation of Hungary in such regional groupings as, might seem to promote its economic welfare and political security, so long as they are not in conflict with the purposes and practices of a general international organization, and are consistent with the policies of this government and with the best interests of the United Nations.

II. *AMERICAN POLICY IN THE TRANSITION PERIOD*

12. The Hungarian people should be encouraged to resist the German invaders by assurances of future political independence and of future participation in international economic and political arrangements.

13. Hungarian surrender should be accepted from any group which will be in a position to effect surrender, although the political desirability of accepting surrender from the groups responsible for participation in the war against the United Nations should be kept in mind.

14. The principle of unconditional surrender still applies to Hungary. If the Hungarian people resist the Germans and establish a more

democratic government friendly toward the United Nations, the United States and its Allies will have to determine whether occupation and military government are necessary. If military government is not set up, they must nevertheless be established a commission or other agency should be established to control such matters as disarmament, reparation and the punishment of war criminals.

15. If it becomes necessary to occupy Hungary, the supreme authority in Hungary should rest with the commander-in-chief of the armed forces which will operate in that area on behalf of the United Nations. Yugoslav and Czechoslovak participation, if admitted, should be limited to token forces.

16. Full opportunity should be afforded during the occupation period for the establishment of a provisional government representative of all democratic groups in Hungary as the best means of insuring a permanent government of representative character. The United States should disapprove the restoration of the Habsburgs to the throne of Hungary or the continuance in power of those Hungarian political forces which brought Hungary into war against the United Nations.

17. In accordance with its general policy of not recognize the acquisition of territory by force, the United States should favor the return to Czechoslovakia, and Yugoslavia, immediately upon their liberation, of the territories taken by Hungary in 1938-1939 and 1941. The return of these territories to Czechoslovakia and Yugoslavia during the transitional period should not prejudice subsequent adjustments as indicated in paragraphs 3, 4 and 5 above.

18. Hungary should be required to provide reparation in accordance with a general agreement among the United Nations. Any stores requisitioned during the period of control in Hungary should be credited to Hungary's reparations account.

Originally prepared and reviewed by the Inter-Divisional Committee on the Balkan-Danubian Region.

Reviewed and revised by the Committee on Post-War Programs, May 26, 1944.

Revised to conform with papers on Rumania and Bulgaria, July 26, 1944.

Box 142

****

§ Document 3 §

PROGRESS REPORT ON POST-WAR PROGRAMS. HUNGARY. SEPTEMBER 1, 1944.

Book I.

HUNGARY

The following policies, in addition to the general objectives and program for all three satellite states, apply specifically to Hungary:

1. *Military Occupation*

Yugoslav and Czechoslovak participation in any military government for Hungary, if admitted at all, should be limited to the provision of token forces under United Nations command.

2. *Territorial Adjustments*

We should take the following positions with respect to territorial questions affecting Hungary:

a. We should favor the return to Czechoslovakia and Yugoslavia immediately upon their liberation of all territories taken by Hungary in 1938-1939 and 1941.

b. In the interest of the peace and stability of the Danubian region, consideration should be given to the ethnic claims of Hungary in the area of the *Grosse Schuett* and the Little Hungarian Plain. We should be prepared to look with favor upon any settlement of these claims, and of the frontiers of Ruthenia, reached through free and direct negotiations between Czechoslovakia and Hungary or through other peaceful producers.

c. We should be prepared to favor any future adjustments of the Yugoslav-Hungarian frontier reached through free and direct negotiation between Yugoslavia and Hungary or through other peaceful procedures.

d. We should favor the preservation of the existing frontier between Austria and Hungary.

e. We should favor an adjustment of the Hungarian-Rumanian frontier in Transylvania along ethnic lines which would transfer a small strip from north of Arad to Szatmár to Hungary. The territory in dispute between Hungary and Rumania should be placed under United Nations control pending subsequent adjustment.

3. *Establishment of Government*

We should use our influence to reorient the political structure of Hungary by:

a. disapproving of the restoration of the Habsburgs to the throne of Hungary or the continuance in power of those political forces which brought Hungary into the war against the United Nations;

b. encouraging electoral and land reform which would open the way for the peaceful development of social and political democracy.

4. *International Position*

No variation from general program

5. *Economic Measures*

No variation from general program.

Box 145

****

§ Document 4 §

DEPARTMENT OF STATE BRIEFING PAPER.[1*]
AMERICAN POLICY TOWARDS HUNGARY

Secret [Undated]

The Hungarians have failed to take any realistic action to withdraw from the war, thought they have repeatedly avowed their desire to do so. The difficulty has been their hope that the "Anglo-Americans" would protect them against Soviet Russia, and their unwillingness to part with territories acquired with German aid. The country is now in ferment, however, and events may move rapidly.

Draft armistice terms for Hungary, having the approval of the Joint Chiefs, were sent to the European Advisory Commission several months ago.[2] Subsequently revised terms, including certain inducements to the Hungarians while maintaining the principle of unconditional surrender, were sent forward.

The United States does not contemplate participation in military operations in Hungary or in the occupation of that country. American troops in that area could probably be used more effectively, in the political sense, than either British or Soviet armies, but such participation would inevitably involve this Government as an active agent in the political questions of Southeastern Europe. Although planning for civil affairs administration in Hungary after surrender is under the jurisdiction of AFHQ in the Mediterranean Theater, American representatives have taken no part in whatever planning has been done. The United States will, however, desire political representatives in Hungary in the period after surrender. Such representation is desirable for the execution of the political terms of the armistice, for supporting our general objectives of promoting a just and stable political and territorial settlement, as well as for securing accurate first-hand political and economic information, and protecting American interests.

As a long-term objective the United States favors the establishment of a broadly-based provisional government, designed to carry through by democratic means the transition to a permanent regime. There are revolutionary forces in Hungary working for land reform, electoral reform and the overthrow of the present ruling group. We acknowledge

---

* This document was published in, *Foreign Relations of the United States of America. The Conference at Quebec* (Washington, 1972), 214-215.

the need and the strong public demand for changes in the Hungarian system, and must expect that these reforms will not be accomplished without some violence.

In regard to the territorial settlement, the United States favors, as a matter of principle, the restoration of the pre-Munich frontier, and any consideration of the boundary disputes between Hungary and its neighbors should start from that point. However, we do not regard the pre-Munich boundaries as unchangeable and believe certain changes to be desirable in the interest of a stable settlement.

Thus, in the case of the frontier with Czechoslovakia, if an opportunity arises for revision by agreement which would leave to Hungary certain overwhelmingly Magyar-inhabited districts, the United States would favor such a solution. In the case of the frontier with Yugoslavia, the United States sees some merit in a compromise solution which would leave to Hungary the northern part of the Voivodina, although this Government should not, we feel, press for such a solution. In the case of the frontier with Rumania, the American position will be more or less frozen by our agreement to the armistice terms for Rumania which provide for the restoration to that country of "all or the major part of Transylvania, subject to confirmation at the peace settlement."[3] In the final settlement the United States would favor, at the least, a revision of the pre-war frontier on ethnic grounds, transferring to Hungary a small strip of territory given to Rumania at the end of the last war.

NOTES

[1] Annex 8 to Hull's memorandum to Roosevelt dated September 6, 1944, which was sent to the White House under cover of a further memorandum of September 8. See ante, p. 120.

[2] See *Foreign Relations*, 1944, Vol. III, pp. 883-887.

[3] See *Foreign Relations*, 1944, Vol. IV, pp. 170, 173.

Maps

European Series Map 1

Compiled and Drawn in Ge. April 15, 1943

2. Slovak - Hungarian Frontier
Population in thousands

Figure 1

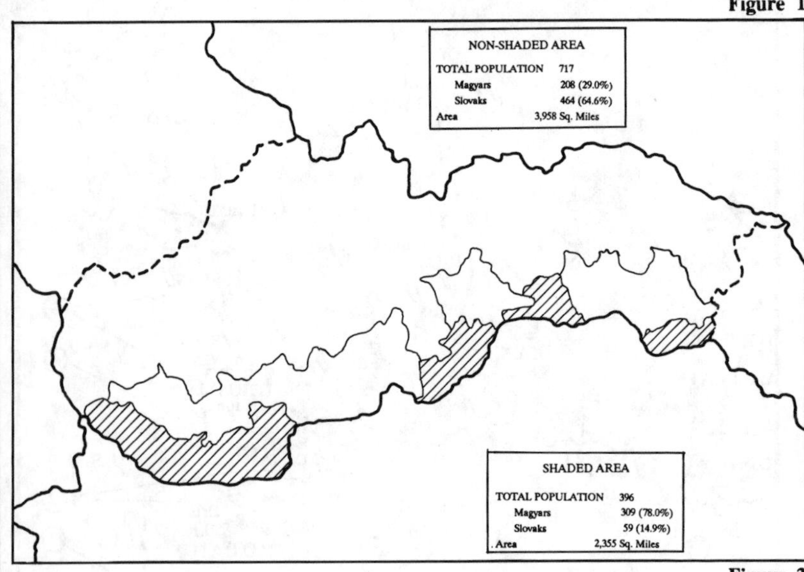

Figure 3

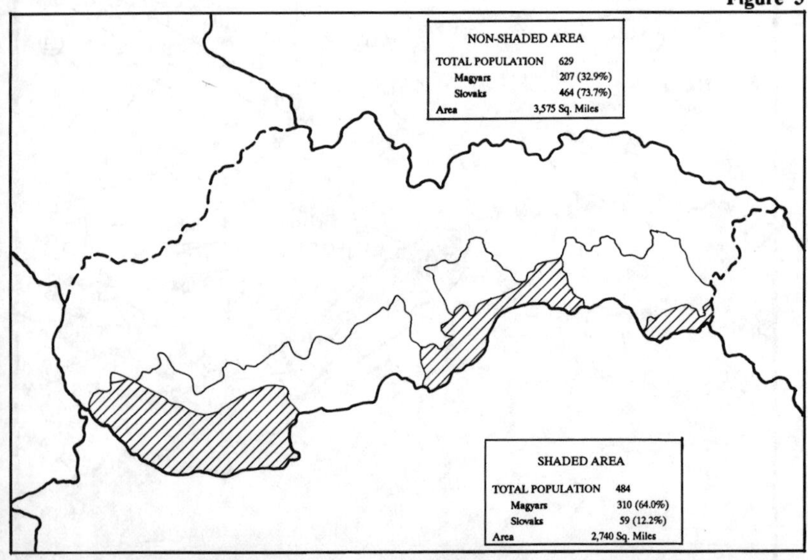

Drawn in the Department of State, Division of Geography and Cartography Dec. 13, 1944 1522 E

Cartogram A to Accompany Czechoslovak Series Map 3

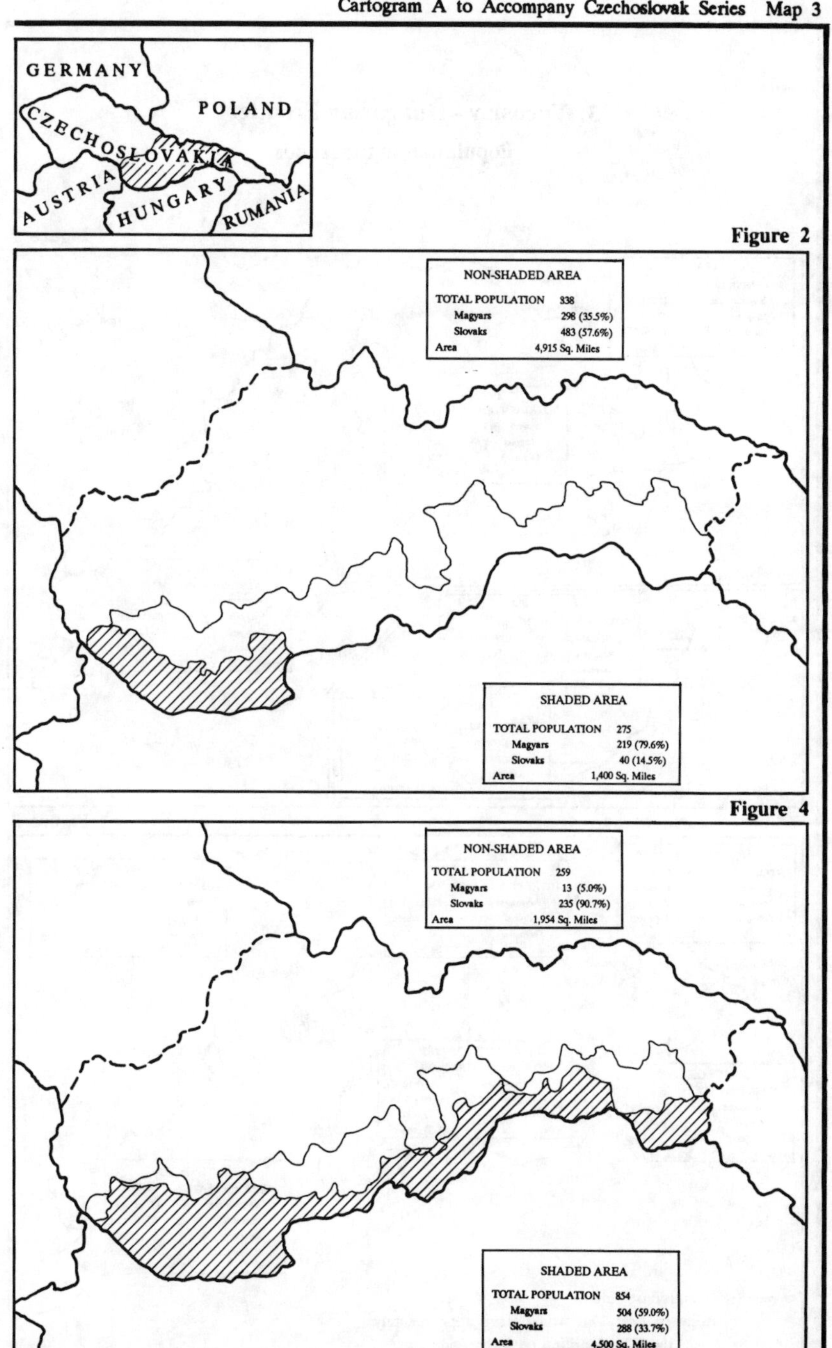

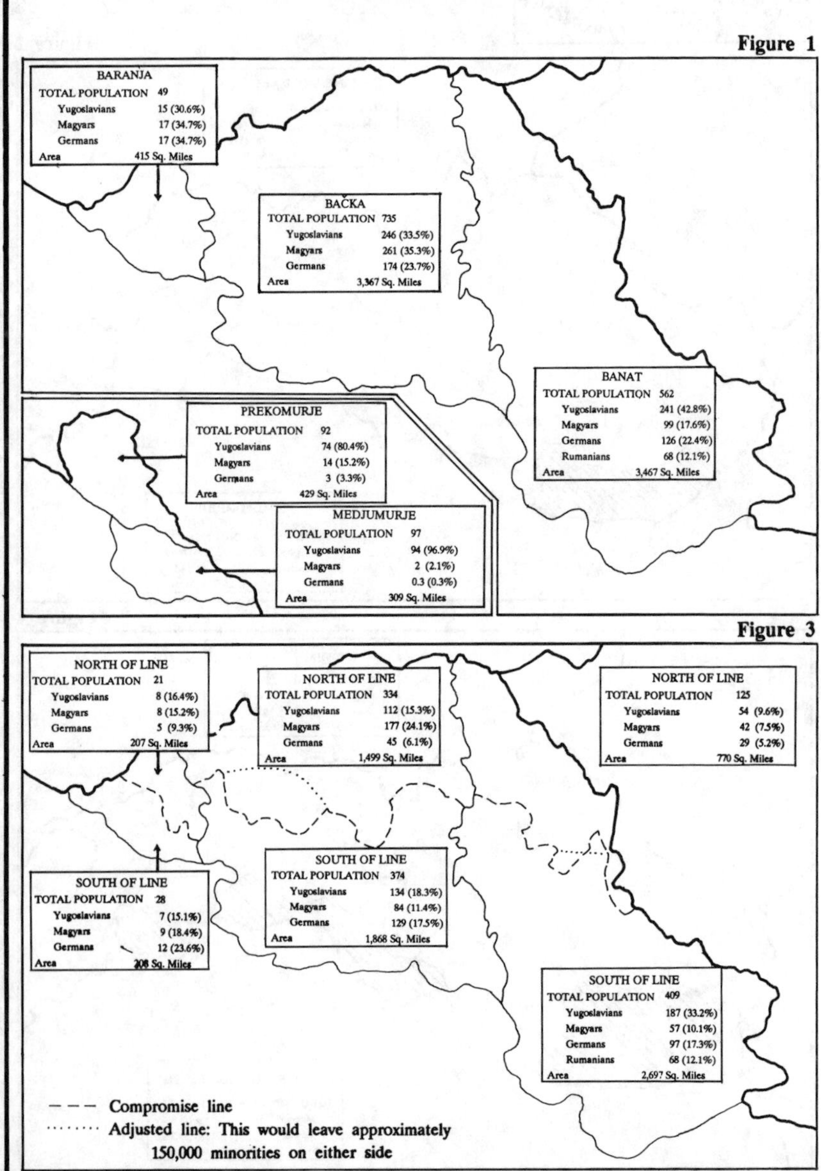

Drawn in the Department of State, Office of the Geographer Nov. 4., 1943 1139 E

Cartogram to Accompany Yugoslav Series Map 3

AUSTRIA
HUNGARY
RUMANIA
YUGOSLAVIA
BULG.
ITALY
ALB.
GREECE

Source of data:
Yugoslav census of 1921,
Language distribution

Figure 2

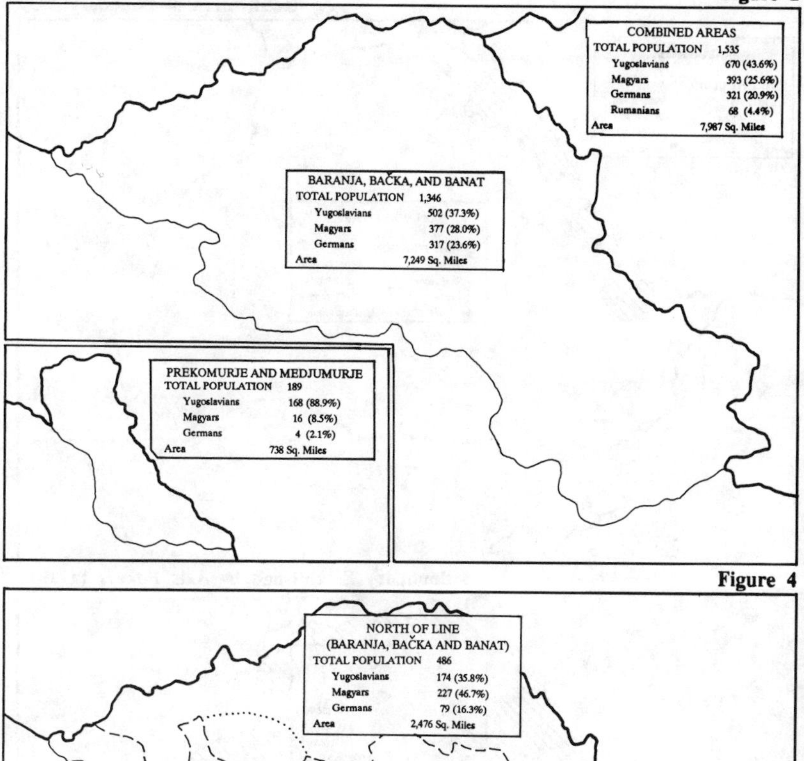

COMBINED AREAS

TOTAL POPULATION	1,535
Yugoslavians	670 (43.6%)
Magyars	393 (25.6%)
Germans	321 (20.9%)
Rumanians	68 (4.4%)
Area	7,987 Sq. Miles

BARANJA, BAČKA, AND BANAT

TOTAL POPULATION	1,346
Yugoslavians	502 (37.3%)
Magyars	377 (28.0%)
Germans	317 (23.6%)
Area	7,249 Sq. Miles

PREKOMURJE AND MEDJUMURJE

TOTAL POPULATION	189
Yugoslavians	168 (88.9%)
Magyars	16 (8.5%)
Germans	4 (2.1%)
Area	738 Sq. Miles

Figure 4

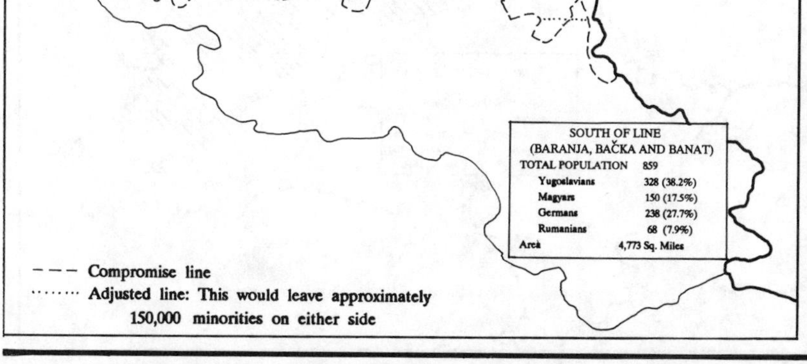

NORTH OF LINE
(BARANJA, BAČKA AND BANAT)

TOTAL POPULATION	486
Yugoslavians	174 (35.8%)
Magyars	227 (46.7%)
Germans	79 (16.3%)
Area	2,476 Sq. Miles

SOUTH OF LINE
(BARANJA, BAČKA AND BANAT)

TOTAL POPULATION	859
Yugoslavians	328 (38.2%)
Magyars	150 (17.5%)
Germans	238 (27.7%)
Rumanians	68 (7.9%)
Area	4,773 Sq. Miles

– – – Compromise line

········ Adjusted line: This would leave approximately 150,000 minorities on either side

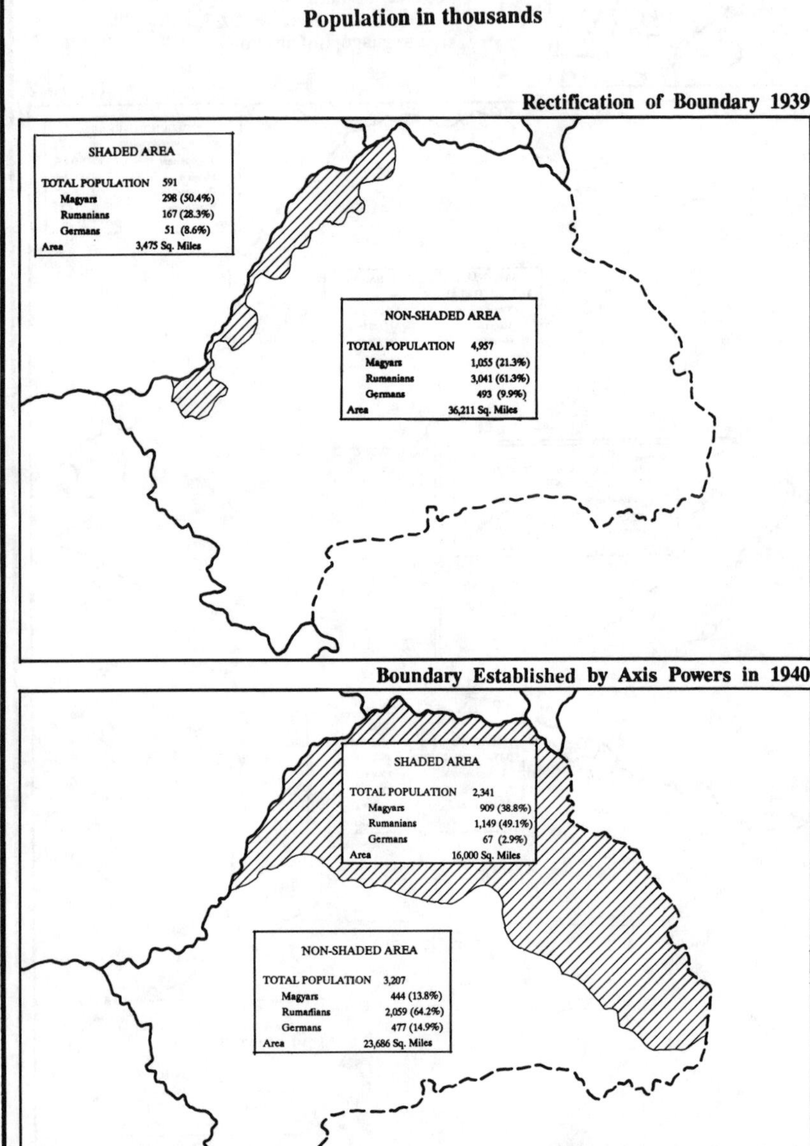

Drawn in the Department of State, Division of Geography and Cartography June 2, 1944 1307 E

Cartogram to Accompany Rumanian Series Map 5

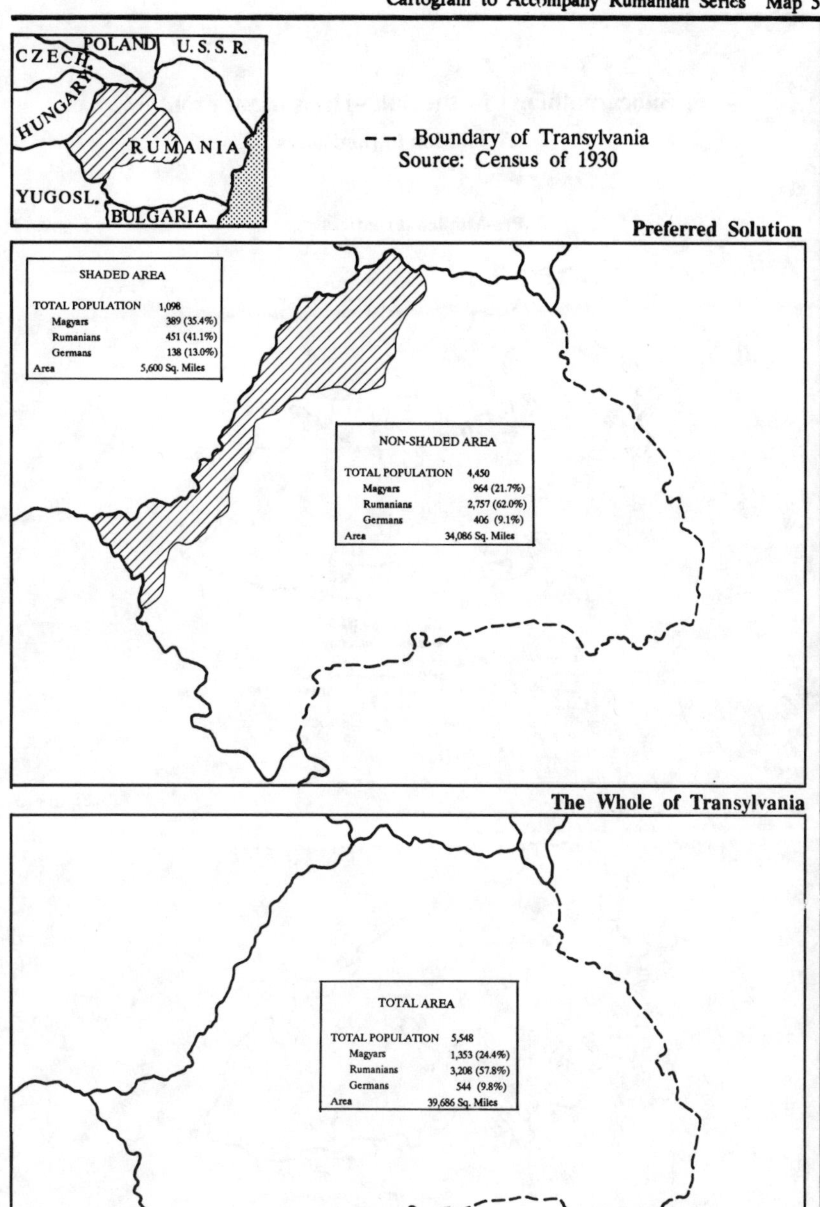

5. Subcarpathian – Ruthenian – Hungarian Frontier

Population in thousands

Pre-Munich Frontiers **Figure 1**

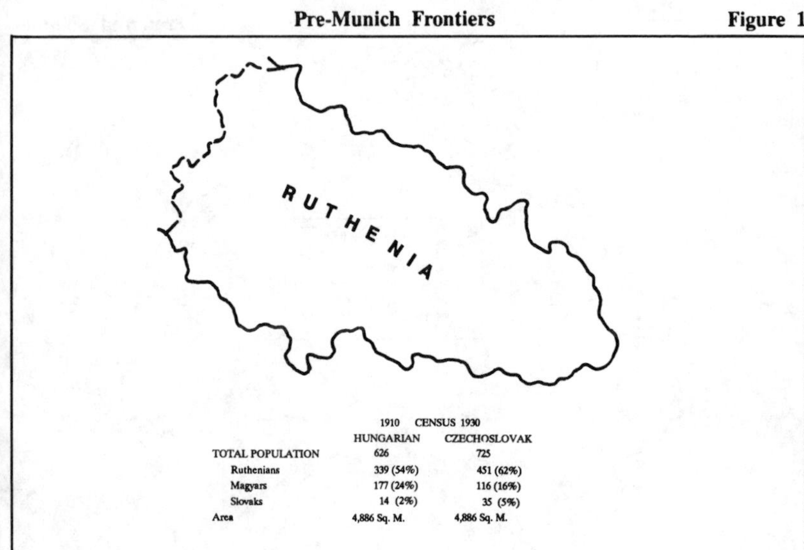

	1910 CENSUS 1930	
	HUNGARIAN	CZECHOSLOVAK
TOTAL POPULATION	626	725
Ruthenians	339 (54%)	451 (62%)
Magyars	177 (24%)	116 (16%)
Slovaks	14 (2%)	35 (5%)
Area	4,886 Sq. M.	4,886 Sq. M.

Figure 3

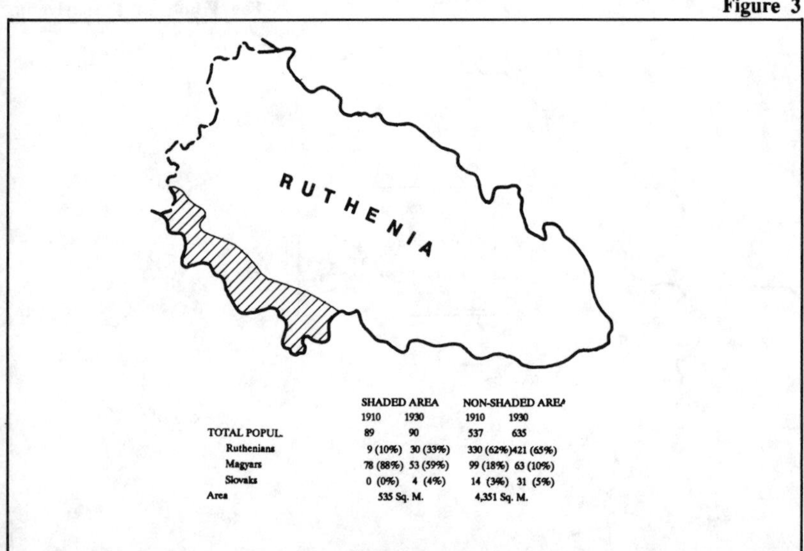

	SHADED AREA		NON-SHADED AREA	
	1910	1930	1910	1930
TOTAL POPUL.	89	90	537	635
Ruthenians	9 (10%)	30 (33%)	330 (62%)	421 (65%)
Magyars	78 (88%)	53 (59%)	99 (18%)	63 (10%)
Slovaks	0 (0%)	4 (4%)	14 (3%)	31 (5%)
Area	535 Sq. M.		4,351 Sq. M.	

Drawn in the Department of State, Division of Geography and Cartography Oct. 18, 1944 1483 E

Cartogram B to Accompany Czechoslovak Series Map 3

POLAND
CZECHOSLOVAKIA
HUNGARY
RUMANIA

Cession by Vienna Award **Figure 2**

RUTHENIA

	SHADED AREA		NON-SHADED AREA	
	1910	1930	1910	1930
TOTAL POPULATION	207	172	419	553
Ruthenians	19 (9%)	38 (22%)	320 (76%)	413 (74%)
Magyars	178 (86%)	87 (51%)	0 (0%)	29 (5%)
Slovaks	2 (1%)	17 (10%)	33 (8%)	18 (3%)
Area	731 S.M.	612 S.M.	4155 S.M.	4274 S.M.

Figure 4

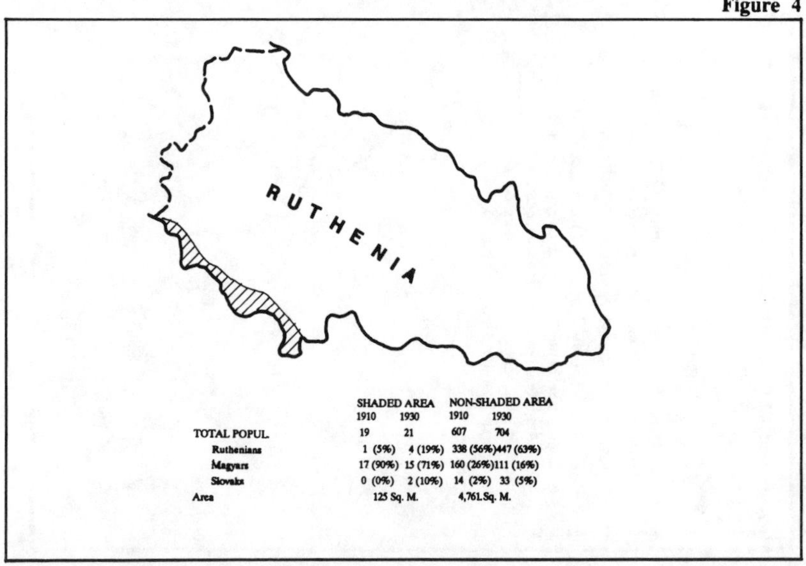

	SHADED AREA		NON-SHADED AREA	
	1910	1930	1910	1930
TOTAL POPUL.	19	21	607	704
Ruthenians	1 (5%)	4 (19%)	338 (56%)	447 (63%)
Magyars	17 (90%)	15 (71%)	160 (26%)	111 (16%)
Slovaks	0 (0%)	2 (10%)	14 (2%)	33 (5%)
Area	125 Sq. M.		4,761 Sq. M.	

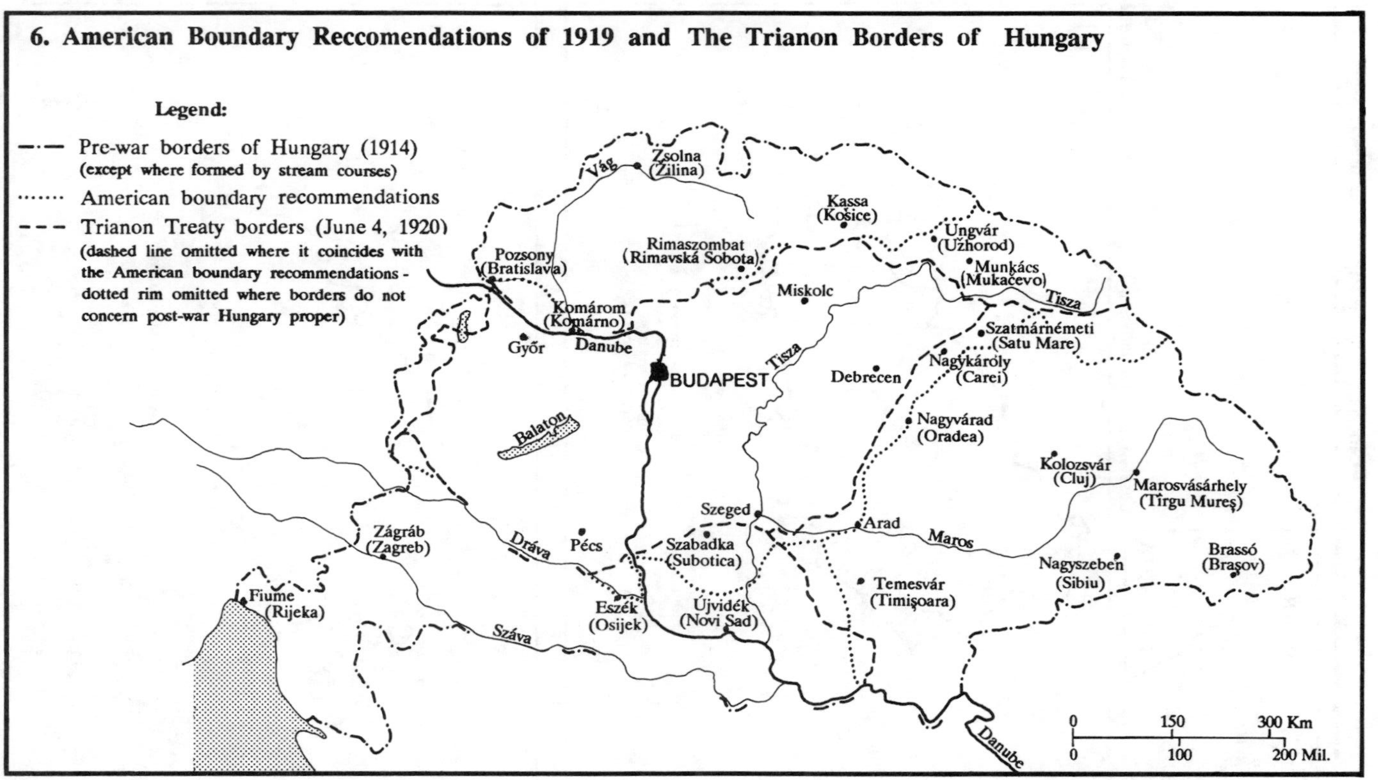
6. American Boundary Reccomendations of 1919 and The Trianon Borders of Hungary
Legend:
Pre-war borders of Hungary (1914)
(except where formed by stream courses)
American boundary recommendations
Trianon Treaty borders (June 4, 1920)
(dashed line omitted where it coincides with the American boundary recommendations - dotted rim omitted where borders do not concern post-war Hungary proper)
Zsolna (Žilina)
Vág
Kassa (Košice)
Ungvár (Užhorod)
Munkács (Mukačevo)
Tisza
Rimaszombat (Rimavská Sobota)
Miskolc
Pozsony (Bratislava)
Komárom (Komárno)
Győr
Danube
BUDAPEST
Tisza
Debrecen
Szatmárnémeti (Satu Mare)
Nagykároly (Carei)
Nagyvárad (Oradea)
Balaton
Kolozsvár (Cluj)
Marosvásárhely (Tîrgu Mureş)
Szeged
Arad
Maros
Zágráb (Zagreb)
Dráva
Pécs
Szabadka (Subotica)
Nagyszeben (Sibiu)
Brassó (Braşov)
Temesvár (Timişoara)
Fiume (Rijeka)
Eszék (Osijek)
Újvidék (Novi Sad)
Száva
Danube
0 150 300 Km
0 100 200 Mil.

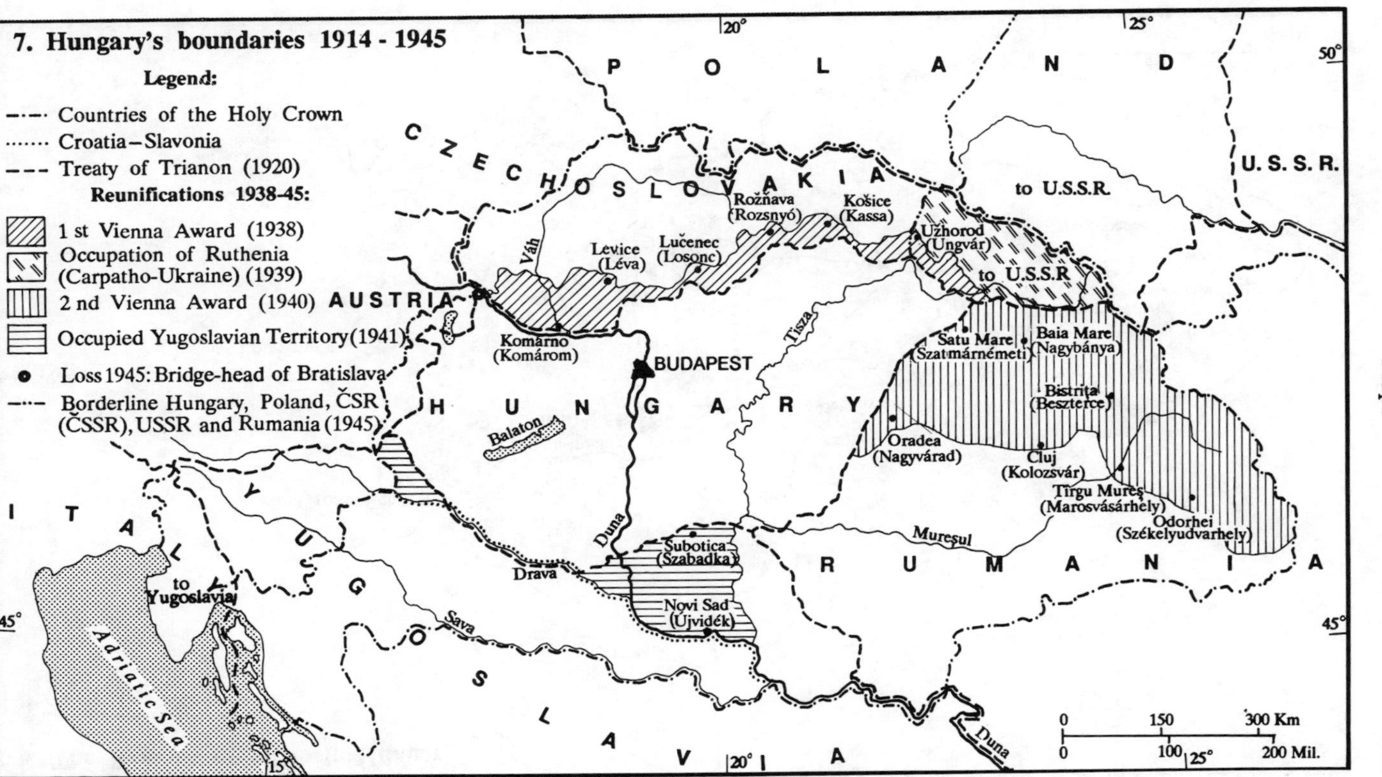
7. Hungary's boundaries 1914 - 1945
Legend:
Countries of the Holy Crown
Croatia–Slavonia
Treaty of Trianon (1920)
Reunifications 1938-45:
1 st Vienna Award (1938)
Occupation of Ruthenia (Carpatho-Ukraine) (1939)
2 nd Vienna Award (1940)
Occupied Yugoslavian Territory (1941)
Loss 1945: Bridge-head of Bratislava
Borderline Hungary, Poland, ČSR (ČSSR), USSR and Rumania (1945)
P O L A N D
U. S. S. R.
to U.S.S.R.
to U.S.S.R
C Z E C H O S L O V A K I A
A U S T R I A
H U N G A R Y
R U M A N I A
Y U G O S L A V I A
I T A L Y
to Yugoslavia
Adriatic Sea
BUDAPEST
Komárno (Komárom)
Levice (Léva)
Lučenec (Losonc)
Rožňava (Rozsnyó)
Košice (Kassa)
Užhorod (Ungvár)
Satu Mare (Szatmárnémeti)
Baia Mare (Nagybánya)
Bistrița (Beszterce)
Oradea (Nagyvárad)
Cluj (Kolozsvár)
Tîrgu Mureș (Marosvásárhely)
Odorhei (Székelyudvarhely)
Subotica (Szabadka)
Novi Sad (Újvidék)
Váh
Tisza
Duna
Mureșul
Drava
Sava
Balaton
50°
25°
20°
45°
15°
0 150 300 Km
0 100 200 Mil.

8. The Regions of Historic Hungary

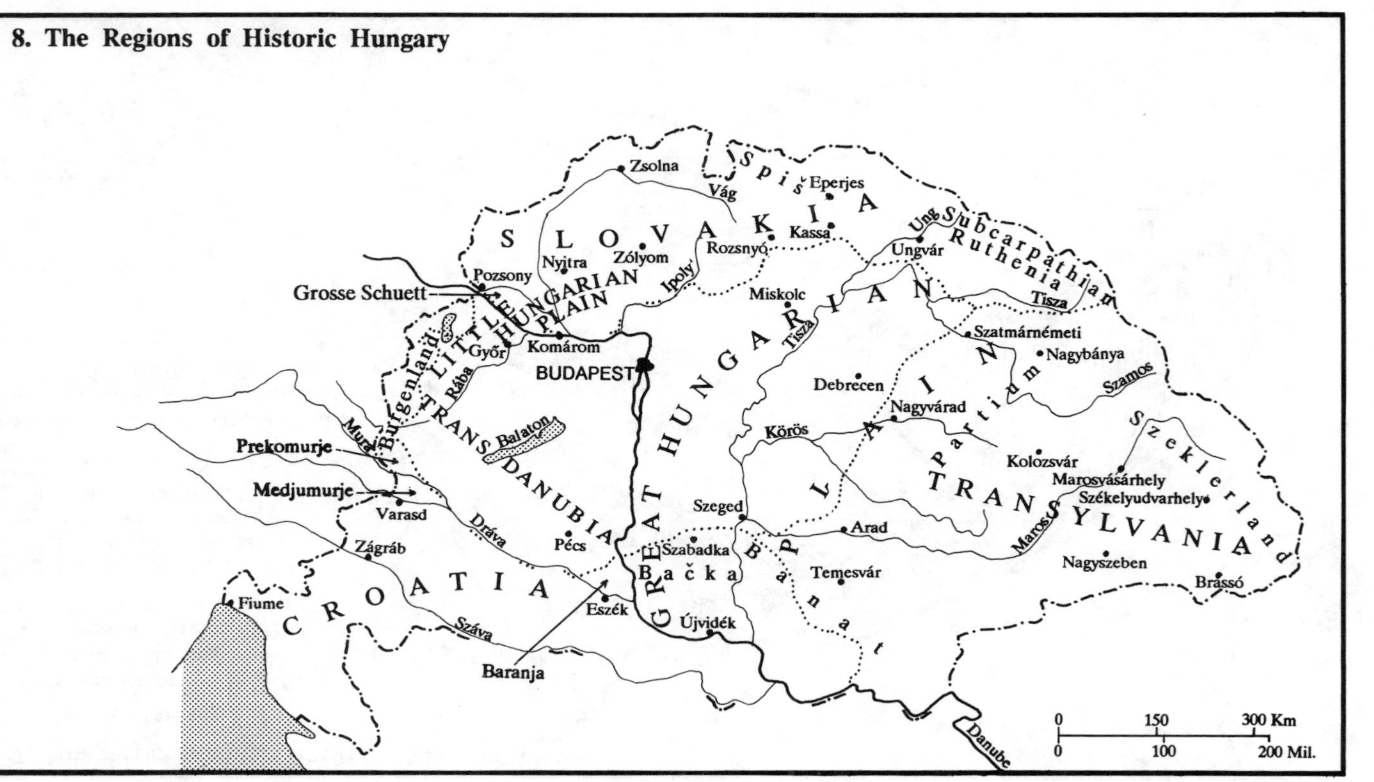

Name Index

Place Index

Volumes Published in "Atlantic Studies on Society in Change"

No. 1 *Tolerance and Movements of Religous Dissent in Eastern Europe.* Edited by Béla K. Király. 1977.

No. 2 *The Habsburg Empire in World War I.* Edited by R. A. Kann. 1978

No. 3 *The Mutual Effects of the Islamic and Judeo-Christian Worlds: The East European Pattern.* Edited by A. Ascher, T. Halasi-Kun, B. K. Király. 1979.

No. 4 *Before Watergate: Problems of Corruption in American Society.* Edited by A. S. Eisenstadt, A. Hoogenboom, H. L. Trefousse. 1979.

No. 5 *East Central European Perceptions of Early America.* Edited by B. K. Király and G. Barány. 1977.

No. 6 *The Hungarian Revolution of 1956 in Retrospect.* Edited by B. K. Király and Paul Jónás. 1978.

No. 7 *Brooklyn U.S.A.: Fourth Largest City in America.* Edited by Rita S. Miller. 1979.

No. 8 *Prime Minister Gyula Andrássy's Influence on Habsburg Foreign Policy.* János Decsy. 1979.

No. 9 *The Great Impeacher: A Political Biography of James M. Ashley.* Robert F. Horowitz. 1979.

No. 10 Vol. I* — *Special Topics and Generalizations on the Eighteenth and Nineteenth Century.* Edited by Béla K. Király and Gunther E. Rothenberg. 1979.

No. 11 Vol. II — *East Central European Society and War in the Pre-Revolutionary 18th-Century.* Edited by Gunther E. Rothenberg, Béla K. Király, and Peter F. Sugar. 1982.

No. 12 Vol. III — *From Hunyadi to Rákóczi: War and Society in Late Medieval and Early Modern Hungary.* Edited by János M. Bak and Béla K. Király. 1982.

No. 13 Vol. IV — *East Central European Society and War in the Era of Revolutions: 1775-1856.* Edited by B. K. Király. 1984.

No. 14 Vol. V — *Essays on World War I: Origins and Prisoners of War.* Edited by Samuel R. Williamson, Jr. and Peter Pastor. 1983.

No. 15 Vol. VI — *Essays on World War I: Total War and Peacemaking, A Case Study on Trianon.* Edited by B. K. Király, Peter Pastor, and Ivan Sanders. 1982.

No. 16 Vol. VIII — *Army, Aristocracy, Monarchy: War, Society and Government in Austria, 1618-1780.* Edited by Thomas M. Barker. 1982.

No. 17 Vol. VIII — *The First Serbian Uprising 1804-1813.* Edited by Wayne S. Vucinich. 1982.

No. 18 Vol. IX — *Czechoslovak Policy and the Hungarian Minority 1945-1948.* Kálmán Janics. Edited by Stephen Borsody. 1982.

---

* Volumes Nos. I through XXVIII refer to the series *War and Society in East and Central Europe.*

No. 19 Vol. X — *At the Brink of War and Peace: The Tito-Stalin Split in a Historic Perspective.* Edited by Wayne S. Vucinich. 1982.

No. 20 — *Inflation Through the Ages: Economic, Social, Psychological and Historical Aspects.* Edited by Edward Marcus and Nathan Schmuckler. 1981.

No. 21 — *Germany and America: Essays on Problems of International Relations and Immigration.* Edited by Hans L. Trefousse. 1980.

No. 22 — *Brooklyn College: The First Half Century.* Murray M. Horowitz. 1981.

No. 23 — *A New Deal for the World: Eleanor Roosevelt and American Foreign Policy.* Jason Berger. 1981.

No. 24 — *The Legacy of Jewish Migration: 1881 and Its Impact.* Edited by David Berger. 1982.

No. 25 — *The Road to Bellapais: Cypriot Exodus to Northern Cyprus.* Pierre Oberling. 1982.

No. 26 — *New Hungarian Peasants: An East Central European Experience with Collectivization.* Edited by Marida Hollos and Béla C. Maday. 1983.

No. 27 — *Germans in America: Aspects of German-American Relations in the Nineteenth Century.* Edited by Allen McCormick. 1983.

No. 28 — *A Question of Empire: Leopold I and the War of Spanish Succession, 1701-1705.* Linda and Marsha Frey. 1983.

No. 29 — *The Beginning of Cyrillic Printing—Cracow, 1491. From the Orthodox Past in Poland.* Szczepan K. Zimmer. Edited by Ludwik Krzyżanowski and Irene Nagurski. 1983.

No. 29a	*A Grand Ecole for the Grand Corps: The Recruitment and Training of the French Administration.* Thomas R. Osborne. 1983.
No. 30 Vol. X	*The First War Between Socialist States: The Hungarian Revolution of 1956 and Its Impact.* Edited by Béla K. Király, Barbara Lotze, Nandor Dreisziger. 1984.
No. 31 Vol. XI	*The Effects of World War I, The Uprooted: Hungarian Refugees and Their Impact on Hungary's Domestic Politics.* István Mócsy. 1983.
No. 32 Vol. XIII	*The Effects of World War I: The Class War After the Great War: The Rise Of Communist Parties in East Central Europe, 1918-1921.* Edited by Ivo Banac. 1983.
No. 33 Vol. XIV	*The Crucial Decade: East Central European Society and National Defense, 1859-1870.* Edited by Béla K. Király. 1984.
No. 34 Vol. XV	*War, Revolution, and Society in Romania. The Road to Independence.* Edited by Ilie Ceausescu. 1983.
No. 35 Vol. XVI	*Effects of World War I: War and Communism in Hungary, 1919.* György Péteri. 1984.
No. 36 Vol. XVII	*Insurrections, Wars, and the Eastern Crisis in the 1870s.* Edited by B. K. Király and Gale Stokes. 1985.
No. 37 Vol. XVIII	*East Central European Society and the Balkan Wars, 1912-1913.* Edited by B. K. Király and Dimitrije Djordjevic. 1986.
No. 38 Vol. XIX	*East Central European Society in World War I.* Edited by B. K. Király and N. F. Dreisziger, Assistant Editor Albert A. Nofi. 1985.
No. 39 Vol. XX	*Revolutions and Interventions in Hungary and Its Neighbor States, 1918-1919.* Edited by Peter Pastor. 1988.

No. 40 Vol. XXI — *East Central European Society and War, 1750-1920. Bibliography and Historiography.* Complied and edited by László Alföldi. Pending.

No. 41 Vol. XXII — *Essays on East Central European Society and War, 1740s-1920s.* Edited by Stephen Fischer-Galati and Béla K. Király. 1988.

No. 42 Vol. XXIII — *East Central European Maritime Commerce and Naval Policies, 1789-1913.* Edited by Apostolos E. Vacalopoulos, Constantinos D. Svolopoulos, and Béla K. Király. 1988.

No. 43 Vol. XXIV — *Selections, Social Origins, Education and Training of East Central European Officers Corps.* Edited by Béla K. Király and Walter Scott Dillard. 1988.

No. 44 Vol. XXV — *East Central European War Leaders: Civilian and Military.* Edited by Béla K. Király and Albert Nofi. 1988.

No. 46 — *Germany's International Monetary Policy and the European Monetary System.* Hugo Kaufmann. 1985.

No. 47 — *Iran Since the Revolution—Internal Dynamics, Regional Conflicts and the Superpowers.* Edited by Barry M. Rosen. 1985.

No. 48 Vol. XXVII — *The Press During the Hungarian Revolution of 1848-1849.* Domokos Kosáry. 1986.

No. 49 — *The Spanish Inquisition and the Inquisitional Mind.* Edited by Angel Alcala. 1987.

No. 50 — *Catholics, the State and the European Radical Right, 1919-1945.* Edited by Richard Wolff and Jorg K. Hoensch. 1987.

No. 51 Vol. XXVIII — *The Boer War and Military Reform.* Jay Stone and Erwin A. Schmidl. 1987.

No. 52 *Baron Joseph Eötvös, A Literary Biography.* Steven B. Várdy. 1987.

No. 53 *Towards the Renaissance of Puerto Rican Studies: Ethnic and Area Studies in University Education.* Maria Sanchez and Antonio M. Stevens. 1987.

No. 54 *The Brazilian Diamonds in Contracts, Contraband and Capital.* Harry Bernstein. 1987.

No. 55 *Christians, Jews and Other Worlds: Patterns of Conflict and Accommodation.* Edited by Phillip F. Gallagher. 1988.

No. 56 Vol. XXVI *The Fall of the Medieval Kingdom of Hungary: Mohács, 1526, Buda, 1541.* Géza Perjés. 1989.

No. 57 *The Lord Mayor of Lisbon: The Portugese Tribune of the People and His Twenty-four Guilds.* Harry Berstein. 1989.

No. 58 *Hungarian Statesmen of Destiny: 1860-1960.* Edited by Paul Bődy. 1989.

No. 59 *For China: The Memoirs of T. G. Li, former Major General in the Chinese Nationist Army.* T. G. Li. Written in collaboration with Roman Rome. 1989.

No. 60 *Politics in Hungary: For A Democratic Alternative.* János Kis, with an Introduction by Timothy Garton Ash. 1989.

No. 61 *Hungarian Worker's Councils in 1956.* Edited by Bill Lomax. 1990.

No. 62 *Essays on the Structure and Reform of Centrally Planned Economic Systems.* Paul Jonas. A joint publication with Corvina Kiadó, Budapest. 1990.

No. 63 *Kossuth as a Journalist in England.* Éva H. Haraszti. A joint publication with Akadémiai Kiadó, Budapest. 1990.

No. 76 *Yugoslavia: The Process of Disintegration.* Laslo Sekelj. 1992.

No. 77
Vol. XXX *Wartime American Plans for a New Hungary. Documents from the U.S. Department of State, 1942-1944.* Edited by Ignác Romsics. 1992.